LONG LIFE

LONG LIFE

NIGEL NICOLSON

G. P. Putnam's Sons

New York

To my children

G. P. Putnam's Sons
Publishers Since 1838
a member of
Penguin Putnam Inc.
200 Madison Avenue
New York, NY 10016

Library of Congress Cataloging-in-Publication Data

Nicolson, Nigel.
Long life / Nigel Nicolson.
p.   cm.
Includes index.
ISBN 0-399-14363-7 (alk. paper)
1. Nicolson, Nigel.   2. Biographers—Great Britain—Biography.
3. Editors—Great Britain—Biography.   4. Great Britain—Biography.
I. Title.
CT788.N486A3   1998
941.085' 092—dc21   97-30180   CIP
[b]

Printed in the United States of America

1   3   5   7   9   10   8   6   4   2

This book is printed on acid-free paper. ∞

Book design by Jennifer Ann Daddio

CONTENTS

ILLUSTRATIONS

*Unless otherwise credited, all photographs are
from Nigel Nicolson's collection.*

30. Carlo Feltrinelli, Christian Bourgois, Ed Victor, Ryan Victor and Nigel at Sissinghurst, 1994

31. Sissinghurst

Sources

The author and publishers acknowledge the following for permission to use copyrighted material:

[1]Aerofilms Ltd

[2]Punch Ltd

[3]Clare Arron, *Daily Telegraph*

[4]Rob Judges

AUTHOR'S NOTE

Most autobiographies begin with birth and end with approaching death. This one is different. By the end of Chapter 1, I am seventy-five; I am born at the beginning of Chapter 2. This is because I have chosen a thematic, not a strictly chronological, method of dividing up my life. I have changed occupations several times, and each has overlapped or interpenetrated the others. Here I have separated them, and to assist the reader to rearrange everything in order, I have added a Chronology at the end.

Some of the material in this book has previously been published in the *Spectator* and *Sunday Telegraph* during the editorship of both journals by Dominic Lawson, and I am grateful to him for permission to reuse it.

SISSINGHURST CASTLE
CRANBROOK, KENT

ONE

THE SON

It is a midsummer afternoon and I am sitting in the gazebo at Sissinghurst, having locked the door to separate myself from the strolling tourists. The windows face outwards on a familiar view, my favorite since childhood. In the foreground is the angle of the moat flagged with yellow iris, then a hedgerow rose in flower, then the green of growing corn and the darker green of trees, fading into the washy blue of the horizon ridge. I can see from here only two buildings: a white oast and a red roof. The view can be little changed since Jane Austen's day. The only movement is of an elderly lady dressed in white walking toward me up from the farm track.

This is my summer office, but an office without telephone, light or heat, so I cannot use it in the winter. But of all places where I have lived, the Sissinghurst gazebo is the one with which I would most like to be identified. With the help of Francis Pym, the architect, I designed it and dedicated it to the memory of my father, Harold Nicolson, who died in 1968, the year before the gazebo was built. So let me begin with him.

HAROLD

I knew him much better than I knew my mother, Vita Sackville-West, for he was a gregarious, companionable person and she shy, and although he always seemed to be busy, as a diplomatist in our childhood and then as a politician and a prolific writer, he always had time for my brother Benedict (Ben) and myself: reading Sherlock Holmes stories aloud to us, drawing imaginary pictures of what we would become in later life (himself, Viceroy of India; Ben, President of the Royal Academy; I, Lord Chief Justice) and attempting rather clumsily to teach us rural skills like clearing brambles, shooting rabbits and diverting a stream to form a lake. His interest in our schoolwork was rare among fathers. He would read Aeschylus's *Seven Against Thebes,* because it was my set book for that term, and discuss it with me in the holidays. He would write to us every week when we were at boarding school. Our family relationships, it now strikes me, were created more by these intertwining letters than by conversation, for we all wrote avidly back and forth to each other but were reticent when we met.

Harold encouraged us to notice things and describe them—the effect of shifting light on a church tower, how the character of a person is defined by mannerisms of speech and dress, how books are arranged in someone's library, or why a stranger's whispers in a railway carriage are more distracting than normal talk. His wit, his social buoyancy, his gift for anecdote, his self-mockery, are best recaptured in *Some People,* the book to which he attached least value because it had caused him least trouble. His personality contained a feminine streak. If he had a fault, it was not snobbishness, which I will discuss later, but a certain softness. "I have no combative qualities," he once confessed. He held no animosity in reserve. He saw most controversies in shades of gray, and although his political reticence was often taken as a sign of impotence, he brought to politics much that was admirable, decent, shrewd and wise, and to literature a sparkle and irony that aerated his lightly classical style. It was sometimes held against him that he never made up his mind what sort of man he was, a writer who dabbled in politics, or a politician with a literary bent, and that he failed to achieve the highest of reputations in either field because he was regarded, as he wrote of himself, "by the Bohemians as conventional, and by the conventional as Bohemian." His life, like mine, tended to zigzag, but he extracted from it much pleasure, and gave much. He had strong convictions and more than a share of adventurousness. Lovable as a friend, loving as a husband, stimulating as a father, he left behind him in his books, letters and diaries a record of his every mood from exhilaration to despair, in controversy and private happiness.

He was adept at transmitting to his sons his own moral values, though he was not religious. When, as boys, we complained that we were made to go to church every Sunday while he and Vita sat chatting on the terrace with their Bloomsbury friends, he replied that in childhood everyone must be exposed to the Christian faith, giving them the opportunity to embrace it as their own, and understand how deeply it has influenced history, ethics, literature and the arts. If, like him, we found that we could not accept its paradoxes, such as a loving God capable of cruelty, or the symbolism of the wafer and the wine, we must remember that greater men than us, from St Paul to Father Martin D'Arcy, have based their whole lives on these fundamental beliefs. He would never scoff at a person's religion, but in private he might express surprise, as when in 1929 he wrote to Vita about a memorial service which he had been attending in Berlin:

Just imagine that with all the prayer-book, bible and hymn-book to choose from, the chaplain selected a ditty which contained the following verse:

> The Lord, ye know, is God indeed.
> Without our aid he did us make.
> We are his flock, he doth us feed.
> And for his sheep he doth us take.

Now, lines as bad as those would be rejected by Niggs [Nigel] for the *Summer Fields* magazine. The first line is meaningless, the second indecent, and the third is a direct misrepresentation of social conditions, and in the last line alone is there a glimmer of irony.

There is much of Harold Nicolson in this. He could not accept that traditional beliefs should be immune to argument, or that noble sentiments excuse bad verse. He called himself a "good pagan."

He told us that there were many virtues, but only three sins: cruelty, untruthfulness and sloth. All other forms of wickedness were classified as naughtiness, for which we were punished. Sins were so dreadful, we were delighted to hear, that no punishment was necessary: there very exposure was enough. Once we mercilessly teased the weak-minded daughter of the gardener. I never knew Harold more angry, and his anger took the form of weeping with distress. We were more often guilty of the other two sins, always with impunity. There was the "bath episode," when Ben, aged ten, insisted that he had had a bath when he had merely sponged his face, a family legend that lingered far longer than it deserved. Sloth is so endemic in children that, in our minds, it barely qualified as sin. Here the family legend was a remark which one of us was supposed to have made on an empty afternoon toward the end of the holiday—"Mummy, have I had tea?"—when she was struggling to complete a novel or refine a verse. "Why can't you build a hut in the wood or something, just as I used to do?" she said. But did she?

My father's morality was summed up in the simplest of lessons: good behavior is in the long run more profitable and enjoyable than bad behavior. Cruelty poisons the soul, lying leads to the habit of lying, laziness rots the mind. To this day I feel ashamed of behaving, even in minor ways, in a manner of which I know he would have disapproved, like pleading traffic, untruthfully, as an excuse for being late, or smuggling a bottle of wine through Customs. He was conscientious to a fault. Equally, I react against prejudices which he inherited from his parents. Let us remember that he was born in 1886, and I in 1917. He was by birth Victorian, by upbringing Edwardian; I am Georgian all the way through. He had an instinctive dislike of Jews and colored people. He once confessed to me that he would rather not know that a friend had a Jewish ancestry, and like many of his generation, he was strongly pro-Zionist, not only for historical reasons and admiration for Chaim Weizmann but because he hoped that Israel would attract as many Jews as possible to live there. Of his color racism he felt no shame. I was once lunching with him in the Travellers Club, which had just engaged its first black man as a waiter. He was an unusually handsome youth, dignified not only by his looks but by his manner. My father ostentatiously took out a silk handkerchief to wipe the spot on his plate where the man's thumb had momentarily rested. I protested strongly. "Yes, I know," he replied, "but I cannot tolerate the dark races."

Of one failing he and my mother are still periodically accused. They are called snobs. It is to misuse the word. They were not snobs but élitist. Snobbishness is vile because it is unmerited and cruel. Elitism is natural and beneficial, an acknowledgement that some people are more estimable than others, for their achievements or character. It is not a matter of class. We all choose our friends from among people who share our interests and tastes. Harold and Vita did not like Ascot or City people because they had little in common with them. For the same reason, they did not spend their evenings in the village pub. To despise people for their lack of education, or admire them because they inherited titles or money, did not occur to them. Harold's books, particularly *Some People* and *Public Faces*, and Vita's *The Edwardians* and *All Passion Spent*, ridicule the snobs and played some part in the decline of snobbishness. Vita, the only child of Knole, beautiful, clever, an heiress, was courted by every "little dancing thing" in London and could have become mistress of Harewood or Belvoir but chose to marry a penniless third secretary in the Foreign Office. When Harold was knighted for his biography of King George V, and someone addressed her as Lady Nicolson, it was with difficulty that she restrained herself from slapping him. While Harold would have preferred a peerage, it was not because he wanted our cook, Mrs Staples, to address him as "M'lord," but because he hoped for a seat in the Lords, having lost his seat in the Commons. He craved some sort of political platform.

But the charge of snobbishness against both of them has become as indelible as a dye. Typically, it was elaborated in a review of their published letters in the *New York Review of Books* by Robert Craft. By selective quotation he managed to make them out snobs of Edwardian dimensions. When Vita thought that she might die in giving birth to Ben, she wrote a secret letter to Harold bequeathing her jewels to different friends. The list is quoted with a sneer. Harold was a snob because on a lecture tour of the United States in 1933 he found the ladies' clubs uncongenial, just as any American intellectual would have found their British equivalents, but when he wrote with sympathy and liking for the Lindberghs, the Morrows, Thomas Lamont and Archibald MacLeish, these people were dismissed by Craft as "acceptable American yahoos." I wrote in protest that he was confusing class with quality:

> But perhaps quality is no longer an acceptable term. One must not make distinctions between people on the grounds of taste, manners, culture, friendships or occupation if it conveys any suggestion that one person is more commendable than another, instead of simply different. A snob is a person who attaches exaggerated importance to birth or wealth, and claims an unfounded acquaintance with the emi-

nent. In what conceivable sense could this definition apply to Vita or Harold?

But it did no good. He replied that the importance they attached to lineage qualified both of them for my definition. It is true that Vita was shocked to discover that neither Ben nor I knew that the Salisbury family name was Cecil and that Pembrokes were born Herberts, and if she was introduced to someone called Lord Aloysius Cavendish, she would give him the benefit of the doubt until he proved that he was worthy, or unworthy, of it. In her childhood, a name like that was a passport that never needed renewal.

I cannot be entirely impartial in judging this question, but I think it grossly unfair that a social historian like David Cannadine should lampoon Vita and Harold as representative of the arrogance and flaccidity that he finds to despicable in the aristocracy. They came from a world which both, in part, rejected. He picked the wrong couple for his demonstration. They inherited a little but created more, in literature, politics, gardens and their concept of marriage. As James Lees-Milne, Harold's biographer, wrote in reply to Cannadine, "They paid no heed whatever to the social standing of their friends so long as they subscribed to the civilised code of manners in which they had been brought up." But perhaps that phrase in itself will be taken as further proof of what I have attempted to disprove. I shall stick to élitism, which has been practiced to the common benefit in every age in every country in every endeavor known to man. In his wartime diary, Harold put it like this: "I have always been on the side of the underdog, but I have also believed in the principle of aristocracy. I have hated the rich but I have loved learning, scholarship, intelligence and the humanities. Suddenly I am faced with the fact that all these lovely things are supposed to be class privileges."

LADY SACKVILLE

Vita's mother was undoubtedly a snob. She never questioned for a moment that the great majority of people were born to serve people like herself. When, at the outbreak of the First War, all her male staff were called up, she wrote to Lord Kitchener, the Minister of War:

I think you may not realise, my dear Lord K, that we employ five car-penters and four painters and two blacksmiths and two footmen, and you are taking them all from us! I never thought I would see parlour-maids at Knole. I am putting up with them, but it really does offend me to see these women hovering around me in their starched aprons, which is not at all what Knole is used to, instead of liveries and even powdered hair! . . . Do you not realise, my dear Lord K, that you are ruining houses like ours? What can you do about it?

Kitchener did nothing except send an evasive reply. Later in the war, when she was staying at Blenheim, she wrote in her diary: "I like the splendor of this vast house. The spirit of Sarah Jennings possesses me, and I should love McNed [Edwin Lutyens] to build for me something very beautiful and very large." But she did emulate the old aristocracy in her gift of command and appreciation of the arts. She ran Knole like a colonel of Hussars, intro-ducing central heating, bathrooms, electricity, telephones and cars as fast as they were developed, and saved Knole, not ignominiously, by persuading Sir John Murray-Scott to finance her improvements and lawsuits, and bequeath to her a large part of the Wallace Collection, which she sold.

When she left Knole in a huff in 1919, furious that her husband had ac-quired a mistress, she employed Lutyens to throw together three contiguous houses in Sussex Square, Brighton, where she lived alone with servants. Even he could not disguise the legacy of three main staircases, three ballrooms and three front halls, and she sold the houses a few years later at a vast loss. She moved to White Lodge, near Rottingdean, an Edwardian villa which Lutyens enlarged for her, forming in part of the garden a terrace made of slates on edge, and as slates are expensive and very thin, the cost was enormous. She didn't care. Having quarrelled with all her friends, she relied on Ben and me for company. We would be driven to Rottingdean despite our protests, and even in wintertime were made to sit for hours on her balcony huddled in her fur coats and with hot-water bottles on our knees, waiting for lunch at 5 P.M., when it would be served by the undergardener, the cook having given notice that morning. She was always in trouble with servants and tradesmen, refus-ing to pay their wages and bills, and, with a jocularity that only she enjoyed, named her house the Writs Hotel.

She would spin us tales of her extraordinary youth as her father's hostess in the Washington Legation, when her beauty, eccentricity and social daring won her the hearts of innumerable suitors, including that of President Arthur, a widower, who proposed to her, she alleged, during dinner at the White House. To prove to us that her beauty had endured, she would hold out the inside of her forearm for us to stroke and feel the softness of her skin. We hated it. We were either smothered in flattery or scorched by reproach. She would tip us £5 each, then telephone to my mother that we had robbed her. Accustomed to this, Vita confiscated the notes on our return home and patiently returned them by post.

Victoria Sackville died in 1936, leaving instructions that her ashes were to be scattered in the sea opposite White Lodge, a task which my father dutifully carried out from a motorboat three miles from shore, the minimum distance allowed by the regulations. She bequeathed the house and many of its contents to me, including several portraits of herself, one by Sargent, which now give the rooms at Sissinghurst an elegance which is not indigenous to them. I sold White Lodge, and ultimately the sale helped finance the launch of Weidenfeld & Nicolson, publishers.

Vita loved her mother, tolerating her injustices with amazing fortitude. The portrait she drew of her in *Pepita* was by turns affectionate and despairing. Lady Sackville never understood her daughter. Once she wrote in her diary, "I made Vita give up having Taloola [*sic*] Bankhead to luncheon. She is the most accomplished Lesbian in England, and talks in a disgusting way." There was a gap in comprehension that Vita never tried to bridge, and she reacted against all her mother's values except one, her love for Knole.

Vita's father, Lionel, 3rd Lord Sackville, was easier and more conventional, an English gentleman of Edwardian attitudes whom she would not have loved so much had he not been her father and the inheritor of Knole. He died when I was ten years old. I associate him with a single incident. Ben and I had cut the cloth of the billiards table by playing idly with a cue. In the 1920s that was a crime comparable to laming a favorite polo pony. Our grandfather summoned us to his study and, as we waited outside his door in terror, the tall clock in the corridor ticked off the seconds with metronomic insistence. That sound, that interval, has remained with me all my life, so that I can still judge the sixty seconds of a minute with astonishing precision. In fact, he was kind to us and took us tracking deer in the snow-filled park. But I did not love him as Vita did. Grandsons seldom do.

VITA

My mother has posthumously become more central to my life than when she was alive because of the books that I and others have written about her and the growing fame of her garden. I never knew her well, fearing to intrude on her privacies, and she was reluctant to inquire into what she imagined to be mine. I now wish that I had taken more pains to know her, for I believe that she would have responded.

She so much disliked discussing her writing that I would not know the subject, let alone the title, of her current book until I saw it advertized. Only once did she venture to involve me in something so personal to her. I was thirteen when she turned to me at the foot of her staircase and said, "I have written a new poem and would like to dedicate it to you." I replied, unthinking, "Oh, don't do that, Mummy. You know that I don't understand your poetry," meaning that I didn't deserve the dedication. She went up to her tower room without a word, and when she came to lunch I saw that she had been crying. I have never forgiven myself for that cruelty. Ben could hurt her in other ways. Absorbed all morning in the study of Piero della Francesca, he would remain totally silent at meals, reluctant, like many scholars, to discuss his specialty with amateurs like us. It made his companionship awkward, then alarming. Vita would beg my father not to leave her alone with him.

There were moments that showed me how much I missed in this distancing of myself from her. Once she took me to join the hop-pickers at their end-of-harvest party in the fields. I was about eight. They passed her a mug of thick-brewed tea. I knew that she hated tea, and surreptitiously I drank her mug as well as mine and put it empty beside her. She alone noticed my stratagem and gave me a glance of such gratitude and love that I felt momentarily weak-kneed. I treasure that moment. Perhaps she did too. But it ended absurdly. "You drank that very quickly," said the hop-picking lady. "Let me give you another mug." This time I managed to spill it clumsily on the grass, and Vita and I exchanged a conspiratorial smile.

Only once did she and I overcome our mutual reserve sufficiently to create between us a moment of intimacy. I was much in love with Shirley Morgan, the daughter of Charles Morgan, the novelist and critic. My love for her, though never admitted to my parents, could scarcely be disguised. She was to have come to Sissinghurst for the weekend. An hour before I was due to meet her train, her father telephoned to say that she was unwell and could not come. The call was taken by Raymond Mortimer, who was staying with us, and he passed the message to Harold who passed it to Vita, who would have to tell me. She came to my room and told me. My disappointment was so great that I turned away from her in tears. She put her arms round me for almost the first time since I was a small boy and whispered, "I'm so sorry, darling." Then she, too, wept.

That is not quite the end of the story, for a few weekends later Shirley did come to Sissinghurst. It, and she, were looking lovely, and I took her for a walk in the woods, thinking that no mood or circumstance could be more conducive to my success. I proposed to her, not for the first time, under a pine tree, which has ever since been known as Shirley's Tree. To say that she refused me would be to suggest a harshness quite alien to her nature, but the message was unmistakable. We walked back to the house, where we were met by Vita and Harold who had well understood the purpose of our walk and could not conceal that their hopes were identical to mine. They saw us returning, one behind the other, Shirley wearing an expression of regret, I one of despondency. Dinner that evening could have been difficult, but Vita moved us from the dining room into a corner of the White Garden where there were chairs and a table, and as the full moon rose, a white barn owl drifted across it and we all exclaimed with joy. Many years later I dedicated *Portrait of a Marriage* to Shirley. She had married Henry Anglesey and the dedication was simply "To S.A.," but it was widely guessed to be her.

Vita was capable of great tenderness, but she was also strong, stronger than Harold. She would stand no nonsense from editors, trespassers, plagiarists, tenants or the hunt. I once saw her seize a rifle, stride down to the lake where a stag had taken refuge from the hounds and the huntsman was pursuing it across the water in our rowing boat, and she fired not at the huntsman, not at the stag, but at the boat and sank it. Then, shouldering the smoking gun, she strode back to the hose, while Harold looked on, amazed. With animals, young people (like land-girls in the war) and miscreants, her sympathy was profound. She agreed to serve on the local Bench, more for the pleasure she took in its Shakesperean associations than from a sense of seigniorial duty, but felt privileged to the point of shame. "When the wretched delinquent stands before us," she wrote to Harold. "I always feel that here is a wild animal trapped and caged, and there but for the grace of God and my mother's marriage settlement, go I."

She was a profounder person than most modern critics give her credit for: I can still be astounded by the originality and depth of some of her poetry and prose, like her poem "Solitude" or the account of her Persian journey in *Twelve Days*. That was not the Vita we saw at the lunch table, where she was shy, silent, unable to match Harold's wit or cope with Ben's silences, but loving both inarticulately.

Oh Hadji [she wrote in 1919, only six years after their wedding], I ought never to have married you or anybody else. I ought just to have lived with you for as long as you wanted me, because I am a pig really, and you are the dearest and sweetest and tenderest person in the whole world, and I only hurt you. We would have lost nothing, you and I, because we would have been every bit as happy unrespectably or respectably. Women ought to have freedom the same as men when they are young. It's a rotten and ridiculous system at present; it's simply cheating one of one's youth. It was all right for Victorians. But this generation is discarding, and the next will have discarded, the chrysalis.

I shall have more to say about their marriage, which was as remarkable a joint achievement as their garden. This cry from the heart in her youth expressed the lifelong conflict between Vita's desire for independence and her feeling of guilt for desiring it, her deep attachment to Harold and her longing to break away. It led to her behaving cruelly towards him, and then spending the rest of her life making up for it.

In the preface to her biography of Vita, Victoria Glendinning wrote: "Some of her behavior was indefensible. . . . To some readers she will be an inspiration, to others she may seem unlikeable." That is fair. She could be selfish. She always tired of her lovers sooner than they tired of her. She wrote in "Solitude":

> Those cheap and easy loves! But what were they,
> Those rank intruders into darkest lairs?
> We take a heart and leave our own intact.

Was that all that they had meant to her? She could be tough. But she was never jealous, for though ambitious to be numbered among the English poets (she cared little for her novels), she was always "desiring this man's art and that man's scope," like Shakespeare. She felt herself to be "a damned outmoded poet," and dropped intellectual friendships like Cyril Connolly's and Cyril Joad's because she distrusted her ability to catch the conversational ball when it was thrown in her direction. Modesty and reticence were unexpected qualities in a woman who had been so rebellious in her youth and had since achieved so much, but they were central to her nature. She was not, as Peter Quennell once described her, "Lady Chatterley and her lover rolled into one," a soubriquet which stuck because it was short, cynical and untrue.

When we lived at Long Barn near Sevenoaks she was sociable, entertaining weekend parties and delighting in the London gossip, to which she contributed no small share. But when we moved permanently to Sissinghurst in 1932, she renounced all that and was so anxious to avoid social obligations that in restoring the house she carefully omitted any guest room, to the extent that Ben and I were obliged to share a bedroom until we were both at Oxford. "You see," Vita explained, "if you have a bedroom each, and one of you is away, Sibyl [Lady Colefax] might find out, and invite herself for the weekend." It halved the risk. Only once did we give a party. It was in the summer of 1945, when Ben and I returned home after three years in the Army in Africa and Italy.

'Let's give a party,' we said.
'Why?'
'Well, the war's over, we've won it, and now we are safe and reunited. It deserves a celebration.'
'What sort of a party?'
'A cocktail party.'
'But we don't know how to make cocktails.'
'We can find out. People have written whole books on the subject.'

Then she said desperately, "We don't know anyone to ask," which was almost true, as few of our friends lived locally. We said that we knew three people and we would ask them to bring their friends. Everyone who was invited accepted. They wanted to see what happened in this mysterious place.

The party was a disaster. We could not introduce our guests to each other because we did not know who they were. After half an hour, a woman approached Vita and asked her, "I wonder if you could tell me the name of that lady over there, the one in a blue hat?" Oh yes," replied Vita, delighted to identify one of the three women whom she did know. "That's Mrs Hamilton-Smythe and she lives at Biddenden." "No," said the first lady, "I'm Mrs Hamilton-Smythe and I live at Hawkhurst." The party never recovered from that incident and in Vita's lifetime we never gave another.

As we grew into our civilian jobs, Ben an art historian and deputy surveyor of the King's pictures under Kenneth Clark, then for thirty years editor of the *Burlington Magazine,* and I a publisher and MP, we gradually moved away from Vita into the intellectual companionship of Harold. For some years we shared a house with him in Kensington. Our friends were of a new generation, with some of whom Vita felt little sympathy, like Philip Toynbee, Ben's intimate, whose Bohemianism she deplored and to whose brilliance she was blind. She believed him responsible for turning Ben away from her traditional values, like family cohesiveness, conservative stability, love of country and countryside, and Ben, fearing to hurt or scandalize her, became more aloof. Until he married, he treated Sissinghurst more as a pleasant place where he could work than as a home.

In my middle life I had a gentler relationship with my mother, but she did not wish to be known too well except by a few friends like Hilda Matheson, Alvilde Lees-Milne, her sister-in-law Gwen St Aubyn, and a few local ladies like Cynthia Drummond, Vi Pym and Edith Lamont. Of her love affairs we were entirely ignorant. She rarely left Sissinghurst and, if obliged to go to London, she would catch the last train home rather than spend a night away. She did go abroad, to Italy or the Dordogne in preference, and during the last six winters of her life she went on cruises with Harold to the fringes of the three non-European continents, steadily writing on board, even the garden articles which she contributed for fifteen unbroken years to the *Observer.* When I visited Sissinghurst with my growing family she was always welcoming, eager for our news but chary of her own, and watching me, I thought, for any sign that I might become a gardener and pace the woods and fields with her own proprietorial delight. I was the heir apparent, the rural son, and Ben the urban.

When Vita and Harold Died

Vita died in 1962 aged seventy. She remained active as gardener, traveler, estate manager and writer until in the last few months of her life she developed the bowel cancer which killed her. I visited her several times in the London hospital where she had undergone an operation and was shocked by the pathetic sight that she presented, weak and pale, and thin as a reed. She returned to Sissinghurst and died there on 2 June. I was at a meeting with George Weidenfeld in our Bond Street office when the news was telephoned to me that she was unlikely to live through the night. I drove down immediately, to find her in the Priest's House, an isolated cottage in the middle of the garden, to which she had been moved for its better facilities to nurse her, and she occupied the bedroom which Ben and I had shared for many years in the hope of deflecting Sibyl Colefax. She just recognized me. Then she relapsed into a coma and her breathing became unnatural, in deep, inward gasps. She died at 1:15 the next day, without pain, we thought. Harold picked a bunch of her favorite flowers and laid them on her bed.

At the start he seemed strangely unmoved. When I telephoned John Sparrow at All Souls College, Oxford, to invite him to come to Vita's funeral, Harold interrupted, "Tell him to bring A. L. Rowse," whom, as John knew well, Harold had decided to nominate, quite without cause, as his only enemy. As we left the Charing crematorium, he turned to Ben and me and said, "If you look round now, you'll see your mother go up in a little puff of smoke." When we reached home we found, besides John Sparrow, his old friends Raymond Mortimer and James Pope-Hennessy, waiting for us with a buffet lunch. They had dressed in dark clothes and assumed downcast expressions, not knowing quite what to expect, and were surprised, perhaps relieved, to find the widower looking forward to a jolly party. A few days later he collapsed, weeping openly at the lunch table. He never really recovered.

It pained me to watch his gradual decline. He had had two strokes before Vita's death, but only now did they take effect. He stopped writing, then reading, than talking. He would hide behind a newspaper when friends like Gerry Wellington, Robin Maugham, Gladwyn Jebb or Richard Church came to visit him, and he would watch television all afternoon and evening, whatever the program, moved to tears by any emotional scene, even when a goal was scored by Wolverhampton Wanderers, of whom he had never previously heard.

Once he asked me, "What's all this business in Vietnam?" when the war had been reported on television every evening for years. I cared for him as best I could, with the help of a male nurse. He had often said to me that he would not want to live in the condition to which he was now reduced, but when the indignities of old age came upon him he seemed not particularly to mind.

We were very short of money to keep him in relative comfort, for he had saved nothing from his considerable earnings, and Vita had been able to leave him no more than £10,000 and the South Cottage for his lifetime. He had given up his book reviews and other journalism, and my own income was reduced to a low ebb by the demands made upon it by school fees and other family expenses. We had to make some extra money, and I suggested to my father that we should publish his diaries and I would edit them. He demurred that they would be of no interest to anyone, for they were typed at top speed and never revised, but he was in a mood to agree to anything. I obtained an advance of £3000 from Collins, and £6000 from the *Observer* for the serialisation rights.

I edited a volume a year for three years, 1965–7, taking time off from my own books. I had on one side of my desk the folders of his diary and on the other his letters to and from Vita, and I would select passages from one or the other, for in the main they covered the same episodes from different angles. I checked facts and references from standard books and biographies, then typed out the extracts and footnotes directly. There was never a manuscript. Although it was done quickly, and with nothing like the care that Joanne Trautmann and I later devoted to our six-volume edition of Virginia Woolf's letters, the result was adequate and the material marvelous.

Harold was of little help. He could not remember names or dates, even from the latest period. I asked him about a discussion he had had with Vita in 1955, only ten years earlier, when they had debated what had been the happiest single moment of their joint lives. He had told her that it was when he found her in the tobacconist's shop in Smyrna. What had happened there? He hadn't the faintest idea. He read the typescripts and my introductions, and his only request was that I should omit a reference to the Prince of Wales's support for Oswald Mosley. Having read volume II and returned it to me without comment, he asked me a week later to show it to him before publication. "But you've just read it!" "Oh no, I haven't." It was like that. I felt obliged to consult other people, if they were mentioned in the diary, like Sir Alan Lascelles on the Abdication crisis, Anthony Eden, Harold Macmillan, Violet Bonham

Carter (whose son Mark was my editor at Collins), and my correspondence with them is now interleaved with the original diary which Harold bequeathed to Balliol College, Oxford.

The three volumes were published at yearly intervals. They were best-sellers, and I suddenly found myself enriched by £30,000, of which I kept one third and devoted the balance to sustaining poor Harold for the rest of his life. He was pleased by his success, but said to me with a flash of his old humor, "It's rather sad to think that of all my forty books, the only ones that will be remembered are the three I didn't realize I'd written." The reviews amounted to obituaries. Praise was heaped upon him for the diversity and generosity of his life, and I do not think he noticed the rare comments that his career as a diplomatist, politician and writer had been, by the highest standards, unful-filled.

He died very suddenly, on 1 May 1968, at Sissinghurst, of a heart attack as he was undressing for bed. His coffin was placed on trestles in his book room and they called me as soon as it was in position. I put my elbows on it with hands clasped, hoping that some thought or silent words would come to me but found only tears. I do not think that I have ever wept so profoundly. Then we took him to Charing, to join Vita in the clouds.

Six weeks later we held a memorial service for them jointly in St James's Church, Piccadilly. John Sparrow gave the address and Cecil Day-Lewis, the poet laureate, read the poem which Vita had written for Harold in the middle of the Second War, looking back on their lives:

> I loved you then, when love was Spring, and May.
> Eternity is here and now, I thought.
> The pure and perfect moment briefly caught
> As in your arms, but still a child, I lay.
> But now when autumn yellows all the leaves,
> And twenty seasons mellow our long love,
> How rooted, how secure, how strong, how rich,
> How full the barn that holds our garnered sheaves!

PORTRAIT OF A MARRIAGE

In my book of this title I described how I found in Vita's writing room, after her death, a locked Gladstone bag which contained a flexible notebook in which she had written, forty years earlier, an account of her childhood and her love affair with Violet Trefusis. In a large Italian cupboard which stood under the tower archway, exposed to the weather and the curiosity of any stray visitor, she had stored the letters which she had received from Violet and many other lovers. With her diaries, and the 10,000 letters to and from Harold, there was clearly material for a full record of her life, but it should be allowed to simmer.

I showed her manuscript to Ben but not to my father, fearing that he might destroy it, or it him. Neither he nor Vita had ever spoken to me about the Trefusis affair, but I knew the gist of it from hints which Lady Sackville had dropped, inexcusably, to Ben, and he to me. After Harold's death I lent the precious manuscript to a few other people like James Pope-Hennessy, John Sparrow, James Lees-Milne, Raymond Mortimer, Enid Bagnold, Hugh Thomas and Billy Collins. I was gathering opinions on whether it should be published, suppressed or destroyed. Jim and Alvilde counseled delay; so did Raymond. Sparrow said go ahead, as did James, and Diana Crawfurd, his literary agent, who also became mine and one of my closest friends. A typical letter of approval came from Peter Quennell:

I feel no doubt that it ought to be published, and that it would be the greatest pity if it weren't. It is one of the most remarkable things that your mother ever wrote. You need not fear damage to her reputation. It might have been so in 1950 or 1960. But not now. And don't worry about V[iolet] T[refusis]. She is among the stupidest and most conceited women I have ever come across, and I suspect that she would be highly flattered.

All the same, there could be no question of publication in Violet's lifetime. Her sister, Sonia Cubitt, survived her for a few years, and although she and Violet had quarrelled incessantly since their childhood she felt a posthumous obligation toward her and responded coldly to my letter, referring to "this distasteful book" and causing me great trouble with her intellectual friends. One of them, Cyril Connolly, who had reacted kindly when I asked him for advice, was strongly influenced by her and cut me dead at James Pope-Hennessy's memorial service.

Violet changed in character in later life. She wrote some clever novels (one of which, *Broderie Anglaise,* was a fictional version of her affair with Vita) and became a *grande dame* in the intellectual society of Paris and Florence, forming intimate friendships with people like the Princesse de Polignac, Harold Acton, Christian Dior and François Mitterrand. But nothing could excuse her youthful selfishness. She attempted to destroy the happy marriage of her closest friend, and herself married a decent man, Denys Trefusis, with the sole intention of humiliating him. She despised marriage, thinking it a hypocritical façade for infidelity, like the marriage of her own mother, Alice Keppel, the mistress of Edward VII. She never believed in the conjugal felicity of Vita's marriage, calling it a fraud. All that mattered to her was total physical and emotional love such as she enjoyed with Vita for three years, and she saw no evil in marrying Denys in order "to oblige her mother, distract society and provoke the woman she loved into claiming her," as Diana Souhami put it in her book about Mrs Keppel and her daughter.

I was more concerned about my father. For although his part in the affair was wholly creditable—by love and patience he rescued his wife from a seductress—it was his own infidelity that had triggered off the whole affair. Vita did not mention the incident in her autobiography, but it was evident from the letters that Harold had contracted a venereal infection from a male fellow guest while staying with Lord Lytton at Knebworth in November 1917. His confession to Vita was his de profundis:

> I can't laugh over it all. I am so frightened about it. It will be such an awful business if the doctor's report is not satisfactory. I simply dread it. Darling, if you hated me today, how much will you hate me if it really does come? . . . I shall know what you will suffer and it will be my fault, my fault—and that eats into my brain like some burning acid. It is too horrible. Dear one—let's face it together and bravely.

I did not mention this distressing event in *Portrait,* nor did James Lees-Milne in his biography of Harold. Victoria Glendinning referred to it, legiti-

mately, in her life of Vita, and the confession, not the incident, was featured in
the BBC's dramatization of my book.

Still, my suppression of the story did little to assuage my feeling of betrayal toward my father. With Vita it was different. The conviction grew in me
that she wanted her memoir to be published. She could have destroyed it. It
presumed an audience. She explained things that she would have no need to
explain if she were writing purely for herself as an act of catharsis, like "We
bought a country cottage where we spent the summer and Harold went up to
London every day"; or, "Edward, who was my cousin, ten years younger than
I." There were passages which suggested that she thought her memoir might
be of help to other people. She referred to "possible readers" of it. Shortly before her death, she told a friend, Elizabeth Taylor, the novelist, that she had
left a partial autobiography which I would find, and she would trust my judgment whether to publish it. The story, which was already familiar to many
people of her generation, would be bound to surface in biographies, letters
and diaries, and what excuse would I have for Victoria Glendinning or James
Lees-Milne if I destroyed the manuscript, the crucial evidence of this central
incident in their lives?

So the decision was made, with Ben's full approval, and he and Diana
Crawfurd agreed with my suggestion that I would place the Trefusis affair,
which lasted three years, in the context of a marriage that lasted fifty. I would
confirm and elaborate Vita's account by details drawn from the correspondence and Violet's letters, which her executor, John Phillips, allowed me to
quote, and I would add my own commentary, both on the affair and the later
years of Vita's marriage until passion was (almost) spent, making it clear that
having survived the crisis, their marriage, though physically aborted after the
birth of their sons, was one of great happiness to both. I called the book *Portrait of a Marriage*, not, as Vita's contribution alone would have suggested,
Portrait of an Affair, in order to clarify my motive.

Having finished my research, I wrote the *Foreword* in Bath in January
1973. In the middle of that month I went to Switzerland for the wedding of
Joanna Caruso to Donald Hess (an all-night wedding, in a snowstorm, followed by a ball), and from Berne I went to Gruyère, where they make the
cheese, and for three weeks stayed in an inn, writing 6,000 words a day. I finished the book at Sissinghurst on 1 March.

Tony Godwin, the editor at Weidenfeld, was pleased with it, as was Mike
Bessie, of Atheneum, New York. The book was serialized in the *Sunday*

Times, and although I was allowed, exceptionally, some degree of control, it was probably a mistake to present it initially in this form. Readers judged the whole by its startling extracts and ignored the calm conclusion. I had evidence of coming opposition. When I went to the *Sunday Times* to discuss the serialization with Godfrey Smith, he said, "I've read your book," then paused. I expected him to make some comment, but he remained dumb. "You experienced it?" I suggested. "Yes," he replied, relieved. "It was some experience." In a preemptive review in the *Washington Post,* Malcolm Muggeridge called the book "regrettable." Lionel Sackville was said to be displeased. When I spoke to our representatives at a Weidenfeld sales conference, most of them were delighted to be given so hot a property, but the Scottish rep said, "I wouldn't have treated my *mither* like that," to which I could only reply lamely that his mother was probably different from mine. When the first part had been serialized, I went to a party of John Murray, the publisher, to test the water, and a man looked at me across the room as if he had just seen Crippen enter it. I was interviewed by Ludovic Kennedy live on television on the eve of publication and he asked me, "Violet had a sister, didn't she? What does she think of it?" Knowing that Sonia must be watching, I replied that I hoped that when she had a chance to read it as a whole, her judgment would not be too severe. But remembering her condemnation of "this distasteful book," it was a dicey moment.

Portrait was published on 23 October 1973. I was alone at Sissinghurst. I came down that morning to find *The Times* lying on the kitchen table. It was minutes before I could bring myself to open it. When I did, I found a review by Michael Ratcliffe which made me dance into the garden with delight. Anthony Powell in the *Telegraph* was also appreciative. But the best was Kay Dick's review in the *Spectator*: "He recaps this marvellous story (moving and funny), filling in the gaps with infinite wisdom and understanding." That was the sunshine. Then came the thunderclaps. Frank Kermode: "Something rather shocking about it." Rebecca West: "It's a pity it was not left in the Gladstone bag." Bernard Levin: "This ludicrous story . . . He should have put his mother's manuscript in the fire," and so pleased was he by this verdict that he reprinted it in a volume of his collected essays. Its reception in America was more favorable, except in the journal which I most respected, the *New York Review of Books,* where John Richardson called it "a tasty, not to say gamey, club-sandwich of a book." I also received some pained letters. Reaction, as they say, was mixed. I was told that the Queen had bought several copies to give away as Christmas presents. Elated at one moment, I was in despair the next. The *Bookseller* reported that it had taken up more column inches in the press than any book in their experience. It stayed near the top of the bestseller list in London and New York for months on end. Soon foreign publishers, from the Japanese to the Serbs, were competing for the translation rights. The British paperback sold for £20,000. I was sore but temporarily rich.

THE BIOGRAPHIES

It soon became clear that something more would be required. I received several requests from authors to write the biographies of Harold and Vita, and chose James (Jim) Lees-Milne for Harold, and Victoria Glendinning for Vita. I had known Jim since childhood. He had been an intimate friend of my father. They had worked together at the National Trust, Harold as Vice Chairman and Jim as the now famed acquisitor of many of its most treasured country houses. He had written Harold's entry in the *Dictionary of National Biography,* and one evening, when he was staying with his wife, Alvilde, at Sissinghurst, he said that there ought to be a full biography. "Why don't you write it yourself?" I said on the spur of the moment. "Do you really mean that?" he asked. I did. He was the ideal biographer, himself a graceful and witty writer, an intimate of his subject, and while he may have thought Harold's left-wing opinions bizarre, he was wholly in sympathy with his cultural and aristocratic background. He began his research immediately, in the Foreign Office archives, in King's College library, in *Hansard,* but his main sources were Harold's diary and his vast correspondence with Vita. Oral evidence he found less useful. After lunching with Gladwyn Jebb he wrote to me, "He was very nice and chatted away, but somehow I get little out of people who knew Harold in the early days. It is the written word that really matters." In this case the documents were unusually full and rich, and he found the book extending to two volumes of four hundred pages each. At first, the publisher, Norah Smallwood of Chatto, was dismayed. Would Harold Nicolson really stand up to such lavish treatment? Jim pleaded with her: "What other Englishman of this century led so varied a life, and wrote so constantly and arrestingly about it?" She was persuaded. I read each volume in typescript, learning much. It was like stirring a bowl of long-settled potpourri. I encouraged Jim to allow his voice to be heard more often, as he was an excellent commentator as well as recorder, and in volume II he did so.

Toward the end of that volume, he described a conversation with Vita, alone at Sissinghurst, which showed me what I could have meant to her as a son:

> From six o'clock until long past midnight we talked without stopping.
> . . . Never in my life have I known anyone, male or female, with whom, once the mutual preliminary shyness were dispelled, I have felt more at ease or whose companionship I have found more congenial . . . No topics were barred. Her curiosity about and understanding of human nature in all its aspects were limitless. Her sympathy with every human frailty and predicament was all-embracing. This was the Vita I knew and most dearly loved.

I had to restrain him. He was not writing Vita's life but Harold's, and before he finished his own volumes, I had already asked Victoria Glendinning to tackle Vita. I had not known her as well as I knew Jim but had much admired her biographies of Elizabeth Bowen and Edith Sitwell. After talking to her at one of George Weidenfeld's parties, I telephoned her, offering her the job. She was delighted. I took her to lunch with Lord Sackville at Knole and to meet Ione Martin at Long Barn. I arranged a biographers' weekend at Sissinghurst, for she and Jim had never met. She returned there many times, often with Terence de Vere White, whom she married in the course of writing the book, and took away in batches armfuls of the same documents that Jim had already sampled. I heard of her in the Berg Collection in New York, at the Humanities Research Center at Austin, Texas, nosing out Vita material and even one of Vita's former lovers, Evelyn Irons, now an old woman living in some Midwest town. The book was published by Weidenfeld in 1983. I reviewed it in the *Spectator*, thanking Victoria for interpreting Vita's life as an adventure story, for it was an adventure, and Vita was far from saintly. It would have been a travesty to present her as the meek, modest, aristocratic, reclusive nature worshipper whom a visitor to her garden or a reader of *The Land* might assume. "She would have wanted her posthumous portrait painted by a Rembrandt," I wrote, "not by a Gainsborough." Victoria was that Rembrandt and I loved her for it.

When I consider what tensions have arisen between biographers of the recently dead and their widows/widowers and children, I count myself fortunate to have had Jim and Victoria as my parents' ghosts. With each of them my relationship was the happiest symbiosis and their books put into the perspective of their whole lives the torrid events of 1918–20.

THE DRAMATIZATIONS

It was a different matter with the various attempts that were made to dramatize their lives. I was moving from a world of mutual confidence and discretion into one where spectacle was more important than truth.

I first saw Vita on the stage in Edna O'Brien's play *Virginia*. Then came Southern Television's proposal to film a documentary about Vita and Sissinghurst, supported by readings from her books. I recorded several talks about her in different parts of the garden and lent them old photographs to insert as stills. Months passed, and I'd almost forgotten it. Then I was told that the program was to be screened on 7 August 1981. I watched it. I appeared at the start, briefly describing how we found Sissinghurst in 1930. That was all there was of me. My photographs were not used at all. An actress, posing as Vita, swam into the shot, and mumbled about rose-red bricks. Then she was joined by a second actress—guess who? Violet Trefusis. The two women cuddled each other like tadpoles at the bottom of a tank, while the most passionate phrases from their love letters were read voice-over. Next came "Harold," typing: "I hate that woman. She is like some evil orchid poisoning the air." After half an hour of this, Vita dies. We were shown her poor dead face, while Harold typed a review, apparently indifferent.

I wrote Southern Television a strong letter of protest and returned their fee. I suggested that they had deliberately concealed their intentions from me, knowing that I would object. They refused an apology, so I appealed to the Broadcasting Complaints Commission (it was their first major case) and gave evidence before them. I said that the main thrust of the program—the dramatic portrayal of my mother's sex life—had never been revealed to me. STV replied that the program had "evolved" during the course of production and that my contributions had been "disappointing." I believe, from some of the questions they put to me, that the Commission thought I had been naive to trust the filmmakers, but they agreed with me that the changes had resulted in a program completely different from the one proposed to me. They upheld my complaint, and I hoped that STV felt ashamed. In any case, it was soon afterward that they lost their franchise.

The STV episode was nothing to the furore created by the BBC's dramatization of *Portrait of a Marriage.* I had turned down some fifty previous offers, including a musical and an opera, being unwilling to see my parents portrayed by actors in the circumstances that the book described and which STV had tried to visualize. Then I heard that a large American film company was planning to make a version of *Portrait* without asking my permission, in the hope (fully justified) that I could not afford to sue them for breach of copyright. I was considering the idea of preempting their film by another over which I would have some degree of control, and it was at that moment, in March 1985, that I received from Ned Sherrin, the television writer-producer and chat-show host, an invitation to meet his friend Patricia Hodge, the actress, who had long wanted to promote a film or television series based on the book, and perhaps act the part of Vita herself. The three of us were joined at lunch by Victoria Glendinning. It was a highly enjoyable occasion. Our discussion turned on the problem of how to present a lesbian affair in a way that would leave no doubt that Vita and Violet were passionately attracted to each other but would not cause offence to many people. The public, I thought, was not yet ready for scenes of explicit sexual love between women, and I felt sympathy for the young actresses who would have to enact them in front of scores of film crewmen. The others agreed. Next day I summed up my proposal in a letter to Ned Sherrin:

Vita and Violet should not be shown making love. There must be no pawing or mutual undressing or passionate embraces ... Their elopement was a crazy escapade from which Vita recovered just in time, largely owing to Harold's extraordinary gentleness and understanding. At the end it might be suggested (I don't know how) that this crisis in their marriage made it all the more successful and secure. In other words, the drama must show the triumph of love over infatuation.

This last sentence became my leitmotif. I believed profoundly that it was true, and that any dramatization must emphasize it.

For three years negotiations hung fire. Then in 1988, the BBC showed an interest in the story and I was asked to meet two producers, Colin Rogers and Colin Tucker. I repeated to them what I had said to Sherrin, and they were given a copy of my 1985 letter to him. I thought that we were in full agreement that the story should be handled on this basis, and Colin Rogers wrote to me afterwards: "Both Colin Tucker and I are glad that you feel our views coincide, and we are grateful that you are happy to leave our agreement on this as a matter of trust." So convinced had I been that we saw eye to eye that I never put in writing to them that the two essentials: that there should be no overtly sexual scenes, no nudity, and that the series should end by showing the happiness of Vita's and Harold's later life together.

Penelope Mortimer, the novelist and mother-in-law of Colin Rogers, was commissioned to write the script and they came to Sissinghurst together to discuss her draft. From the start it was quite clear that she disliked Vita and Harold. She called them "silly people." Penelope was not silly. She regarded Harold as "hen-pecked." John Mortimer was not hen-pecked. She was determined to tell the story her way, not my way, and I had the impression that she had never been fully alerted to my reservations. She had little patience with my suggestion that the love between the two women could be indicated by looks, words and gesture more than by touch. With the support of her son-in-law, and the director, Stephen Whittaker, she had written into her script three scenes where Vita and Violet were filmed semiclothed or naked, in and out of bed. Nor was she taken with my idea that Vita and Harold should be shown living happily ever after. I suggested that at the end of Part 4 there should be a culminating scene indicating this, and I even tried my hand at the script. Their conversation had turned to Vita's elopement with Violet:

VITA   It was crazy of me. It is the sort of thing that happens only once in a lifetime. You should have stopped me.

HAROLD   But I tried. I really tried. But you can't stop someone who's off her head, as you were.

VITA   I know. But if you'd been a Spaniard, you'd have dragged me back by the hair.

HAROLD   But I'm not a Spaniard.

VITA   (*laughing*) Anyhow, we've got this now (*and she waves a trowel round the White Garden*).

Mrs. Mortimer didn't think that this would do at all. It was sentimental. I said that sentiment is nothing to be sneezed at. She said it was her script. I said that it was my book. She had to think of her reputation. I had to think of mine. We did not come to blows. I told her that apart from my reservations about the sex and the marriage she had dramatized the book brilliantly. I gave her a cigarette case which had belonged to my mother, and she held out three fingers to be squeezed in a gesture of reconciliation.

The actors playing the three main parts came to Sissinghurst for the night. Vita was played by Janet McTeer, Violet by Cathryn Harrison and Harold by David Haig. It must have been a strange experience for them to sit down to dinner with a "son" three times their age, and I felt awkward in suggesting to them mannerisms and tones of voice characteristic of my real-life parents, for the personality of an actor inevitably dominates the personality of the person whom he or she is trying to represent and has never met. All three gave excellent performances, but they were not Vita, Harold and Violet. Janet could be as formidable as Vita occasionally was, but I missed her tenderness. David was less intelligent than Harold (but the script gave him little opportunity to exercise his wit), but Cathryn, whom I at first thought too pretty for Violet, did convey her feline seductiveness with great artistry. Peter Birch, whom I never met, was utterly convincing as Denys Trefusis. The scene where he confronts the two women in a London drawing room was the best in the whole series.

I deliberately avoided much of the filming, because I sensed that my presence, and possible protests, might be off-putting. I could catch an occasional glimpse of the scenes which they shot at Sissinghurst, but when the crew moved to Hever Castle (for Knole), to Stoneacre (for Long Barn), to Folkestone (for Dover and Calais), to Nice (for Monte Carlo and Amiens) and to the Elstree studios for a mock-up of Vita's tower room and other scenes, I rarely accepted Colin's invitations to follow them. Once I went to Hever, as they were filming Vita and her mother dining alone together at Knole in 1910. They were sitting at opposite ends of a twenty-foot table in full evening dress, loaded with jewels, and discussing Vita's father's performance as a lover in front of three footmen in livery and a butler in tails. The men's faces remained utterly impassive. It would never have happened like that, I said. I was reminded that this was not fact but drama. The scene suggested the period as most viewers would imagine it to have been. I shut up. I had no right or talent to interfere, and indeed I thought the whole production brilliantly staged and executed.

But that did not remove my fundamental objections. When I saw the rough cuts, I gasped inwardly at the sight of Janet and Cathryn in the nude (how they must have hated it!) and of my father in old age, writing a soppy letter to Violet immediately after Vita's death. I was now associated with all this. I had heard of authors who protested that their books had been badly distorted by script writers. Penelope Mortimer was one of them. She had recently complained that Harold Pinter's screenplay of her novel *The Pumpkin Eater* "had no connection whatsoever with what I'd written." I did not feel as strongly as that, but she had turned a portrait of a marriage into a portrait of an affair. I told the producers that I felt bound to make my disappointment known. They had not kept to the spirit of our agreement. So I gave an interview to Sally Brompton for the *Radio Times,* and she honorably reported that I "would have preferred more emphasis on the long-term success of his parents' marriage," and that I was "embarrassed" by the sex scenes.

I had my own say in a long article which I wrote for *The Time*'s Saturday review of 22 September 1990, and it was published to coincide with the showing of the second part of the four-part series. I was then in America, editing the Vita–Harold letters which I had sold to the Lilly Library, Indiana University, and I received the reactions there by fax. Michael Wearing, a BBC executive, told the *Sunday Times* that I must be "a very old-fashioned guy who probably hadn't watched TV since 1953." Colin Rogers wrote to *The Times* that "final editorial judgments on matters of taste and content must be left to us," which I had never disputed, and he denied that the Sherrin letter ever formed part of our agreement. He was suspicious that I was trying to have my cake and eat it. It was perfectly true that I had accepted a large slice of cake. I did not reply. *Le combat cessa faute de combattants.* I was happy to allow the dispute to rest with the headline attached to the *Spectator*'s review of the series: ARS BREVIS, VITA LONGA.

ON HAVING FAMOUS PARENTS

I am often asked whether it is a handicap or an advantage to have had well-known parents. Undoubtedly it is an advantage. It is not simply a firm platform on which to construct a life but a trampoline from which to bound. Parental fame implies success, which for their children normally brings with it security, a comfortable home, a good education, a childhood nurtured by stimulating parents and family friends, and help with the founding of a career, quite apart from the tangible benefits that the child may inherit.

To bear a famous name is not too inhibiting. The "chip off the old block" notion is outdated. Children can escape into different occupations. If I were Mary Moore, I would not try to sculpt: Richard Olivier has wisely taken to directing, not acting. An author's son has a wider choice. He can follow his parent's path, but need not tread in his footsteps. He can write on different topics in different ways. In my case, I became a publisher, as well as an author and editor of other people's diaries and letters. In politics I joined a party, the Conservative Party, which my father denounced.

The disadvantage is that one can be saddled with a fame that is not of one's own making. If strangers know anything about me, they will probably call me Vita's or Harold's son. I have benefited greatly from their joint notoriety. It placed me against an identifiable background. It opened doors. It provided me with an inheritance, not large in money terms but rich in influence, example and contacts. It is nonsensical for parents to demand gratitude from their children, who in the long term are more benefactors than beneficiaries, but I am happy to think that in my case our lives, generation to generation, interpenetrated, like a handshake that signifies mutual affection and support but which can instantly be released.

Two

THE BLOOMSBERRY

182 EBURY STREET

The letters which I had been selecting and annotating in the University of Indiana were published in 1992 under the title *Vita and Harold*, and it did something to broaden public understanding of their marriage after the hectic scenes on television. English Heritage suggested that a plaque be affixed in their memory to the outside wall of 182 Ebury Street, Pimlico, where I was born on 19 January 1917, and where Virginia Woolf was first entertained by Vita, rather nervously, to dinner. I unveiled the plaque by pulling aside a little pinafore of a curtain. It recorded simply that Vita and Harold had once lived there and that they were "writers and gardeners," the most suitable joint description that we could devise. There was some discussion whether the inscription should also state that they were married, for only Vita's maiden name was given, but it was decided in the negative because passers-by would either know or guess it, and for those who did not, it would add a note of mystery, scandal and romance to a street which epitomizes Pimlico's respectability.

The owner of the house, Fionn Morgan, allowed me to explore it in search of the room where I was born. As a guide I had a page of photographs from a 1915 copy of *Vogue*. In one of the bedrooms on this page I recognized the silver brush, comb and mirror which Vita kept all her life, and in the corner of the same room the bed in which I was born. The room has been slightly changed since then. The doorway, at some period, was shifted by six feet and the paneling has gone. Still, there was enough left to establish that my first breath was drawn from this very cube of air, and one cannot trace a long life further back than that.

Lady Sackville, who owned the house in 1917, also bought the house next door (commemorated by another plaque recording that Mozart lived there as a boy of eight) and connected the two by doors driven through the party walls. She commissioned Lutyens to build in the garden a large dining room, of which only relics of the pavement survived the bombs of 1940. We left the house when I was three or four, and I remember only two things about it. On the opposite side of the street there was, and still is, a block of flats with a staircase built into the facing wall, like Azay-le-Rideau's but less decorative. As the tenants mounted it, they would disappear for a moment, only to reappear on the next landing, if they had not entered their flat in the interval. From my nursery window I would watch this vanishing act for hours, hoping that the topmost tenants would come home and I could watch their progress up all six storeys.

This performance, which remains my earliest memory, continues to this very day, but now I find it less enthralling than the Ebury ghost. I never met the ghost myself, but my mother told me long afterwards that once she had felt a warm feminine hand close over her own as it rested on the banister rail outside my nursery. Turning round, she found nobody. Who was this lonely woman who implored her company? No tradition of her was attached to the house and she has never reappeared to its present occupants.

LONG BARN

This ancient house, down the hill from the village of Sevenoaks Weald, was only a mile from Knole, and I was taken there when I was a few weeks old. When Vita bought it for £3,000 in 1915, it was a tumbledown fifteenth-century farmhouse, held together more by gravity than structural design, the floor of the main bedroom tilted at such an angle that any piece of furniture placed on it appeared crippled, and a rubber ball let go in one corner would roll with gathering speed to the other. My parents made of it a surprisingly comfortable house, adding a wing at right angles to the original cottage, formed from the timbers of a long barn at the foot of the hill, which gave the place its name. A gallery extended the full length of this wing on the ground floor and above it were three bedrooms with bathrooms attached, but by an oversight (my father was the amateur architect) there was no corridor linking them, so that the occupant of the central bedroom could only escape through the bedrooms of his neighbors on either side. This arrangement led to an unfortunate incident when I was six and Ben eight. Geoffrey Scott, the architectural historian and Vita's very temporary lover, was changing for dinner when we burst into his bedroom, forgetting that he was there. He was stark naked. Neither of us had ever seen a grown man naked before. We were appalled by the sight. He was furious.

We did not sleep in the main house. We lodged in a cottage a hundred yards from it. Our bedroom window opened conveniently on the flat roof of a garage, from which it was a simple matter to climb by drainpipes to the ground. Our guardians were at first nannies, then governesses, and it was with these harassed women that we spent the greater part of the day. One of them was a Miss Cherry, who was so strict that we assumed (so recent was the First World War) that she must be German and therefore an enemy. But the governess who stayed longest was a Frenchwoman called Mlle Nadré, and by us, for some inexplicable reason, Goggy. French words and expressions soon mingled with the English in a comic language that Goggy, in despair, called français-japonais, as in "I'm going to *laver ma* face," but we retained more of her language than she thought, winning most of the French prizes at school. For Vita, who was bilingual, and my father, whose diplomatic career made French his second language, this was not good enough. He advertized in the *Figaro* for a tutor to spend two months with us in the summer holidays of 1927. A young man called Maurice Couve de Murville, fresh from the Sorbonne, applied for the job and got it. He came to Long Barn dressed in tweeds and we found him totally ignorant of the laws of cricket. We were not kind to him, and it is to this experience that I attribute his Anglophobia when he became Foreign Secretary and then Prime Minister, under de Gaulle. I met him only once in later life, at a reception in the French Embassy in London. He was not specially affable to his old pupil.

The custom in families like ours was that the children would be brought down once a day to meet their parents, and the traditional time was 6 P.M., between tea and bed. It was also the time of day when Vita's poetry flowed most freely, and I think of her bent over her writing table as we burst in, patiently laying down her pen and spectacles to amuse us for half an hour. Only after her death, when I found the manuscript of *The Land*, did I realize what it must have cost her in concentration. In the summer the rules were relaxed. We were free to wander round the garden or act as ball boys when the grown-ups played tennis, and if Harold was at home we would cut brambles with him or go for walks. But we were not easy children. Given that Ben was to become one of the most distinguished art historians of his day, it now seems to me extraordinary that we never looked at a picture and seldom read a book. We had no friends and few occupations. Desperate to amuse us, or induce us to amuse ourselves, Harold made a swimming pool out of a pond, one half of which was only six inches deep, while the other half was four feet. Perversely, we bicycled round the shallow end.

FAMOUS FRIENDS

Very seldom were we allowed to join the grown-ups for meals, and it was on one such occasion that I made my first acquaintance with Bloomsbury. Thirteen people were sitting down to lunch and, even in that sophisticated company, thirteen was considered unlucky. I was told to join them and sat on a cushioned chair next to my mother. Seated opposite me was an extraordinary woman, camouflaged in paint and feathers like a parakeet. She was Ottoline Morrell. Transfixed by this apparition, I whispered to Vita, "Mummy, is that lady a witch?" and my whisper coincided with one of those pauses that suddenly occur at even the most garrulous parties. Everybody heard it. There was an appalled silence, broken by Clive Bell from the far end of the table: "Of course she's a witch. We have always known she was, but nobody had dared say so." It did not quite restore the party's composure.

A happier, non-Bloomsbury occasion was the visit of Charlie Chaplin. Vita, who was then in her social phase, persuaded Edward Knoblock, the dramatist, to bring him to Long Barn for lunch. As a special treat, I was allowed to attend. The conversation turned to jokes. Each of us was asked in turn to tell our funniest story. Mine was: "What's the difference between a cricket team and a small packet of cigarettes?" Answer, "One Player." That did not go down too well and everyone turned to the world's greatest comic genius. His story did not seem at all funny to me. It was this:

A man in a teashop orders a cup of coffee and a piece of shortbread. On paying the bill he compliments the manager on the excellence of the shortbread and asks if it could be made in any shape. "Why, sure." "Well, if I come back tomorrow, could you make me a piece in the shape of the letter e?" "No trouble," replies the manager. Next day, on returning to the shop, the man looks aghast. "But you've made it a capital E," he cries. "I meant a small e." He arranges to come back another day, and then expresses complete satisfaction. "Where would you like me to send it?" asks the manager. "Oh, I won't give you the trouble to send it anywhere. I'll sit down here, if I may, and eat it now."

Then there were expeditions. One was to lunch with Sir Philip Sassoon at Lympne. It was a large party at a very long table, and I sat at one end, squashed like the Dormouse between my parents. "Observe," my father said to me, "the man sitting on the left of Sir Philip. Never forget that you have seen him." I saw a small man with a hatchet face and gimlet-blue eyes, dressed in the rough uniform of a private in the RAF. "Who is he?" "He is T. E. Lawrence, better known as Lawrence of Arabia, but now he likes to be called Aircraftsman Shaw." I wondered then, as I wonder now, why, if he was so memorable, he held so humble a rank, and if he wanted to hide from his fame, why did he attend parties like this where he was certain to be recognized and adulated? I much preferred Rex Whistler, another guest at the party, whom we found up a ladder, stripped to the waist, decorating a room with fantastic townscapes that still survive.

The most frequent expeditions were to Dorothy Wellesley's houses, first Sherfield Court near Basingstoke, then Penns-in-the-Rocks in Sussex, a lovely seventeenth-century house associated with the family of William Penn, which I still often revisit now that it belongs to Pat and Dione Gibson, who have restored to it the serenity that in Dottie's day it lacked. She had two children of our age, Valerian and Elizabeth. With the fatal optimism of most parents, Vita and Dottie assumed that their children would become instant friends. There survives a photograph of us taken at Sherfield, scowling at each other in a punt, clear evidence of our mutual hostility, but it worsened at Penns. Valerian and Elizabeth were exceptionally beautiful children, of whom we were secretly jealous. We sank his toy boats in the swimming pool and induced the bulldog to play havoc among his Angora rabbits. Whether Valerian, the present Duke of Wellington, remembers these incidents I do not know, but if he does, he shows no animosity toward me. We have met only three times since then, once and most appropriately on the battlefield of Waterloo.

Duncan Grant and Vanessa Bell were then painting panels and furniture for the dining room at Penns, and it was the first time that I ever set eyes on their daughter Angelica. I was amazed by her beauty and became suddenly aware (aged fifteen) of girls as objects of admiration and desire. When I was over seventy, I confessed to her this moment of enlightenment. She was unimpressed.

With Lady Dorothy our relationship declined further. Although she was a poet much esteemed by Yeats, and edited the series of modern poets for the Hogarth Press, to us she was a terrifying figure. She walked in her sleep and would enter our bedroom in the middle of the night with a torch turned on her face, now with the green shutter, now the red, making horrible grimaces. In later life she was more of a burden to Vita than a friend. She joined a health farm near Sissinghurst and demanded my mother's constant attention. In writing Dottie's obituary for the *Dictionary of National Biography*, Vita put it tactfully: "Her health, never very robust, considerably deteriorated."

The sad truth is that Vita wished that Ben and I had more of Valerian's qualities. He rode, he fished, he shot, he stood manfully on the bridge of a bucking fishing boat beside the skipper, and he was beautiful. Although Ben was handsome in his teens, neither of us matched his other qualifications. It must have been at this period that Vita bought a large painting of a naked boy sitting astride a tiger. It was known to us as "Peter Scott," because we were forced into an uneasy friendship with the real Peter, the future naturalist, and Vita believed that his father, Scott of the Antarctic, obliged his son to play with dangerous animals and spend most of the day, summer and winter, stark naked, to harden him. She admired him for his boldness. I hated Peter Scott, the painting, and one day took my toy sword and stabbed him between the shoulder-blades. The rent is still visible in the picture that hangs in Vita's tower room at Sissinghurst, opposite the doorway where visitors group, wondering that the National Trust can take so little care of their possessions.

KNOLE

My grandfather's great house near Sevenoaks was an important feature in our lives. We had a permanent nursery on the first floor overlooking the Green

Court, bicycles and a pony, and the full run of the house. We came to know all
the staff and their children. It was still very feudal. My mother told me that
when she was a child, her father stopped a housemaid in the passage and asked
her to give a message to Miss Vita. The girl bobbed a curtsy and asked, "What
name shall I say, sir?" She had been in Lord Sackville's employ for two years
and had never previously set eyes on him.

Between the wars there was a smaller staff and less formality, and it was
only at Christmas that the old tradition surfaced. Every year my grandfather
threw a party in the Great Hall for the children of the staff and tenants, and
Ben and I were enlisted as junior representatives of the family. I do not look
back on those occasions with any pride. Even then I was vaguely aware that
our jovial mingling with the tenantry was tinged with falsehood. We played a
game called Nuts and May, when a small girl was selected as the May Queen,
and the refrain, sung by the housekeeper, went like this:

> We'll make Mary Dibbins Queen of the May,
> Queen of the May, Queen of the May.
> And who shall we send to pull her away.
> Pull her away?
> We'll send . . .

That was the moment that I dreaded, for while it might be,

> We'll send little Freddie to pull her away,

all too often it was,

> We'll send Master Nigel . . .

and I would advance in my sailor suit, blushing at the snobbishness implied,
and take Mary's hot little hand in mine. Once I had to make a speech: "Would

a strong boy help me to pull this giant cracker, please?" No, I was not designed by nature or aptitude to play the role of Little Lord Fauntleroy.

It was the habit at Knole to allow the children to come down to the library for tea. It was always a delicious tea, cucumber sandwiches and sticky cakes, but there came an inevitable moment when my mother said that it was time to return to the nursery, some five hundred feet of corridors distant from the library. "You're sure that you can find the way? You don't want me to come with you?" "Of course not, Mummy." But it was hell. I knew that at the bend of the final staircase I would be confronted by Van Dyck's full-length portrait of Frances Cranfield, dressed in oyster-white, mystic, wonderful. She terrified me.

There was in fact no ghost at Knole, and in daylight it was a wonderful house to explore. Few restrictions were imposed on us. Once I was found fast asleep in the Venetian Ambassador's bed which nobody had occupied for two centuries. The collegiate design of the house, court leading into court through arches in the cross-wings, increased its intimacy the deeper you penetrated. The courts both divided and linked, forming many external façades, each different, each a surprise, courts to cross, treading on grass, stone, gravel or cobbles, and courts to look into from upstairs windows. From the park you surveyed a cataract of roofs and towers, and the courts were lost between them, trebling the area covered by actual buildings.

I inherited Vita's love of the place, and when her uncle Charles died, the present Lord (Lionel) Sackville invited me to join him as a Trustee of the settled estates, but I remained a Trustee for only a short time, as I had little knowledge of finance and he had much. I came to know his brother, Hugh, and Hugh's wife, Bridget, better than I knew Lionel, and Hugh's son Robert joined my son Adam as founders of Toucan, a successful publishing firm. Thus our families remain linked, as they were centuries ago, when Cecilie Baker, the daughter of the owner of Sissinghurst, married Sir Thomas Sackville and became chatelaine of Knole. But the most enduring bond of all is Virginia Woolf's *Orlando,* which she wrote for Vita, about Vita, with Knole as its background and centerpiece.

VIRGINIA WOOLF

Virginia first entered our lives in 1924. Although she had met Vita two years earlier, their intimacy was slow to develop. There was much in Vita that was alien to Bloomsbury. She called it "Gloomsbury." To Vanessa Bell, Keynes and Lytton Strachey she was interesting only because Virginia fell in love with her. Vita was clever and had rebelled against the philistinism of her parents, but she was not as quick and bright as the Bloomsberries. In conversation she lacked wit and a gift for anecdote. Virginia adored her because she adored Virginia, and had been daring to the point of recklessness in her private life. As a writer she was by no means negligible, possessing as Virginia once put it, "a rich, dusky attic of a mind," and was capable of great fluency and variety in her writing, from poetry to travel books, religion to architecture, gardening to biography, none of which, except the last, Virginia attempted, and even her fiction, which Virginia once described to Jacques Raverat as written "with complete competency, and a pen of brass" (a phrase which idle critics have enjoyed copying from each other in order to condemn Vita's books to insignificance), could excite her admiration, particularly *Seducers in Ecuador*, which reflected Virginia's own elusive style.

It was her lineage and her body which disarmed Virginia most. She was a self-confessed snob. If asked to choose between Einstein and the Prince of Wales as a dinner companion, "I would plump for the Prince every time," but that may have been because he would be easier to talk to, while Einstein would sit silent, enveloped in his fame. Virginia read Vita's *Knole and the Sackvilles* soon after their first meeting, and in the same letter to Raverat described her delight in her mere association with such an heiress. "She descends from Dorset, Buckingham, Sir Philip Sidney, and the whole of English history, which she keeps, stretched in coffins, one after the other, from 1300 to the present day, under her dining-room floor." Every word of this, except Dorset, was untrue, but it illustrates the fantasy that Virginia wove around Vita, endowing her with a sort of dominance, a quality that Vita never really possessed, calling her "virginal, savage, patrician," only to remind herself that Vita had two children and that her savagery had been satisfied with the eclipse of Violet Trefusis. In her diary she wrote, "Snob as I am, I trace her passions five hundred years back, and they become romantic to me, like old yellow wine."

It puzzles me that Virginia should have been physically attracted by Vita. Virginia was sexually cold, if not exactly frigid. From that angle, her honeymoon with Leonard had been a failure ("Why do people make such a fuss about copulation? Certainly I find the climax immensely exaggerated," she wrote from Spain to Ka Cox) and though she always slept under the same roof with him, it was rarely under the same ceiling. Her long flirtation with Violet Dickinson had never progressed beyond a little hand-holding, nor with her brother-in-law, Clive Bell. Why, then, at the age of forty-four did she embark without hesitation, apprehension or remorse upon a love affair with Vita? It lasted, on and off, about three years, without, I surmise, great passion on either side. They slept together perhaps a dozen times, at Long Barn or Rodmell, making no secret of it from their husbands, who were neither shocked nor indignant but feared that the excitement might trigger in Virginia another attack of madness. "For heaven's sake be careful," Harold warned Vita. "It is like smoking over an open petrol tank."

Ben and I were unaware of all this. Once an older woman, who should have known better, said to me, "I suppose you realize that Virginia loves your mother?" and I remember replying, "Yes, of course she does. We all do." To us Virginia was as delightful as a favorite aunt. "Virginia's coming to stay." "Oh good." We knew that there would come a moment when she would take us aside and interrogate us about our simple lives. "Go away, Vita. Can't you see I'm talking to Ben and Nigel." "Now," turning back to us, "what's the French mistress like?" We would mutter, "Well, she's all right." "That won't do. What sort of shoes does she have? Does she wear scent in the classroom?" Gradually we learned to adopt her manner, veil truth in half-truth, fantasize. Once I traveled alone with her to London and she whispered to me as the train drew out of the station, "See that man over there?" "Yes." "Well, he's a bus conductor from Leeds. He's been visiting his uncle who has an apple farm at Marden." "But, Virginia, how can you possibly know that? You've never seen him before." "No question about it," and then, for as long as the journey lasted, she told me the man's life story, while he sat in his corner, smoking his pipe, unaware that he was the subject of her impromptu novel.

More seriously, she turned to me once as we were butterfly hunting through the woods and fields of Long Barn and said, "Tell me, what is it like to be a child?" I replied, "You know what it's like, Virginia. You were a child once, but I have no idea what it's like to be you, as I've never been grown-up." That was the only time that I managed to silence her. She was writing *To the Lighthouse*, in which a boy of my own age, James, plays a significant part, and I liked to think that she was seeking copy, which I, to my lasting regret, failed to supply, for James is not in the least like me. She was patient with us, as she seldom was with older people, encouraging us to think in words. Keep a diary, she advised us, and write letters, because—and this is the phrase that rings in my memory—"Nothing has really happened until you have described it."

I never saw any sign of her insanity, but an incident at Monk's House might have suggested it to me. Vita took me there one evening and, besides Virginia and Leonard, there were only Keynes and his wife, Lydia, present. They started a discussion in which Virginia joined with great animation, standing by the fireplace. Leonard, watching her, slowly rose and touched her on the shoulder. Without inquiry or reproach, she followed him from the room and they returned together some fifteen minutes later. Nobody made any comment; all but myself knew exactly what had happened. Leonard had seen danger signals in her agitation. She must calm down. Whenever I read in some feminist tract that he ill-treated his wife, was jealous of her genius, and even that he drove her to suicide, I think of that moment, and the tenderness with which he touched her shoulder and the trust with which she followed him.

Monk's House, I recall, was very shabby in their day. The only attractive pieces of furniture were designed by Vanessa or came from the Omega workshop. There were saucers of dog food on the floor and books on every step of the narrow staircase. Neither Virginia nor Leonard had much visual taste, nor desire for comfort. At first, their only lavatory was an earth-closet in the garden and when they made a water closet out of the profits of *Mrs Dalloway*, they were so delighted by the novelty that its flushing had to be regularly demonstrated to the guests. Leonard extruded an ugly verandah from the roof and for Virginia he designed a bedroom which could only be approached from outside in such a position that the gardener would stare at her as she lay in bed. The garden hut where she wrote was doubled in size after her death by the addition of a studio for Trekkie Parsons. It should now be removed. But the garden was not her territory. Once she ventured to ask Vita what she thought of Leonard's creation. Vita hesitated, then said, "Well, one shouldn't try to recreate Versailles on a quarter-acre of Sussex. It can't be done."

Then came *Orlando*. We know the exact moment of its conception because Virginia described it for Vita in a letter dated 9 October 1927:

> Yesterday morning I was in despair . . . I couldn't screw a word from me, and at last dropped my head in my hands, dipped my pen in the

ink, and wrote these words, as if automatically, on a clean sheet: Orlando. A Biography. But listen. Suppose Orlando turns out to be Vita,
and it's all about you and the lusts of your flesh and the lure of your
mind (heart you have none, who go gallivanting down the lanes with
Campbell) . . .

Pause there, because these last words betray Virginia's secret motive for
the book, jealousy. She would reclaim Vita from Mary Campbell by writing
her a love letter, so long, so fantastic, so flattering, that it would be irresistible.
It worked. Vita replied, "My God, Virginia, if ever I was thrilled and terrified,
it is at the prospect of being projected into the shape of Orlando. You have my
full permission."

So began an amazing year. I was only eleven but was let into half the secret. Virginia was writing my mother's life. She took my brother and me to
Knole, walked us through its galleries, interrogated us about the portraits and,
taking our ignorance for granted, supplied her own make-believe answers on
the spot. Some of the characters in *Orlando* were born that day, but we did not
know it, and the two fantasies, that Orlando ages only twenty years in three
hundred and fifty, and changes from man into woman halfway through, were
hidden not only from us but from Vita, too, until a finished copy, and the manuscript, arrived by post on publication day. She wrote to Virginia, "I am completely dazzled, bewitched, enchanted. . . . How you could have hung so
splendid a garment on so poor a peg." But when Ben and I read it, loud were
our complaints. "You've given Orlando only one son! There are two of us!"
To which she replied, as Humpty Dumpty might have done, "In my books one
person counts as two." It was all the more insulting when in the film of *Orlando*
the one son turns out to be a girl.

The novel is full of family jokes, like Vita's adventurous driving habits,
whether in a four-in-hand or a Rover, and her ineradicable belief that rivers
like the Nile which flow north must run uphill. But in the filmed version the
most poignant real-life event could not be hinted at. In January 1928, when the
book was half finished, Vita's father died, and an uncle, not she, inherited
Knole. The dancing wit of the early chapters acquired a more sombre note.
Orlando became a memorial mass and gave Knole back to Vita by identifying
her with it for ever. It was wholly appropriate that when she died, she left a
note for me with her Will, "I think that the manuscript of *Orlando* should go

to Knole." There it will remain in perpetuity, the property of the National Trust.

Orlando defused their love affair. In the 1930s they drew apart. Vita immersed herself in poetry, gardening and new friendships where Virginia could not follow her. She came only three or four times to Sissinghurst, always with Leonard and never for a night. Their letters became gradually fewer, until the Second War stirred the embers of their old love. But not sufficiently to save Virginia from suicide. Long afterwards, Vita wrote to my father, "I think I might have saved her if only I had been there and had known the state of her mind." I do not believe this. If Leonard and Vanessa were both unaware of her intention, she would have been unlikely to reveal it to Vita. The reason why she killed herself was not that she feared madness or found the stress of war unendurable but that she thought she had lost the gift of writing, and what was the purpose of life if she could not describe it?

EDITING VIRGINIA WOOLF'S LETTERS

This was the tentative conclusion that Joanne Trautmann and I came to as we annotated the second of her suicide notes to Leonard, late one night at Sissinghurst in 1979. We had dreaded that moment, knowing that we must bear witness to the horrifying death of the woman whom we had come to know better than our own mothers. In fact, we became so engrossed in interpreting the evidence—when was the first suicide note written? Was there any change in her handwriting to indicate madness? Where did she leave the notes?—that having drafted an appendix with our conclusions, we separated, quite calmly, for bed.

But I am anticipating. In 1971 Joanne Trautmann was an American academic on a year's leave of absence in England, studying aspects of Virginia Woolf's life, and she consulted me on Virginia's relationship with Vita. We first met in May of that year. I saw a young woman with sleek black hair, eager, scholarly, merry, and I immediately took to her. She sent me her chapter on Vita–Virginia. I thought it admirable. When Quentin Bell invited me two years later to edit Virginia's letters, I accepted on condition that I could have an American collaborator, because over half the surviving letters were in United States libraries, primarily the Berg Collection in New York, and I could not always be crossing the Atlantic to inspect them. Jo Trautmann was my first choice. She was very familiar with Bloomsbury literature, totally reliable as a researcher and delightful as a companion. By then she was Professor of Literature at Penn State's College of Medicine at Hershey and could spare only two months a year to edit the volumes. I offered her credit but not much money. She immediately wrote back, "Let's do it!"

The first two-month marathon was spent in accumulating the letters and arranging them in chronological order. Our mentor was Olivier, Quentin Bell's wife, who had done the research for his two-volume life of his aunt and was the world authority on Bloomsbury, its ramifications, chronology and liaisons. She was about to edit Virginia's diaries, a lap behind us, for which we were paradoxically grateful, since if her five volumes had appeared ahead of our six we would inevitably have plagiarized her notes, for she was unequalled in tracing Virginia's most obscure allusions and acquaintances. Her first act of generosity was to supply us with her own datings of the letters and the names and addresses of all Virginia's surviving friends or their heirs, whom we would entreat to search their attics. When I was at school I received half a dozen letters from Virginia and threw them away when I had answered them, so I was in no position to reproach others, but most people had kept them from an early age, and the letters to her four major correspondents, Vanessa, Vita, Ethel Smyth and Violet Dickinson, had been preserved almost intact, with very many of their replies. Olivier also made available the typescripts of Virginia's diaries, which were essential to us as an additional source of information on her friendships and occupations. As we completed each volume, she checked it for accuracy. That was not all. Her unfailing cheerfulness buoyed us through occasional troughs of despair. Quentin, the wise old counselor, was Nestor to her Helen.

Jo Trautmann has published her own account of our collaboration in the *Charleston Magazine* of spring/summer 1996. There she makes out that I was a Holmes among literary detectives. In fact, most of the information that we needed was available in the small room at Sissinghurst, known ever since as the Virginia Room, where we sat at facing desks surrounded by biographies and works of reference. I would call across to her, "Did she write passable or passible?" and she would ask, "What does pump ship mean in English slang?" When we were stumped, we made lists for our researchers, who would ransack the British Library, the London Library and the Colindale newspaper library for the answers. We and they would take endless trouble to discover the identity of "Phoebe" whom Virginia met once at a party. Who would care who Phoebe was? We did. We wanted to impress Olivier.

For volume III (the Vita volume) we employed as our researcher my daughter Juliet. For volume IV it was an American girl of infinite resource and charm, Jane Lancellotti. For volume V it was Lorraine Helms, another American, who was too old (about thirty) to take kindly to our teasing and goading. And for the sixth volume we employed Kate Stout from Louisville, Kentucky, the best of the lot. In addition, we had a team of typists, Pamela Kilbane (who doubled as the National Trust's administrator at Sissinghurst), Valerie Henderson, Jane Carr and Lyn Dunbar, who was also, for several years in succession, our cook. It was quite an industry, a cottage industry, it is true, but remarkably professional. Jo would come each year for June and July, and the major part of our work on the current volume was completed during those months. It became a matter of pride for me to hand over the corrected typescript to Norah Smallwood of the Hogarth Press on 1 September.

One of our early problems was to decipher Virginia's handwriting. When she was young, it was a spider's scrawl. In her maturity it was elegant but hasty. Pamela Kilbane became an expert at reading it, and it was very seldom that we were obliged to confess *illegible*. One important word totally defeated us, and I reproduce it here to invite the help of cryptologists:

It comes in the postscript of a letter to Leonard in November 1912. 'Shall you get any ******* from Craig?' Craig was her doctor. The word cannot be "onions." Doctors don't supply onions to their patients and there was no shortage of them at Rodmell. In our note we suggested that the word was "'assions"; a private shorthand word for contraceptives, and if we were right it throws a startling new light on Virginia's alleged frigidity. But were we?

Another problem was discretion. Virginia was notorious for her merciless descriptions of friends in writing to other friends. She would call Middleton Murry "a posturing, Byronic little man; pale; penetrating; with bad teeth; histrionic; an egotist; and writes the poetry a very old hack might write." She wrote of Will Arnold-Forster's "little mongrel cur's body: his face appears

powdered and painted like a very refined old suburban harlot's, and his ridiculous little voice." It was all part of the Bloomsbury style. You wrote like that
to X and Y, knowing full well that Y was writing to Z in a similar vein about
you. If the libel were repeated to you, you minded quite a lot, but repetition
was rare. If Clive Bell intended to read aloud a letter from Virginia, he would
be careful to peruse it first and mentally mark passages for excision. This discretion, however, was not always available to the editors of the collected letters. We could sometimes put dots, and explain them by "Twelve words
omitted," which had the immediate effect of sending the person whose feel-
ings we had hoped to spare straight to the original letter in Sussex University
or New York. Frequent victims of Virginia's scorn were Lydia Keynes, whom
all Bloomsbury ridiculed, and Ottoline Morrell, but her cruellest jibes were reserved for Barbara Bagenal, who was unwise enough to call on the Woolfs at
Monk's House in October 1938, accompanied by her husband, Nick, and her
daughter, Judith. Barbara had been very helpful to us, particularly for the
early Asham and Richmond periods, when she had been an assistant at the
Hogarth Press. She retained for Virginia an affection which she imagined to be
reciprocated. This is part of Virginia's letter to Vanessa describing the visit,
with our bracketed attempts to conceal the Bagenals' identity:

A face at the window. A voice. "May we come in, Virginia?" A jersey;
trousers; bright red cheeks; glassy blue eyes. [*Name omitted.*] An interval of sheer horror: of unmitigated despair. So we had them for
four hours by the clock. . . . After they'd gone, we both agreed that
the poor [*names omitted*] are in the lowest rung of life; water-blooded;
blowsy; grumpy; servile; their eyes all flies; [*her daughter*] such a trial;
no friends; boys so stupid; can't pass exams; no money; no servants.
L. Took [*him*] round the garden. He too giggles. Not a drop of hope
or health in them.

Barbara did not live long after this bowdlerized letter was published, and
we hope that she never read it, for to her, if to nobody else, it would have been
plain that the omitted names were hers, Nick's and Judith's.

I faced a more difficult dilemma in the case of Raymond Mortimer. He
was my father's most intimate friend. He was one of the new generation of

Bloomsberries, had known the Woolfs well and we consulted him many times. Imagine, then, my distress at coming across phrases like this in Virginia's letters:

> Vanessa says that she doesn't mind how much it rains [at Cassis]. so long as Raymond 'ain't there.
> He's a male [Lady] Colefax, just out of his shell.
> What a damned snob he is.
> He yapped like a fox-terrier, all about nothing.
> Raymond I can't cotton to, though his virtues are as prominent as his nose.

There were other more flattering references, and I made the most of them in the index under Mortimer, R.: "Very charming"; "Fresh as a lark"; "Flowing, scintillating"; and I buried the insults under a long string of "*mentioned*"s, hoping that Raymond would not bother to turn to the relevant pages. Of course he did, and though he never complained to me, friends told me that he was deeply hurt.

Jo had the "American" letters typed at Hershey, and I the "English" letters at home. When she arrived annually at Sissinghurst, our first task was to interleave our two sets in chronological order, then we sat up, often till midnight, arranging and annotating them. She was so good at her job that the secretaries would bypass the editor with some query and make straight for the co-editor. I admired her quickness, her accuracy, her memory and persistence. She had a sounder knowledge of English literature than I had, while I was more conversant with the history of the period before she was born, and had known many of the characters involved, including Virginia herself. Some of them visited us. The backstairs to the Virginia Room echoed to the footsteps of V. S. Pritchett, George Rylands, Jeremy Hutchinson, Barbara Bagenal, Stephen Spender, John Lehmann, Richard Shone, my brother Ben, James Lees-Milne and, among the Americans, Stanley Weintraub and Jack Willis, the historian of the Hogarth Press. Jo delighted them all. She was the least dry scholar whom I have ever known. She could sing and dance, play badminton. She was excellent at any party, including Juliet's wedding.

Most years, she and I would contrive a holiday from our work. It could not last long and it must not be too expensive, because the six volumes did not earn us much more than the cost of editing them, after we had paid for the xeroxes, the typists, the researchers and the cook. Quentin Bell and his sister, the copyright holders, were entitled to their share of the royalties. Indeed, had it not been for the success of *Portrait of a Marriage* it is doubtful whether Jo and I could have afforded a holiday of any kind.

The first, in 1974, was the grandest, for we were invited to stay with Dan Silberberg, a Wall Street banker, in his villa at St Tropez. The night before we left England we dined with George Weidenfeld, and Jo found herself partnered by Freddie Ayer, whom she asked whether it was true that he was the world's most famous philosopher. "No," Ayer replied, "only the third most famous." He completely fell for her. He pursued her with letters and telegrams to St Tropez, and told her that she was wasting her talents on such a footling occupation as editing someone else's letters. Jo was amused. She met him only twice more, innocently, and Freddie gave up. So did the beach gigolo who fell in love with her at St Tropez, and the postmaster in our local town, Cranbrook, who asked her if she was Liza Minelli.

In the summer of 1975 we went to St Ives in Cornwall to see the lighthouse of Virginia's novel and the house where she had spent many childhood holidays. Next year we went to Wales and walked the clifftop of Manorbier, where Virginia had decided to devote her life to literature. We visited Dylan Thomas's grave at Laugharne and stayed two nights with the Angleseys at Plas Newydd. There were minor trips to Stratford, to a ball at the American Embassy, and frequently to Sussex University to study the "replies" under the eye of the excellent curator of manuscripts, Elizabeth Inglis. When we had finished the last volume we went back to Monk's House and sat on the banks of the Stour to contemplate its ugly waters.

In between her visits we corresponded almost weekly. I would write to her, "Send Amy [Henderson] to Chicago, and tell her to charm that old woman into letting us see the originals of V's letters to Lytton." She would write to me, "There may be some Colefax letters in one of the smaller Harvard libraries. I doubt it, but I will follow up the lead." Our correspondence lengthened into an archive almost as massive as the one we were editing. It continues to this day, for new letters are always surfacing. The most startling of them were found at Sissinghurst itself. A Dutch student, Patty Brandhorst, was sitting at my mother's writing table in the tower, toying with the table top, when suddenly she felt it move. It concealed three drawers, from one of which she pulled four previously unknown letters from Virginia to my mother, which contained some passages that Vita must have thought too saucy for publication, and omitted them when she sold the bulk of the collection to the Berg. Jo edited them for the *Virginia Woolf Miscellany* in 1994. Previously she had edited a one-volume selection from the letters, including many of the "too lates." She married Samuel Banks, a distinguished academic, and they now live in Tierra Verde, Florida. She has made her career principally in the study of the connections between literature and medicine, and lectures, as I have, in many parts of the United States on our favorite subject, Virginia. Of all the by-products of our joint endeavour, the one that I value most is not, as Jo has written, "prolonged contact with the dazzling facets of Virginia's mind," but my friendship with Jo herself.

In the year after the publication of our sixth volume, two American scholars, Louise DeSalvo and Mitchell Leaska, edited Vita's letters to Virginia, which included the best letters, specially those from Persia in 1926–7, that she ever wrote. The two scholars disagreed on editorial priorities and were scarcely on speaking terms at the launch party in New York in 1980. I stood between them like the referee before a boxing match. I took Leaska's side in the dispute, which made me, to my great regret, the enemy of DeSalvo.

MONK'S HOUSE AND CHARLESTON

I played some part in preserving for the public the two sister-houses that will always be associated with Bloomsbury, Monk's House for Leonard and Virginia Woolf, and Charleston for Vanessa Bell and Duncan Grant. I persuaded the National Trust to accept Monk's House as a gift from Sussex University and the Trust quickly raised an endowment of £75,000. Charleston was a different matter. While Monk's House was little larger than a cottage, Charleston was a roomy farmhouse and, while Monk's contained few works of art, at Charleston every wall, every piece of furniture, down to the very log bins had been decorated by Duncan and Vanessa and their painter friends over a period of sixty years. The house was in a very bad condition. In the last years of his life Duncan was almost unaware of its slow deterioration. What was to be done with it? The Bells had been discussing the problem for some time when an unexpected *diva* appeared, in the person of Deborah (Debo) Gage, a young woman related to the owners of Firle Place. Charleston was one of their estate farms, which Duncan rented from them. Debo proposed to Quentin that they should form a Trust to buy the house and restore it, not just as a memorial to Duncan and Vanessa but to preserve the finest example of a particular period of English painting and decoration. The task was colossal. The roof must be rebuilt and part of the foundations, and in several of the main rooms the walls were covered with rotting layered wallpaper, distempered and overpainted by the artists in the 1920s. The Trust was formed in 1980. I joined the Committee, of which Quentin was Chairman and Debo was Secretary. For two years I succeeded Quentin in the chair, before handing it over to Robert Skidelsky, the biographer of Keynes, who lived at nearby Tilton, Keynes's own house.

In the end, we raised nearly £1,000,000. Part of this huge sum was achieved by selling at Sotheby's the Bells' valuable Woolf papers and paintings given by our supporters, but the bulk was raised by Debo herself in America, notably from Mrs Lila Wallace, the widow of the owner of the *Reader's Digest*. As a fund-raiser I was useless. I was the nominal leader of an expedition to Dallas in 1984, where Debo had organized a program of lectures on Bloomsbury-related subjects to be given by Michael Holroyd, Margaret Drabble, Angelica Garnett, Richard Shone, the Duke of Devonshire and myself, and a dinner was held for sixty wealthy people at which I was instructed to make the keynote appeal for funds. Overcome by British reserve, I failed to end my speech by asking the audience for money. As a result, they gave none. Why should they? To Dallas it meant very little that Lytton Strachey had read a chapter of *Eminent Victorians* at Charleston, or that Keynes had drafted *The Economic Consequences of the Peace* in an upstairs bedroom. More interesting to them was the visit to Dallas of Princess Margaret that coincided with our own. Though their hospitality was generous, I suspected that they were growing tired of Brits coming to Dallas to beg.

We persevered. The costs were enormous. Wallpaper which might have been decorated with a sponge in a single afternoon, cost £20,000 to restore. Creeping damp was a constant drain upon the walls and our resources. But gradually it all came together. Richard Shone, the authority on Bloomsbury painting, with Peter Miall as his adjutant, supervised the restoration of the works of art, and equal care was given to the garden. We opened the house to the public in 1986, and it has since become the chief visual memorial to the Bloomsbury Group.

We offered the restored building to the National Trust. They said that they could only accept it if we raised an endowment of £600,000. I suspected that the Trust's Executive Committee, then under the chairmanship of Lord Gibson, did not greatly care for Bloomsbury and doubted whether its fame would survive. They had done their duty by accepting Monk's House. For Charleston they set a target which they knew would be beyond our means. But between us we managed to save both. Charleston, as it turned out, is more visited than Monk's, but it is to Monk's that I more frequently return. Once, in the summer of 1995, it was with Denis Healey and his wife, Edna, when we recorded a talk for Radio 4. We wandered round the house, chatting amicably, he about Leonard, I about Virginia, and when we came to the spot in the garden where their ashes are buried, Denis began to read a passage from Virginia's diary. After a few sentences he broke down in uncontrollable sobs, which the BBC duly broadcast a month later. I was much moved myself. There can be no greater justification for preserving the houses of artists of genius than this demonstration of their lasting significance to men and women of his quality.

VIRGINIA AND VITA ON STAGE

The British public are ambivalent about Bloomsbury. Reviews of Bloomsbury books in the literary journals are apt to start by saying that all such books are boring, except this one, which is unexpectedly fascinating. The legend that they were a self-admiring, decadent clique died hard, in spite of Quentin Bell's life of Virginia, which showed, among much else, how self-critical they were, and Holroyd's biography of Lytton Strachey, which demonstrated how profoundly they affected public attitudes to religion, sex, art, politics, literature and much else. We are still the inheritors. They were exceptional people, who in several fields achieved the most difficult of human ambitions, to give an art (and in the case of Keynes and Leonard Woolf, a political doctrine) a new form which was valid to contemporaries and of lasting influence.

Of all their multi-faceted relationships, those between Strachey and Carrington, and Virginia and Vita, continued to arouse the greatest speculation and astonishment. The first to dramatise the Vita–Virginia affair was the novelist Edna O'Brien. She had allowed me to read the script. It seemed to me magical. Nervously I asked her if she really intended that the two women should appear on the stage in the nude, as the script indicated. At one point Virginia takes a bath, and at another Vita removes her dressing gown. "Oh no," replied Edna. "In those days women wore shifts." "But surely not when they were having a bath or making love?" "Well, the lights will go out," said Edna. When the play was eventually staged in 1980, no such scenes were performed. Maggie Smith played Virginia, giving every nuance of her character with an accuracy that astonished me, and the actor who played Leonard had exactly his chunky, defensive, tolerant, nervous charm. But the woman, Patricia Connolly, who played Vita was badly cast, a combination of Eva Peron and Mae West. It was so outrageously wrong that I laughed. I met her afterwards at Edna's party. She told me that she had been conscious of me sitting there, and wondered what I thought of her performance. I didn't dare tell her. Maggie Smith had read everything about Virginia Woolf and was eager to know more. We were getting on famously, when Claire Bloom, the actress, came up. Maggie Smith, turning to me, said, "Claire, I'd like you to meet Quentin Bell." I said nothing.

Next came Eileen Atkins's adaptation of the Virginia–Vita correspondence at Chichester, when she played Virginia and Penelope Wilton was Vita. It was ingeniously done. Only fragments of a letter are normally written in direct reply to the other person's, but by a judicious selection and some legitimate transposition Eileen had shaped their correspondence into a dialogue, most of it spoken face to face, and some, ruminatively, apart. To see one's mother portrayed by an actress less than half one's own age is not as weird an experience as one might imagine. One reason was that Penelope Wilton was not like Vita. She couldn't be and didn't need to be. No actress can totally shed her own personality in reproducing that of another woman whom she has never known. Besides, the Vita of the early 1920s, when most of the action took place, was not the Vita that I remembered. She was at the stage of her life when she was pouring out novels and poetry in a spate of creativity, planting her first garden at Long Barn, packing her bags for Persia or Italy, and falling in and out of love. She toyed with Virginia half flirtatiously, half apprehensively, wondering all the time why this gifted woman should have picked on her. Penelope conveyed all this superbly. Eileen Atkins played Virginia with the affectionate raillery that I well remember in her, judging to a nicety the degree to which she could provoke Vita without losing her, now languid on a *chaise longue*, now striding about the stage masterfully, with a great deal of gesticulation to indicate where the words would have been italicized. I attended the first performance at Chichester, and the director, Patrick Garland, led me to the stage for a sort of curtain call. I was able, quite genuinely, to congratulate both actresses, who had been kept unaware that I was there.

The play moved to London, but it was not well attended. Then in 1994 it moved to New York, where it was a triumph. Penelope had not been able to get the necessary permit to perform in America, and Vanessa Redgrave took her role as Vita. With my daughter Rebecca I attended a rehearsal in the Union Theatre, just off Broadway. "How," Vanessa Redgrave asked me from the stage, "would they have pronounced the word 'trough?'" "Troff," I replied firmly. "Was it Long *Barn* or *Long* Barn?" The stress should be equal on both words. Would a sophisticated New York audience know who Tom [Eliot] was, or Lytton? Yes, they would. And then, "If Vita was announced by a flunkey at a very grand reception, would he have said 'Mrs Harold Nicolson' or 'Miss Victoria Sackville-West'?" He would have said Mrs Harold Nicolson and she would have hit him.

Eileen Atkins again impressed me how closely she resembled the Virginia Woolf whom I had known, languid, with spurts of fire and fun. But Vanessa Redgrave was like Vanessa Redgrave. In appearance and manner she did not resemble Vita, but the Vita that Vita would have wished to have been. In fact, the play was an improvement on real life. Vita was rather scared of Virginia. But if she had been made to seem subordinate the play would never have worked so well. It was a duel. One could hear the distant click of rapiers. But it was also a relationship animated by deep mutual attraction, and that is exactly how it was in life.

THREE

THE STUDENT

I t is strange that I cannot see the child-me in the man-me. A biographer imagines that he can detect characteristics, tastes and opinions early in life, but the autobiographer knows that these things take time to develop, like my interest in books, architecture, maps, archaeology, history, nature. As for opinions, I had none. I suffered as a small child from a lack of guile, an uncompetitive spirit, hoping to be loved, fearing rejection. I was known in the family as "sweet little Niggs," in contrast to Ben, who was thought moody. So it was as sweet little Niggs that I was propelled at the age of eight into the concentration camps of boarding schools. We did not consider this practice cruel. It was an inevitable stage through which one had to pass, and it is only sixty years later that I have come to realize that parents like mine were relieved to be free from their troublesome children for eight months in the year, while congratulating themselves on giving us a great start in life.

My first school was a square, yellow house up the hill from Long Barn where I was taught the rudiments of reading and writing. First I had to learn to talk, and I am still filled with amazement when contemplating my grandchildren that they achieve this miracle so quickly. Never can mental alertness be so sharp than at the age of four. Before they have even heard of Shakespeare, they can frame sentences as complex as: "I'll let you down if you give me up," which they can never have heard spoken by an adult. Equipped with these three essential tools, speaking, reading and writing, I went to a London day school, Mr. Gladstone's, off Sloane Square, where Harold Macmillan also started his schooling, and from that moment I followed in his footsteps to Summer Fields, Oxford; Eton College; Balliol College, Oxford; the Grenadier Guards; and the back-benches of the House of Commons. Thereafter, our paths diverged.

SUMMER FIELDS

Ben was already there, which was some consolation. I was Nicolson mi. Like most other boys I was deeply unhappy when abandoned by my mother in the same room where I abandoned my son Adam forty years later, and unlike him, I cried myself to sleep for the first three nights. I can still feel the coldness of the sheets on which I dried my tears. The experience was worsened by the ridicule aroused by the gray shorts which Vita had packed for me instead of trousers. I tried to hide my bare knees behind the desks, but when I came to stand in line to enter the dining room for breakfast, there was no disguising their incongruity.

I was happy at Summer Fields. It taught me the pleasure of sustained effort, even if it ended only in a second prize for Latin. But one's small triumphs were always spoiled by greater fears—the fear of unpopularity and unpunctuality, of humiliation in class or on the cricket field, of losing a library book, of being found out stealing a sweet, of the coming swimming race—all of which fears we concealed from our parents. They kept my letters, and rereading them, I can still detect the little lies, the little boasts, with which I tried to cover up my anxieties. "I've started boxing. It's quite easy, really. I knocked out a boy yesterday." And this, aged nine:

My dearest, darling family,
    In Greek I am really flourishing. Although I was bottom in the exam, and hardly know a word of Greek, I have got a treble remove.
    Your loving son,
        Nigel Nicolson

Two things puzzle me about that letter: the contrast between the affectionate opening and the formal ending; and the paradox of my undeserved promotion.

Life was spartan. Although we were by no means starved, food meant so much to us that we would carefully count out an equal number of peas served with Sunday lunch—sometimes it was thirty-three, sometimes twenty-six—and the greatest treat of the year was a strawberry tea on the headmaster's lawn at the end of the summer term. The most primitive of the facilities was the lavatory. A row of twenty pierced seats was flushed by a sewer in continuous flow. It was known as the vinery rush. The great joke was to light a bunched-up newspaper and drop it through the aperture of seat 1. It would float down the alley, toasting all nineteen bottoms as it passed. The masters never knew of this, because the vinery was the one place that they never entered. Otherwise, discipline was strict. The severest punishment was a caning on the bare behind: more often it was three strokes on the hand, which one must not withdraw after the first stroke for fear of incurring a fourth. Once I caught out the headmaster in an injustice. He sent for me to his study, the place of maximum execution, and upbraided me for a crime that I had not committed. He ended, "Bend over, Nichol-Smith." "Please, sir, I'm not Nichol-Smith. I'm Nicolson mi." It was the first time that I became aware that grown-ups, too, could blush and apologize.

As we slowly ascended the school, small privileges bolstered our self-esteem. We became "league-leaders." We wore a badge on the breast pocket of our rugger shirts to signify membership of the First XV. We sat in the Fifth Form room where the hand-caning was administered to other boys sent there from junior classes. And we said grace before lunch in the dining hall: *Agimus tibi gratias omnipotens deus pro his et universis donis tuis,* it began (Thank you, Almighty God, for this and your other manifold gifts), and went on for quite some time. At the end of the meal, the Almighty was thanked again in a different speech, again in Latin. We had to learn both by heart. That was no problem. It was the terror of hearing one's own voice ringing out in front of one hundred twenty masters and boys, identical to the terror I experienced on rising to my feet to make my maiden speech in the House of Commons.

Among the masters were Leonard Strong, the novelist, and Cecil Day-Lewis, the future poet laureate. Among my contemporaries were a few whom I continued to know in later life: Dickie Paget-Cooke, whom I count as my oldest friend; Alfred Shaughnessy who later achieved fame as the script writer of *Upstairs, Downstairs;* Francis Egerton, of Malletts, the antique dealers; Archie Wavell, son of the Field Marshal; and most glamorous of all, Julian Amery, already a statesman in embryo, who was alleged to speak Latin on weekdays and Greek on Sundays, read *The Times* daily, smoothed his hair with brilliantine, and when he was aged ten started a speech to our debating society, "Mr. President, I am in favour of conscription; I have been so all my life," according to Nicholas Henderson, another star, who became in turn British Ambassador in Warsaw, Bonn, Paris and Washington, a record.

I was not a star but advanced far enough to be nominated as the boy most likely to sustain the school's unbroken tradition of winning a major scholarship to Eton. We were taken by the classics master, Geoffrey Bolton, to stay for the four days of the exam at the White Hart Hotel, Windsor, and each morning he walked us down Eton High Street to the Examination Rooms and waited outside for two hours until we emerged. He would then grab the exam paper, rapidly scan it for any question to which he had failed to teach us the answer, and others on which he had thoroughly briefed us. "Oh, sir," I said. "I got *Works and Days* right. It was written by Homer, wasn't it?" "Hesiod, boy, Hesiod," he said in despair. The honours board in the school dining room at Summer Fields bears the name Nicolson, B., for Ben's minor scholarship two years earlier. There is no mention of Nicolson, N.

Ben was generous to his brother. When he was already at Eton, and I still at Summer Fields, he posted me a book every month. The parcel felt like a book and passed scrutiny. In fact, it was hollowed out and filled with sweets. I posted it back to him ("How splendid of Nicolson to take such an interest in his brother's lessons"), and it circulated undetected between us, and made me extremely popular in the dorm.

ETON

On my last evening at Summer Fields, the headmaster, Cyril Williams, invited the school-leavers into his study not for a caning but for a glass of port and a lecture on the facts of life. In the early 1930s, boys of twelve were still very innocent. A junior master was discovered snuggling up to a boy after lights-out and was sacked next day, but none of us had any conception of the enormity of his sin. We thought that he was merely showing unusual affection. So when Dr. Williams began his dissertation we stared at the floor, scarcely comprehending it and deeply embarrassed. I forgot what terms he used. Probably elliptical, like "your thing." He talked about puberty and its consequences, but said nothing, as far as I can recall, about homosexual love.

When we arrived at Eton we were still very ignorant. Dr. Williams's homily had not been supplemented by any parental advice until I wrote to my father, who was in America, about masturbation. He replied in a six-page letter (distance overcoming his diffidence), of which the gist was "Only on Saturdays." He, too, said nothing about homosexuality, which was rampant at Eton as in all boarding schools, and he could not bring himself to discuss with me the question of girls, of whom he had had but limited experience himself. In any case, girls were never mentioned at school. A sister's photograph might sometimes be observed on a boy's desk, but it was never subjected to scrutiny or inquiry. An unusually attractive girl regularly attended evening chapel in order to excite the admiration of the older boys, but they responded only with sidelong glances, never a provocative stare. That would not happen now. Two years ago I revisited my old room to find its walls covered with pin-ups. The present occupant, aged seventeen, was unabashed.

There have been other changes. Fagging, the system which obliged younger boys to be servants of the older, cleaning their boots, cooking their suppers, running their errands, was abolished many years ago. I benefited from it to the extent that I learnt how to fry sausages and scramble eggs, and in return I was helped by my fag-masters with my own work and problems. One of them was Charles Villiers, the future Chairman of the British Steel Corporation, whom I never saw again until he gave evidence for Lord Aldington in the famous Tolstoy trial of 1989. Another revolution was the abolition of flogging. In our house, the senior boy carried out the caning (Villiers was very good at it), and for major crimes the headmaster applied the birch while two senior boys held the culprit down. Ben endured this. I never did. It still astonishes me that so humane a man as Robert Birley, assistant master while I was at Eton and Head Master after I left, could bring himself to hurt young boys so brutally. I once asked him the reason, and he replied that abolition was so strongly resisted by Old Etonians, who had enjoyed their floggings, that it would have caused an upheaval to do away with it. That upheaval has now taken place.

We did not work so intensively as we had at Summer Fields. For much of the time we studied unsupervised in our own rooms. There were "saying-lessons," thirty lines of poetry which I would read over twice before going to sleep and repeat word-perfect next morning. There were Sunday Questions, and Extra Work. There was that peculiar Eton system called Private Business, when two or three of us gathered in our tutor's study to discuss a book or a play, and he would treat us much as an Oxford tutor would treat undergraduates. Then there were societies, like the Essay Society, which met in Robert Birley's house, and one of us would read a paper on a subject of our choice. Mine was on Pytheas, the first Greek to discover Britain, for I was fascinated by Greek literature and history, largely owing to the encouragement of another master, George Tait, who taught Greek archaeology, and Francis Crusoe, who once told us to abandon the word-by-word construing of Plato's *Phaedo* and put away our books, while he read to us in English the concluding chapters describing Socrates' death. This, I thought then, and believe even more strongly now, is how the classics should be taught. What one loses by translation, one gains in intelligibility. That was a great moment in my education.

One Sunday evening the lights failed in the school chapel, and Cyril Alington, the Head Master, mounted the pulpit to deliver his traditional "Bedtime Story." His beautiful Gothic face was illuminated by a solitary candle. He told us the story of the fall of the Romanovs. It was a performance deliberately designed to arouse fear and pity, and admiration for the speaker, and it aroused all three. That was a rare contact with one so eminent. It was Robert Birley who gently pulled me out of childhood. He would often dine with my housemaster, A. H. G. Kerry, and afterwards come to my room, and hands behind his back, bounced off the wall, shy at first, as I was, and then he would ask a question, "What are you reading?," "Is that your house?" and we would talk. He was the only Eton master with whom I formed a friendship in later life. When I was twenty-one, he told me to stop calling him "sir." "Try 'Robert.' You'll find that it will come quite easily after the first dozen times." "Yes . . . sir."

I was a swot. I was someone who enjoyed his work and took more trouble over it than was strictly necessary. That was considered bad form at Eton except for King's Scholars and boys who hoped to win a prize or scholarship and were reduced to reading with a torch under the bedclothes after lights-out. I usually gained a distinction in Trials (no great rarity), but when I eventually attained the Head Master's division and was taught by that great scholar Walter Hamilton, I often found myself out of my depth in the company of brilliant boys like Stubbs, whose first name I never knew and of whom none of us has heard anything since.

Sports meant a lot to me. When I was sixteen, we had just sat down to supper in my house when the captain of our football team, passing behind my chair, dropped into my lap a cap—my house colors. Everyone laughed and cheered, and I felt that life could have nothing more to offer. In the summer I was a wet-bob, an oarsman. The pleasures of rowing are ineffaceable. There is nothing like it for rhythm except dancing. The apparatus is beautiful—the long, slender shell of a racing eight, the subtle curve of the oar's blade. The scenery is beautiful, on the stretch of the Thames between Maidenhead and Windsor. The motion is beautiful—the seat running on tiny wheels, telescoping and straightening the body, and the oval described by one's rotating hands. And the company is beautiful, all eight striving in unison toward a common end. It could also be terrifying. I have never experienced such tension as at the start of a race, knowing that utter relaxation must be replaced in a split second by maximum and unrelieved exertion—and the fear of catching a crab.

I never did catch a crab in a race, but I once suffered a far greater humiliation. As a very junior boy I was idly turning my sculling boat in mid-river. There was much shouting, but I paid no attention. Then suddenly I caught sight of the flash of pale-blue oars as they dug violently into the water not twenty feet away. It was the school's eight, halted by me at the climax of their trial course. I feared an eight-tanning, an ordeal described to me by an earlier victim. He was summoned to the Eights Room, where the crew was assembled, every one of them a hero, and each of them in turn, from bow to stroke, delivered on his bent bottom a stinging swipe of the cane. He counted the blows, ". . . six, seven, eight," and then got up. "Get down again!" shouted the Captain of Boats. He had forgotten the cox. At last able to compete in virility with his crew, the cox hit hardest, hurt most, said my friend. I was spared this ordeal.

My holidays from Eton are memorable for three events. The first was in 1933, when I went to Sanary in southern France to stay with Aldous and Maria Huxley as a companion for their son Matthew. We had not met before. I described the encounter in a letter to Ben:

I was met at Bandol station by Mrs. Huxley, a very painted, brightly dressed young woman, speaking with a strong French accent. She drove me in a bumpy car over bumpy roads to their villa, and a little boy in shorts and a green blazer with a crest on it opened the door. This was Matthew. He took me to my room carrying my suitcase. I said, 'Are you sure that's not too heavy for you?' That was my first mistake. Then he showed me his model railway, and I asked, 'Is it electric?' 'Of course it is,' he replied nastily. Next I messed up the points. Then I saw Aldous. He has the fattest lenses in his specs that I have ever seen, but even so, he has to bend right down to read anything and looks so close that he has to move his whole face to follow a line of print. At lunch it was all very embarrassing. Matthew asked his father, 'Is your wireless guaranteed, Aldous?' (he calls him Aldous). Aldous didn't answer. Matthew repeated his question. 'Quiet, child,' said Aldous. Then Maria smoothed things over. Aldous terrifies me.

Things improved after that. The Huxleys took me to visit the Noailles in their house on the Iles d'Hyères, and I was shocked to see the Count applying lipstick to the lips, toe-nails and nipples of a nude statue of Cleopatra.

It was on my return from Sanary that I nearly died of appendicitis. I thought that my internal pains were due to nothing more than a surfeit of cherries, until they grew so acute that I moaned in agony. The exams in which I hoped to shine were about to start, and when asked about my condition I lied. I said it was only a tummyache. The house dame, Nancy Hichens, did not believe me. She fetched the school doctor. He diagnosed acute appendicitis. Vita and Harold were told, and rushed to Eton. I was driven to London wrapped in a blanket and operated on immediately by the surgeon, Lancelot Barrington-Ward. The appendix was found to be twisted and exceedingly dangerous. When I recovered, I had a lovely time. I was showered with presents and visited by many people, including John Sparrow, Robert Birley and, to my delight, Gerald Heard, Bloomsbury's scientist, who examined my wound with flattering intensity. And it was then that I discovered Anthony Trollope.

In 1935 we went on a cruise to Greece with Irene Ravensdale (Curzon's daughter) and the novelist Hugh Walpole. Early one morning my father woke me up and took me on deck. Pointing to low hills on the horizon, he said, "Look, that's the Peloponnese." I had never seen Greece before and was in my most emotional philhellenistic phase. We stood there in silence and there was no moment in our relationship when we felt closer together. Next day, the ship grounded on a sandbank outside the Gulf of Corinth and Harold lectured to the passengers on Byron's last journey to Missolonghi, which was visible on the port bow. Tugs from Piraeus eventually pulled us off, but we lost three days.

To make up for missing Mycenae I returned to Greece alone three years later, and walked from Athens to Olympia via Corinth and Sparta. I had no money. I needed none, as I lived off the fruit and bread tossed to me by the peasants, and slept under olive trees. In those prewar days the wilder parts of Greece were roadless. I was making my way in moonlight through the gorge of the Taygetus mountains. The path, cut into the cliff face, with a sheer wall on one side and a precipitous drop on the other, was narrow and treacherous. Rounding a corner, I confronted a huge dog barring my way. Whether I advanced or retreated, it growled with horrible ferocity, and for four hours we faced each other till dawn and the shepherd came. Fifty years later I passed that same spot in a tourist coach and told my story to Sue Baring to impress her. But the mildness of the scene, the comfort of the coach, the smoothness of the new road, diminished its appeal.

From Kalamata I walked to Phigalea and climbed the mountain slope to visit the temple of Apollo at Bassae, one of the loveliest and most remote of fifth-century temples, designed by Ictinus, the architect of the Parthenon. I lost my way when darkness fell and lay down to sleep on a bed of corn husks. In the dawn I saw the temple, only two hundred yards away, shimmering in the half-light. I pressed on to Olympia, crossing the River Alphaeus by a ford to which small boys guided me, and entered the ruins to find myself alone. Those were magical moments.

OXFORD

I did not win a scholarship to Balliol, but was admitted in the autumn of 1935 on the strength of my exam papers. At first I was lonely and alarmed. The school chapter of an autobiography is allowed to be a fairly gloomy record, but by the time the author reaches university he is expected to show, by anecdote and deft allusion to names that subsequently became famous, that he was at last in the swim, and that the university meant a sudden flowering of talents and lifelong influences and friends. From me such an account would be false. My letters home were sprightly, but I remember all too well, during the first terms, that I was making the most of small successes and magnifying acquaintances into friendships. How often did I sit miserably beside a miserable fire, hitting at dead coals with a poker and hearing shouts of friend to friend across the quad, and the banging of doors that signified my exclusion.

It was parental expectation that became a burden to me. Harold, too, had been at Balliol. Throughout his life, he said, the very name of Oxford, even on a pot of marmalade, made his pulses race. He wrote to me on the eve of my first term:

The main thing to remember is that Balliol is half a school, and half not a school. In other words, you cannot treat it as a Summer Fields boy would treat Eton when he first goes there. Balliol does not care overmuch for the extent of a man's knowledge: it cares dreadfully for his state of mind. Remember that what they want to find out is whether you are *intelligent*, not whether you are *learned*. They judge intelligence by the extent to which you avoid saying something stupid, rather than by the extent to which you manage to say something bright.

So anxious was I not to say anything stupid, that I hardly said anything at all. I was still very shy. Shyness at nineteen may be a pathetic quality, but it is not stimulating. On arrival at Balliol I found an invitation to lunch with a senior Fellow, Roger Mynors. He greeted me affably, even warmly, but I noticed a quick glance at my eyes for any indication of that intelligence which my father said was essential for a Balliol man. My fellow guests were the Pope-Hennessy brothers, John and James, both undergraduates, whose social and intellectual gifts far exceeded my own. The conversation turned to Piero della Francesca, of whom I had heard, just, but could think of nothing to add to John's flow of erudition and analysis. James took all this in his stride, poking his brother's fires with caustic comment, while I sat silent. Eventually Mynors turned to me:

"What have you been reading lately?"
"*Emma.*"
There was a slight quickening of interest.

"And what did you think of *Emma*?"

"Rather snobbish," I said.

They resumed their discussion of Italian art.

I found John Pope-Hennessy intimidating. At the beginning of my second term, when I had just returned from France, he asked me how I had traveled. "By the ferry from Boulogne." "And what did you think of the new Sassetta in the Boulogne museum?" "I didn't go there. I was late catching the boat." "You mean to say that you were in Boulogne and didn't . . ." He was like that. Throughout his life he alarmed people but owed his distinguished career to the superiority not only of his manner but of his intelligence and learning.

John was more Ben's friend than mine. Ben blossomed at Oxford, while I, at least for the first year, wilted. He had been unhappy at Eton. Later he told me that the only time he had laughed there was when his pious housemaster, the Rev. J. C. Chute, pinned up a notice: "Mrs. Chute cannot conceive why the lower boys are making so much noise" and a wit added a period after "conceive" and a question mark after "why." At Balliol his friends were men whose quality revealed something of Ben's own. Apart from John Pope-Hennessy, they included Stuart Hampshire, Jo Grimond, Francis Graham-Harrison, Jeremy Hutchinson, Lionel Brett, Pat Gibson and three stars who were killed in the war, David Wallace, Jasper Ridley and Guy Branch. Several of them shared lodgings with Ben at 7 Beaumont Street, where I later succeeded him with my group of less scintillating companions, including Rohan Butler, Christopher Hohler and a jovial Portuguese, Peter Bon de Sousa Pernes.

It was James Pope-Hennessy who lifted me from my trough of despond and remained as long as he lived my closest male friend. He took me by the scruff of the neck, declaring my solemnity absurd, and forced me to bicycle with him through Normandy. That was the turning point. I learnt to laugh with him, quarrel with him and enjoy excess. We found ourselves in Bayeux Cathedral, and I observed, "How odd it is that the descendants of the people who built this glorious church can fill it with such hideous effigies in painted wax." James turned on his heel without a word, his Catholic susceptibilities outraged, and took the next train to Paris. A week later I caught sight of him in Notre-Dame. I crept up behind him. "How odd it is . . ." I began. He turned, laughing, and we resumed our journey together without referring to the incident again. That was the James I knew, quick to anger, quick to for-giveness, never sullen, expecting welcome because he was always welcoming, assuming the best in people until confronted by the worst. He was outwardly frivolous, but applied himself to his work with deep seriousness. He was a scholar, treating facts with a respect that he seldom accorded to his friends. He seemed made for Balliol, with his cleverness, slenderness and willowy charm, but he was one of the few among us not to last the course. He left Oxford af-ter two years without taking his degree. He thought the place stuffy. There was the occasion when a delegation of undergraduates waited on him (it now seems incredible) to complain that his gaudy ties were giving the college a bad name. And then there was his essay on the Star Chamber in the reign of Queen Elizabeth I, which I heard him read to our tutor, Kenneth Bell. It was based on the Queen's personality and appearance, starting with her slippers and mounting to her jeweled hair. He was told to do it again, properly. He re-fused. He left the university in a huff and wrote, with Clarissa Churchill as his foil, *London Fabric*, which won the Hawthornden Prize. Though he was "a deal of Ariel, just a streak of Puck," as Henley described R. L. Stevenson, the subject of James's last biography, he was too mature for Oxford. While I found it too free, he found it too restricting. His departure was a terrible blow to me, but his example left much behind.

I began to enjoy myself. I spoke at Union debates; I was Secretary of the Bryce Club; with Niall MacDermot, a future Financial Secretary to the Trea-sury, I organized the university branch of the National Labour Party. I counted among my friends two future political stars, Edward Heath and Denis Healey. I remember Heath playing the organ with great gusto and his laugh, which even then shook his entire body, his undeviating gaze and the touch of puritanism which has persisted in him. Once we went for a walk along the banks of the Cherwell and came to the spot, known as Parson's Pleasure, where undergraduates had for centuries bathed in the nude. Ted had never heard of it and was shocked. "Why," he said, "anyone might come along. *Girls* might come along," and nothing would reassure him. Subsequently, when he was Chief Whip, he did me a great service. He lacked the common touch, but he was a stalwart character, whom history will treat with greater admiration than his contemporaries. Denis Healey was very different. I recall his gift for mimicry and comic ballads, the wide range of his interests, his xenophilia, but nothing of the ruthlessness which he was to show in his political life.

Women were lacking from our lives. We knew that they existed somewhere in the outer suburbs linked academically to our great monastery, but we never met them. In all those years I never once entered a women's college, and never knew a single girl well enough to call her by her first name. We took our cue from the dons, who discouraged heterosexual love as irrelevant to our purpose in being there, and treated girls as bluestockings who could not be expected to understand our male society. There was a don at Hertford who lectured on Edward II. About fifty of us attended his first lecture, including six girls. He looked down the hall, wrapped his gown protectively round him like a toga, and declared, "I do not lecture to *undergraduettes*" (the word was expelled with mordant sarcasm, heavily italicized). Spontaneously, we all rose and walked out. Next week we returned, including the girls, and he surrendered. On our part, it was more a gesture of romantic chivalry, on which we greatly flattered ourselves, than one of university solidarity.

None of us spoke to the girls whose champions we had so unexpectedly become. In the whole of Oxford there was only one woman who ignored the taboo which the women's colleges accepted as their sad lot. She was a White Russian called Tatiana Voronoff. She had heavy artificial eyelashes and long white fingers ringed in amethyst and tapered to lacquered nails. She filled our rooms with strong scent and sexy laughter. There must have been some who loved her, but she was no Zuleika, the goddess who paraded nightly in my imagination, after her creator, Max Beerbohm, suddenly appeared at Balliol and gave me a copy of his book. He had asked to see me because he knew my father. I was the only person in the entire university whose name he knew, and here was a man, I thought, whose name was known to the entire university.

One method of overcoming my shyness was to join the college boat club. I had enjoyed rowing at Eton, rising to the Second Eight, and was a natural candidate for Balliol's crew. It included two Americans, and a Canadian, Hart Massey, as cox, and we were successful enough in the bumping races to be chosen to row at Henley Regatta. Our coach was R. C. Sherriff, author of *Journey's End*. We were in competition with the best crews of several nationalities, and at no moment of my life have I experienced so sustained a wish to excel. For those few days we lived in dread of the next race, discussing tactics, grooming the boat, eating enormously, sleeping long—and then the race began in distant privacy to end ten minutes later between banks of parasols and tumultuous acclaim. Those were ecstatic moments.

Though we never advanced further than the semifinals of the Ladies Plate, Henley was the crux of my rowing career. I was awarded an oar, as a matador is awarded an ear, to hang above my mantelpiece, and the much-coveted membership of Leander entitled me to wear its lovely tie, monochrome in salmon pink. But I was still too reserved to enjoy the bump-suppers, which ended the college races and entailed heavy drinking. I have always suffered from *le vin triste*. At the climax of the evening the Balliol Eight would line up on our side of the wall that separated us from Trinity and yell "Bloody Trinity!" at which the Trinity Eight, on their side, would yell back "Bloody Balliol!" After this duet had continued for some time, we would shout, "Bring out your black man!"; for Trinity had a negro in its crew. And they, with creditable spontaneity and wit, shouted back, "Bring out your white man!"; since Balliol was famous for its African and Indian students. When the film *Sanders of the River* was shown in an Oxford cinema, and a canoe manned by eight natives shot across the screen, there was a shout, "Well rowed, Balliol!" and the audience erupted into applause. That was the extent of undergraduate racism in the 1930s.

But work. Surely I worked? Yes, in spasms timed to the climax of the weekly essay, which I would read to my tutor, Humphrey Sumner. He was the epitome of Balliol's clipped austerity. My first interview with him went like this:

"You were at Eton?"

"Yes."

"Where did you spend your holidays this summer?"

"At Tours."

"Nice place, Tours. Where did you go when your parents were in Persia?"

He seemed to know all about me.

"I stayed with my uncle in Devonshire."

"Nice uncle?"

"Not too bad."

Really, I felt, this is absurd and rather cruel. But what was Sumner doing except fishing for an interest, a character, a peg on which to hang something? He was a difficult, admirable man. Tall, wiry, pipe-smoking, he had a prodigious capacity for work and set his pupils unattainable standards. He distrusted generalizations, disliked epigrams. He elicited opinions but seldom expressed one. Once he asked me, "Do you like Napoleon?" "Quite," I said. "I hate Napoleon," he said. There was a dead silence. Humphrey had committed himself. His statement became famous and so, momentarily, did I. I was the man to whom Humphrey had said that he hated Napoleon.

With so much discouragement under the guise of encouragement, so much freedom, such an excess of opportunity, I grew lazy, which I had never been at school. I would attend fashionable lectures which had nothing to do with my course and skip my own. I listened to Dick Crossman on Plato, Roy Harrod on population control ("Every one of you in this hall must have at least two and a half children"), but not to Vivian Galbraith on Stubbs's Charters. There were days, however, when I felt myself gripping something, and I associate them mainly with the Codrington Library in All Souls, the loveliest, coolest room in Oxford, to which I was given privileged access. The long gallery was almost empty of students. The few of us sheltered in alcoves between the book stacks, and we read in silence. Under pressure of confinement, I began to learn what study is, the delight of original documents, the mean pleasure in finding scholars wrong, and to form opinions of my own which I could test against Sumner's pouncing mind, argue my case, and feel the muscularity of his response.

Too late. I approached the final examinations with apprehension, learning by rote quotations that might fit in somewhere, memorizing my past essays in the hope that the same subjects would recur, and then scribble, scribble, scribble in the Examination School, twisting questions to admit prepared answers, but knowing all the while that deception of this kind is always detectable, as it was. When it was all over, a group of us ran along the Ridgeway on the Berkshire Downs to celebrate our release, among them Rex Whitworth, who became a major-general and commanded the British troops in Berlin, and John Bury, the authority on Spanish-American architecture, who of all my Balliol friends has remained closest to me.

I aimed for a Second in Modern History. I got a Third. The news reached me in Glasgow, where there was a great international exhibition. With me was Rohan Butler, later a Fellow of All Souls. We decided to separate at the entrance to the exhibition and meet three hours later to compare impressions. When Rohan returned, he was carrying a copy of that day's issue of *The Times*. Casually I asked him if the Schools results were published in it. He said they were. "What did you get?" "I got a First." "And what did I get?" "You'd better have a look." I looked. I searched expectantly down the Seconds, failed to find my name, and then the Thirds. It was there.

"Get in," I said. We drove for an hour in silence. Then Rohan said, "We are going the wrong way. We're driving south. It should be north." He was infinitely kind.

RETROSPECT

Thus ended my formal education, for which Vita had paid by writing *The Edwardians* and *All Passion Spent* when she wanted to be writing poetry. I was never sufficiently grateful to her, for I took for granted this method of passing from boyhood to manhood, and I had not particularly enjoyed it. My letters reveal how much I longed for the holidays, even when I was a senior boy at Eton. I would not have turned out any differently if I had been, say, at Repton and Caius College, Cambridge. The stresses would have been the same, and though I would have missed Birley, Tait and Sumner, there would have been comparable influences, and I now know that parental example and home environment, if not genes, shaped my character more permanently than my schools.

I have seldom revisited them. I went to Summer Fields once or twice, but not often enough, when Adam was there, and once I was persuaded to take part in a cricket match against the school as a member of the Prime Minister's XI, composed of peers and MPs. Harold Macmillan, our captain, did not show up, and I was bowled first ball.

Nor have I often revisited Eton. Old boys—which means old men who were once young boys—no longer feel the same devotion to their schools that their great-grandfathers felt. Attempts to raise a football team to play against their successors have faltered from mutual embarrassment. The reunion habit is obsolescent because people develop differently, drift apart and have no wish to witness their appearance reflected in the awful faces of men whom they have not seen for thirty years. I did return to Eton in 1992 to give a lecture and stayed the night in my old house of which Nigel Jaques, the son of my old tutor, was now housemaster. I found that the ethos had not greatly changed. Tradition clings. Tail-coats are still worn, and when it was suggested some years ago that they were anachronistic, the reply was that the boys liked them, because they could not be worn in the holidays and the tails hid holes in the seats of their threadbare trousers. At lunch in College Hall I felt my way carefully to distinguish between Sixth Form boys and the young masters, for in manner they seemed identical. Courtesy and a certain reticence remain characteristic of the Etonian. Do I exaggerate? Probably. Barbarity, ambition and deceit are inseparable from school life, but Eton is good at concealing it.

In my lecture I told the boys a story to indicate that I was aware of this. It was based upon fact, and its purpose was to indicate that the bullying of a younger boy by an older is the most odious of juvenile crimes. I had no need to point the moral. In the 1930s there were two boys in the same house at Winchester. Let us call them Anderson and Bates. Anderson was two years older than Bates, and made his life intolerable by physical beatings and humiliating him on every possible occasion. When Anderson left the school, Bates sprang up like a fawn released from bondage. He became captain of cricket and won a scholarship to Cambridge, where he gained a blue and a First Class in classics. War came. Anderson served honorably but ingloriously as a lieutenant in the Pay Corps at Nottingham. Bates won the DSO commanding his regiment in the desert. After the war, he entered the Foreign Office and rose rapidly to become our ambassador in one of the Middle Eastern capitals. Anderson taught mathematics in a comprehensive school in east London. One morning Bates, riffling through the despatches that had reached his embassy overnight, paused when he came to the following telegram: "Doctors tell me that I have only a few weeks to live. Cannot die in peace unless you telegraph forgiveness for bullying at Winchester." It was signed "Anderson" and he had added his address. Bates contemplated this message for two minutes, then drew toward him a pad of embassy telegraph forms and wrote these three terrible words: "Cannot forgive. Bates."

The problem I put to the boys was this. Was Bates justified? Our immediate reaction must be that his cruelty was inexcusable. But I suggested that he was showing extraordinary strength of character. He had not forgiven Anderson. He could not forgive him. He would not lie for the sake of a charitable convention. There was dead silence in the hall when I had finished. But I had made my point about bullying, from which I had suffered when I was a boy. That was my legacy to Eton.

Returning to Oxford was a different matter. I went there for many reasons other than nostalgia. I had frequent contacts with the Balliol librarian, who had charge of the typescripts of my father's diaries and allowed accredited authors to consult them. I gave a lecture to the University Architectural Society on "Has a house a personality?" Answer: No, only the personality with which its inhabitants endow it. A few years later I took part in a seminar at Balliol with Jennifer Jenkins, Chairman of the National Trust, when I said the opposite. I debated the Suez crisis with Julian Amery. I took a Belgian student to see the Cretan and Egyptian treasures in the Ashmolean. On all these visits I wandered round Oxford enjoying the buildings and entering other colleges, which I had virtually ignored as an undergraduate.

My chief reexperience of Balliol was Harold Macmillan's visit in extreme old age. He was invited to propose the toast of the College at a reunion of Balliol men, very few of whom were of his own generation. At the Master's reception he was almost incommunicable and was helped across the quad and up the steep steps to the hall by young Fellows who must have feared for his survival. He sat at the high table between the Master and a professor of history. We watched him from our benches in apprehension. He seemed dumb. Then he rose to speak. It was an amazing performance. He had simply been conserving his energy. He talked to us for half an hour about what Balliol had meant to him, not the "effortless superiority" of which Jowett's pupils had boasted, but of its scholarship and dignity, its companionship and fun. He spoke without notes, being too blind to read any, but with a wit and authority that Harold Wilson once described as his "tired wisdom." That evening I talked in the Common Room with Denis Healey and other friends about our past, the glasses clinking as they were emptied and refilled.

NEWCASTLE-UPON-TYNE

My education took a sharp turn after leaving Oxford. I had no idea what to do. War seemed imminent in 1938 and I almost looked forward to it, as I would feel wanted, given a job. In the meantime, I eagerly accepted an offer of an unpaid post with the Tyneside Council of Social Service, to which I was introduced by William Adams, the Warden of All Souls, whose son was its Director. I would have the chance to study industry and the poor, of which I had no knowledge whatever. I accompanied social workers as they toured the slums, helped them compile a report on the incidence of tuberculosis, went down a coal mine, toured Swan Hunter's shipyard, attended juvenile courts, read countless blue books, conducted a survey of leisure activities on Tyneside, and guided Humphrey Spender, brother of Stephen, when he came to photograph for *Picture Post* the miseries of the Depression. The mayor of Newcastle strongly protested against the subsequent article, and I wrote him a letter of apology which he contemptuously left unanswered. More successful was my work for Ellen Wilkinson, the left-wing, red-haired MP for Jarrow, about which she was writing a book, *A Forgotten City.* On her behalf I compiled statistics, interviewed local government officers and reported to her what I had learned. That was my most valuable experience in Newcastle. I fancied myself a Socialist, but in the same way that my father fancied himself a Zionist. I professed, as he did, "equality of opportunity," knowing that such a thing is an impossibility.

I had two side-interests in Newcastle. One was the Roman Wall, which I walked on weekends, driving to the point where I had left off the week before, and covered its entire length beyond Carlisle. I wrote an article about it for the *Architectural Review,* my first appearance in print.

My other pleasures were periodic visits to Blagdon, a grand but unlovely house which belonged to Lord Ridley, built over the coal mines that had paid for it. Its garden was designed by Edwin Lutyens, Lady Ridley's father. I associate these visits with a luxury undreamed of in my Newcastle lodging, but also with two painful incidents. One morning I found myself alone with a fellow guest, a man of fifty, who asked me what I was doing. I told him that I was studying the mining industry. As he pretended complete ignorance of the subject, I proceeded to enlighten him, lecturing him for half an hour with statistics derived from my blue books. He nodded from time to time: "Really?" "That's most interesting." Later that day I heard from Lady Ridley that he was the greatest expert on the coal industry in the House of Commons. Then and there I made two resolutions: never show off your superior knowledge; never humiliate the young.

The second incident was even stranger. I came down to breakfast one Sunday, to find that Nicholas Ridley, the younger son of the house, was there before me. I was twenty-one and he was nine. At that age I was the shyer of the two but thought it my duty to open a conversation. The subject which I chose, by bad luck, was the deplorable record of the local football team, one of whose many defeats I had witnessed the week before. I was not to know that Newcastle United were as sacred to little Nick as the Twelve Apostles. He said nothing, walked to the sideboard, picked up the steaming coffee pot and poured its contents over my brand-new suit. At that moment his mother came in. "Good heavens, what has happened to your suit?" "I stupidly upset my coffee over it," I replied, hoping that this would make Nick Ridley my slave for life. I never met him again. When he became a Cabinet Minister, he displayed exactly the same qualities of independence and disdain. His behavior to me, disgraceful as I thought it, was in fact more splendid than if he had simply turned away from me to help himself to kedgeree. That he never thanked me for sparing him his mother's reproaches showed a certain dignity, as if he found it contemptible that I should seek to curry favor with him by a lie.

Third Newcastle lesson: never suppress righteous indignation.

OTHER PEOPLE'S EDUCATION

I seldom tried to interfere with my children's education, other than guide them into it and praise results. Once I thought that Benenden School was unworthy of my daughter Juliet. It was a magnificent school, six miles from Sissinghurst, but I came to think that its accommodation was superior to its education. When she was there, I gave a lecture to a group of senior girls on snobbishness, insisting that no members of the staff be present, and ended by asking how many of them would send their daughters there. None volunteered. In the event, they all did. In another lecture I instructed them on the art of writing personal letters. I extracted from Juliet all the secrets of the dorm and retailed them in a sample letter, to the consternation of the staff and the delight of the girls, who could not imagine how I came to be so well informed. It was not then an academic school. It is now. It fitted girls for life, not for learning. When they were told to write a five-hundred-word essay on the history of Germany up to 1600, they sensibly copied the relevant paragraphs from the *Encyclopaedia Britannica*. When told to walk ten miles for a Duke of Edinburgh's award, they took a bus. I removed Juliet from the school and a London tutor qualified her for St. Hugh's College, Oxford, where she was happy but not exhilarated, until she and Belinda Harley founded the University Literary Society. This gave her self-confidence and prestige. It was much the same with her sister Rebecca, who also went to St. Hugh's. All three of my children found their feet less at university than afterwards, when they met with chance opportunities that determined their future.

Adam found his way through Summer Fields and Eton without my help. Only once did I interfere, when I was about to publish *Portrait of a Marriage* and feared that it might expose him to ridicule. I wrote to the Master in College, Peter Pilkington, to warn him. He replied that Adam was far too sensible to mind the revelation of his grandmother's peccadilloes. He rose in the school to enjoy the last years, and seemed an ideal candidate for Cambridge, for he was popular, nice-looking, industrious and open-aired, but the university did not appeal to him. I have never understood the reason why.

Everyone is learning throughout life and the only difference in adulthood is that the fear of failure ceases to haunt us to such a great extent as in childhood, and that there are no more written exams. My education was continued by reading, listening and traveling, but especially by writing, for nothing concentrates the mind more than the obligation to put thoughts on paper. I kept in touch with the educational world by lecturing at schools and universities, in Britain and America, and by the flow of students who poured in and out of Sissinghurst to study our growing archive and find books, like Vita's early novels, which were unavailable elsewhere. The great majority were foreigners, from universities in the United States, Germany, Italy, Holland, France and Belgium, whose interest in Vita's personality and writings, and in Harold's diaries and essays, far exceeded that of their contemporaries in England. Except for the Americans, all these students were shy at first but soon gained in confidence, and months later I would receive their dissertations, with titles like *Vita Sackville-West: In Tre Suoi Romanzi* or *Sex Roles, Social Class and Love in "The Edwardians,"* and best of all, Angélique Corthals's dissertation on Vita, Violet and *Orlando,* which won her top marks at the University of Brussels. These periodic visitors, and the friends of my own children, put a brake on my advancing years. One in particular became a close friend, Susannah West, who at the age of fifteen introduced herself to me in the gazebo and sent me her poems and short stories. I replied, and six years later, although we only meet twice a year, we still correspond. I take vicarious pleasure in her growing love of learning and delight in her delights.

CRANBROOK SCHOOL

I was brought more directly into touch with modern education by my ten-year Chairmanship of the Governors of our local secondary school. Cranbrook School is an ancient foundation. It boasts a charter of Elizabeth I. During the centuries it declined almost to the point of extinction, but since 1850 it has become one of the leading grammar schools in Kent, with a school population of about six hundred, half boys, half girls, half boarders, half day-children.

I was never quite sure what Governors were for, since the strategy was dictated by Government and County, and the tactics by the Headmaster. The Governors made suggestions—that classical history should be an optional subject in the Sixth Form, that the girls' home-economics class should cook the Governors' lunch—but our amateurishness and the Headmaster's professionalism always surfaced in the ensuing argument. There was one area where the Chairman exercised undoubted authority, the choice of a visiting speaker for Speechday. I managed to entice quite a galaxy, including the American Ambassador, Malcolm Muggeridge, John Julius Norwich, Sir Jack Boles (Director General of the National Trust) and Edward Boyle. The most successful was the Irish novelist, Edna O'Brien. She was so nervous, never having done such a thing before, that she requested a chair so that she could deliver her speech sitting down and conceal her trembling hands beneath the table. We provided a throne. Her speech was wonderful, and when she came to present the prizes she kissed every boy and every girl instead of shaking their hand.

It was the period when grammar schools were under threat. They selected children by their ability, a process frowned on by the Labour Ministers, Shirley Williams and Anthony Crosland. They favored schools and classes of mixed ability. So at Cranbrook we hedged. We selected our pupils by a system known as "Guided Parental Choice," which in effect still meant that the abler children came to us and the less able to the neighbouring Angley School, where they felt inferior, which caused them much distress.

I thought this system intolerable for Angley children and devised a new method of reconciling the nonselected children to their lot, and persuaded the Governors, but not the County, to accept it. The idea was that our two schools, scarcely a quarter-mile apart, would be "jointly comprehensive," each school offering its specialty, Cranbrook the more academic subjects, Angley the more modern and vocational subjects like engineering, business studies and computer sciences. But the division would not be rigid. Both schools would teach basic subjects like English and history, and they would exchange pupils for special classes. In this way we would create two local schools that would gradually acquire equal status. They would supplement each other and collaborate. Neither would be "better" than the other: they would simply be different. I felt it to be wholly unjust that a farmworker or mechanic should be considered socially inferior to a bank clerk or teacher. The snobbishness implied in the distinction should be eradicated at secondary-school age, just as it was, and is, in the primary schools.

My formula failed to catch on. The Angley staff felt themselves to be patronized and the Cranbrook staff preferred to leave things as they were. Even the Headmaster, Peter Rowe, and his deputy, Peter Allen, were not wholeheartedly in support of the Nicolson plan. Moreover, I knew that I was guilty of euphemism: the word "aptitude" applied to Cranbrook, and "less demanding" to Angley, conveyed a distinction between the two schools that could not be disguised. The league tables and university entrance would make it evident. So their intellectual apartheid continues to this day, and when Angley proposed to introduce a grammar-school type of selection in its upper forms there was an outcry. I have come to accept elitism as the natural product of every form of education throughout history. And who was I, who had enjoyed an elitist education myself, to deny its value to others?

Cranbrook School flourished under Peter Rowe's direction. He was an excellent teacher, fostered the arts and music, and made entry into the school so desirable that parents would move house from distant places in order to enter our catchment area. I felt for him and his wife affection and esteem, and when some of the other Governors hinted that it might be time for a change, I told them that if they were seeking a new headmaster, they would also find themselves seeking a new chairman.

Only once did I have to reprimand a boy. It was not my decision, but his mother's. He had stolen a bicycle and lied about it. So his mother, thinking mistakenly that the Chairman of the Governors must be an even more formidable figure than the Headmaster, brought him to my house and told him to apologize. He did, but my reprimand was milder than she had hoped. I suddenly saw myself back at Summer Fields, aged nine, terrified. "Don't do it again, son," I said, affecting the style of Mr. Chips.

FOUR

THE SOLDIER

❧ ❧

I was born during the First War, too late to remember it. My father was exempted from military service by his work in the Foreign Office, a fact of which he felt slightly ashamed, so my knowledge of the horrors of the trenches was transmitted to me through his brother, my uncle Fred, who would say that those were the happiest days of his life. He was not alone. When I came to write the life of Field Marshal Alexander, I discovered that men like him who had suffered abominably did not look back on the experience with any resentment. Indeed, Alexander wrote to his aunt on Christmas Day 1917, "I'm afraid that the war will end very soon, but I suppose that all good things come to an end sooner or later, so we mustn't grumble." When I read those words, I was shocked and amazed. But what Harold Macmillan called "a sense of teamship and a sense of triumph" and even Siegfried Sassoon described as "the honor and glory that made the war such an uplifting experience" explained why Uncle Fred, who never made much of the rest of his life, found war so ennobling. It did not excite in me as a child any feeling of revulsion. I associated it with heroes, and the heroes were to be found in all ranks below that of brigadier. In my war, the roles were reversed. The heroes were the generals, like Alex, Monty and Slim.

THE DICTATORS

I was never a pacifist. In other ways I was nonconformist, like refusing to be confirmed with other Eton boys at the age of sixteen, but I cheerfully joined the Officers Training Corps, and with steady gaze marched past the band as they played "The British Grenadiers" at the end of a field day. The summer camps were fun, at Tyneham in Dorset, where the days ended with singsongs round huge bonfires and we slept ten to a bell tent, our feet pointing toward the central pole. We were pale imitations of our heroes and had no conception that we might be called upon to emulate them.

I rather admired the dictators. When I was eighteen, we returned from a Greek cruise through Rome, and I had the good fortune to see Mussolini and the Pope on the same day. I stood with a vast crowd in the Piazza Venezia watching the Duce distribute medals to the mothers of soldiers who had fallen during the conquest of Abyssinia. Then he spoke from the balcony of the palazzo that overlooks the square, with the diminutive King Victor Emmanuel standing beside him. I forget the speech except for its concluding sentence, when he turned toward the King with a triumphant gesture and said, *"Salute il Re d'Italia e l'Imperatore d'Etiopia!"* The meaning was outrageous—he was usurping the throne of the Negus—but the words were magnificent and every hand was raised in salute, including mine. That evening, my father and I dined at the British Embassy. They were discussing who should succeed Baldwin as Prime Minister. The ambassador eventually turned to me: "Let's hear the opinion of the younger generation. Whom would you choose?" I looked aghast, while a dozen pairs of eyes swiveled in my direction. "Come on, young man. Don't be shy. Who would you like to have as Prime Minister?" "Mussolini," I replied.

I found the Nazis equally attractive. For two years in succession, 1936–7, I spent a holiday in Germany to learn German, first in Göttingen, then in Berlin. At Göttingen my host was the son of the violinist and composer, Joseph Joachim. I spent most of my time with the university students, all Nazis, and joined them in a torchlight procession through the town. Joachim made no protest, but I could sense that he was worried. As a Jew, he had lost his place as the university's librarian. In the Referendum after the Rhineland crisis he was not allowed to vote, and a friend of his, half-Jewish, had his name taken by a stormtrooper who leaned over his shoulder as he wrote *Nein* on his polling card. In reporting this scene to my father, I added, "Nevertheless, I still believe that there is a great deal to be learnt from them in political method," and I sought to reassure Sissinghurst that Hitler was really a very nice man:

> There is something awfully naïve and charming and sincere about him, and I find it very difficult to believe that a man who in some ways is very human can have made all those promises with his tongue in his cheek.

The following year I stayed in Berlin with a family called Hagen. From the very start I sensed that Herr Hagen was reluctant to discuss politics with me. He subscribed to the *Völkischer Beobachter,* the official Nazi paper, wore a party badge in his coat lapel and kept a photograph of Hitler on his desk. Once he took me to a party rally, "to complete your education," at which Goebbels was the main speaker. At the end of the speech, the audience rose with arms extended. I glanced at Hagen. "You'd better," he whispered. "Otherwise there might be trouble." So there I was, standing in line with a thousand others, shouting *"Sieg Heil!"* It was not as painful to me as it should have been. I wrote home:

> I cannot help reacting against the negative criticisms of the régime that one hears in England. Nag, nag, nag the whole time. When one gets here, one is surprised to find that the whole population is not in concentration camps [so I knew about them], that one never hears of a soul who knows anyone who has a son fighting in Spain, that Goering is a very amusing and likeable man.

and I compared the denial of free speech in Germany to our obedience to traffic policemen. "It is only temporary, to give the system a chance of showing its worth."

At Oxford my attitude changed. There I was in the company of German Rhodes Scholars like Alexander Böker, liberals like Heinz Koeppler and Communist friends like Denis Healey and Philip Toynbee who were not so much pro-Stalin as anti-Hitler. The Munich crisis clinched my recantation. We had discovered an enemy. By that time I was in Newcastle. I helped equip the Tynesides with masks to protect them against expected German gas attacks, and when news of the Munich peace reached us,

> there was no rejoicing, no cheering crowds in the streets, not even a cheer in the cinema when Chamberlain appeared on the screen. They all say, 'We let Hitler get away with it too easily.' I'm sure that there's another reason. They would have welcomed war here. It would have given the armaments industry, on which Tyneside largely relies, an immense boost, and made heroes out of the dejected unemployed. A man who was in the last war said to me, 'When I was asked to kill or be killed, that was the only time I felt myself a full human being.' [Letter to Harold and Vita, 2 October 1938].

I was struck by how small a gap divided the will for peace from the will for war. Chamberlain had won great acclaim for his Munich pact; he could have won equal acclamation if he had declared war. I found myself caught in the same trap. Dreading war because war is dreadful, I wanted this war, because it was just and it would give me something serious to do. "Justice" played little part in our emotions once war began. We fought the designated enemies. Germany, Italy, and Japan, satisfied that they were a threat to our liberties, but the motive was soon overshadowed by the function. We hoped not to disgrace ourselves, and to emerge alive.

MY WAR PSYCHOLOGY

I had wanted to join the Air Force, for no better reason than that it was the most glamorous of the three services. I had not yet flown even as a passenger, and they turned me down. So in April 1939 I enlisted in the Officers Cadet Reserve, which involved no duties except a commitment, if war came, to apply for a commission in the Grenadier Guards, a regiment which I chose for much the same reasons as led me later to join the Conservative Party, namely ortho-doxy and the fact that some of my friends joined it simultaneously.

The war broke out while I was at Sissinghurst, and we gathered in the din-ing room to hear Chamberlain's funereal announcement. I was immensely ex-hilarated. While Ben thought the war a tragedy and an interruption to his deepening study of the history of art, I was happy to have a small role in a great drama.

World War Two occupied, with its aftermath, the next seven years of my life, from the ages of twenty-two to twenty-nine, the major part of my youth. Surprisingly, it had little permanent effect on me. I would have matured no differently in an office. It made me less shy but no tougher. Like all soldiers in all wars, my main object was to earn the respect of my peers. I also acquired an interest in the practical side of soldiering, like organizing a road convoy, the study of maps and air photographs, the mechanics of a gun. I experienced moments of acute fear but never a moment of boredom. If nothing much was happening, one could read, write or explore the neighborhood. Campaigning, when out of the line, offers many opportunities denied to the tourist. We had leisure to learn a foreign language, free lodging, free transport, the right to oc-cupy public and private buildings, and make friends with natives who would have ignored us had we not been in uniform and to some extent in control of their lives. Thus I came to learn Italian, to discover the Roman towns of North Africa and occupy, if only for a night, splendid palazzos in Italy. Best of all was the consciousness that we were *winning*. We were liberators. There can be few more thrilling experiences for a young man than to enter a village ahead of the main army and be greeted by a decorative population with wine, garlands and kisses. After one such incident in Tuscany I wrote to my father that the con-quest of a country was a wonderful adventure. He replied. "Hitler feels ex-actly the same." I deserved the rebuke.

As for courage, until you actually face enemy fire you cannot know how brave you are. No civilian experience is comparable to it. In the event, it is the knowledge, derived from war films, that wounds hurt terribly which creates the sickening fear of being hit, and it is only the greater fear of being thought a coward that keeps you rooted to the spot. You can only disguise your fear, not suppress it. The hero invites danger; the coward runs from it; the normal man merely accepts it. The hero must strive for something beyond the call of duty. He must be eager to kill people, while for most of us killing was as much something to avoid as being killed. I was never in a face-to-face confrontation with an enemy soldier, when one of us had to die, and only once did I try to kill a man. I tell the story here as an illustration of the conceit and innocence that war engenders.

In February 1943, my battalion was holding a pass in southern Tunisia against a threat by Rommel's Afrika Korps to outflank the Allied line. We manned two low hills each side of the pass and waited there for two days, unmolested. During that interval we were joined by an American journalist, Virginia Cowles, who had managed to persuade Eisenhower to allow her to visit the front. Her appearance was doubly startling: that she should be there at all at so critical a moment; and that she was the most beautiful young woman on whom, till then, I had ever set my eyes. I was put in charge of her. I took her to our position overlooking the pass, and in that very hour the plain ahead of us began to fill with Rommel's panzer troops. An armored car advanced slowly toward us and halted about two hundred yards away. A young officer raised himself in the turret to scan our position through field glasses. Virginia and I were lying on the ridge with a section of guardsmen on either side of us. I reached for the rifle of the nearest man, took careful aim and fired. This was done solely to impress Virginia. She was not impressed. I missed. The officer withdrew at leisure inside his vehicle. I turned to apologize for exposing her to such danger, but she was less scared than I and had a wonderful story for her newspaper. I did not tell her how glad I was not have killed that young man.

Then companionableness. In memoirs of the First War we are constantly told that the stress of trench warfare brought together Englishmen of different backgrounds. The officer, censoring his soldiers' letters, realized, as if for the first time, that their emotions, their love of country and family, their hopes to behave honorably in battle, were akin to his own. When he next saw the writer of such a letter he looked upon him with a new eye, and mutual confidence and affection grew between them. This did not happen to the same extent in the Second War. We did not censor our soldiers' letters and our experiences were less horrible than our fathers'. The gap between officer and soldier was bridged only by responsibility and sympathy, and on their side by a certain trust. Some officers, like John Nelson in my battalion, managed to create a closer bond, but for most of us there was always a block between the commissioned ranks and the noncommissioned. When I joined my regiment, green as grass, I found myself nominally in command of men whose street-wisdom, experience of the harsher sides of life, knowledge of the Army and an instinctive gift for leadership were much greater than my own.

There was only one method by which a noncommissioned officer could rise to commissioned rank in the Brigade of Guards. A sergeant-major, very rarely, could be appointed quartermaster, with the rank of major. One of them, Fred Turner, was quartermaster of my battalion when we were stationed in Scotland. On the evening before he was due to leave us for another posting, he made an unprecedented speech to the young officers as we sat at dinner. He told us that we were a disgrace to the Regiment. We were idle, ignorant, conceited and did not know our men. He felt anguish at the thought that their lives would soon depend on our leadership. Not one of us had the weight of character to answer him. We thought his remarks in poor taste, a breach of manners. I had made an effort to know the thirty-five men in my platoon. I knew them individually, their tastes and characters, where they came from, what had been their civilian trades, but when I entered their barrack room or billet, they stood to attention. Once I spoke to them about their habit of attaching to every sight, sound, action or feeling the same stupid swear word. I said that if they used that word for everything, nothing would be left for the occasions when it was justified. The platoon stared at their boots, embarrassed. It did no good. A photograph taken of me at the time (illus. 11) is cruelly indicative of my character. Does it reveal an alert, kindly, confident man? Or is it just "sweet little Niggs" in uniform?

We were the officers, all from public schools; they were the Other Ranks. We ate separately, slept in different buildings, talked differently. When invited for a drink in the Sergeants' Mess, it was an occasion for a slight lowering of social barriers, but each group was conscious of making an effort to please the other and would prefer to be apart. The difference was accentuated by the absurd regulations that required officers in the Brigade of Guards to behave like eighteenth-century noblemen. When in uniform we were forbidden to carry a parcel, even a book. We could smoke Turkish, but not Virginian, cigarettes. We must not reverse in waltzing. We must not talk in the officers' mess about women, religion or politics. To women in person we must be exquisitely polite. Asked to define a gentleman, our commanding officer replied, "A gentleman is a man in whose presence a woman feels herself to be a lady."

I was not used to such polished behavior. When I came up to London from Sandhurst where we had been treated like recruits, I was wearing for the first time the uniform of an ensign (2nd Lieutenant) and took my first salute from a passing soldier. At Paddington station I handed my small attaché case to a porter, mindful of the injunction that officers must carry nothing but a walking stick and a pair of gloves. There was laughter behind me, and I turned to see the porter holding up my minute piece of luggage between forefinger and thumb, and following me with mincing steps, to the great entertainment of his friends. I snatched the case from him and ran. That was not the worst. On arriving at Windsor Barracks to join the Regiment's training battalion, I knew nobody and nobody paid any attention to me. Dressed for the first time in my "blues" (evening uniform), I hung around the anteroom till dinner was announced. I had no idea where to sit but considered that the bottom of the table was the most appropriate place. It was not the bottom. It was the top. The commanding officer took his seat beside me, glancing at me with surprise, but without speaking. When the mess waiter came round to take our orders, he approached me first. "What do you wish to drink, sir?" I looked down the long table glittering with regimental silver and at the colors stirring gently against the wall. There could be only one possible answer. "I'll have half a bottle of champagne, please." "Certainly, sir." I heard the responses of other men as he moved down the row of bent backs. "Cider, please." "Half a pint of bitter." "A glass of white wine." My bottle was brought, and detonated behind me. Everyone looked up, then quickly away. The commanding officer still said nothing. On my other side was the only man wearing a different uniform. A guest, obviously, I thought, and I would put him at his ease. "Are you staying with us long?" I asked. "I am the Medical Officer. I have been with this battalion for six years."

I did not suffer so acutely again. My brother officers came from much the same background as myself, and as their uncertainties at the start were much the same as mine, we supported and consoled each other, and in course of time became fast friends. I was best man at the weddings of three of them: John Buchanan, Dick Paget-Cooke and Willie Bell. This was the camaraderie of which I had read, bolstered by the tradition, particularly strong in the Brigade of Guards, that there was no greater crime than to let down a brother officer. So basic was this rule that in the Brigade a special word was applied to any breach of it, to "cart." You could cart a friend by leaving him all evening with a plain girl while you danced off with the belle of the ball (you could also cart the plain girl by abandoning her completely); you could cart him by borrowing his car without permission and damaging it; or in battle by failing to relieve him on time. You must not forget to repay a debt, nor cheat at cards, nor reveal a confidence. Privacy was respected, and variety of tastes and character welcomed. Shyness was considered a drawback, not a deformity, and heartiness was deplored unless allied to adventurousness or wit. If you preferred to paint or read instead of dancing and playing cricket, it was not considered eccentric. In my group there were officers who achieved later distinction in a variety of professions: Mark Bonham Carter in politics; Roly Errington, who as Lord Cromer became Governor of the Bank of England; Marmaduke Hussey, the future Chairman of the BBC; Brian Johnston ("Johnners"), the cricket commentator and broadcaster; and Humphrey Lyttleton, the band leader and trumpeter, in whose company I spent many a disturbed night at Chelsea Barracks. Two of our junior officers, John Nelson and Rex Whitworth, became generals. It was not a bleak, gormless society.

BEFORE THE REAL WAR STARTED

Sandhurst was a crash course in military discipline and tactics, an initiation into a wholly unfamiliar world. The sergeants called us "sir," but never mitigated their normally abusive language. I spent hours polishing my belt, brasses and boots to a standard never expected of me before, not achieved since. There was drill, which I quite enjoyed for its symmetry and rhythm, but I hated bayonet practice with its grotesque imagery, and the conclusion of every gym class, when we were made to drop our shorts and stand naked for a minute, facing each other, before going to the shower, with the sole intention, I suppose, of humiliating us and ironing out conceit.

Our dignity was to some extend restored at Windsor, where I was given command of a platoon, then at Wellington Barracks in London, where the accommodation for officers was even more luxurious than at Windsor. I was once Ensign to the Colours in mounting the guard at Buckingham Palace and there were more warlike activities. I learned to shoot at Bisley, escorted two German prisoners of war to a camp near Kendal, and took a half-company of reinforcements to join our battalions in France. This was marvelous—my first independent command. I led my men down Birdcage Walk and over Westminster Bridge. A few bystanders cheered. On the far side, I mistook the entrance to London County Hall for Waterloo station, where we were due to entrain, and marched my army into the courtyard from which there was no exit at the far end. Typists leant out of the windows and tittered. My sergeant somehow extricated us and we arrived intact at Rouen, where I left them to return home. There was still no war.

It came in May 1940. At Wellington Barracks we were placed on constant alert. As the situation in France deteriorated, the high command feared a sudden parachute descent on London, and we were ordered to build strong points out of sandbags to protect the Palace and Westminster. Mine were at Lambeth Bridge and under the Admiralty Arch. I sited my Lambeth blockhouse on the south side of the river. This was wrong. I must rebuild it on the north, Westminster, side. I protested that the Germans would then be able to capture the bridge. Not at all, I was told. You'll shoot them as they advance over it. So we heaved the sandbags back again. The public sniggered. The men lost confidence in my generalship. I went to the Guards Club for lunch.

The Grenadier officers who had been in France and escaped through Dunkirk trickled back to London, and told us of their experiences with sadness and some shame, in contrast to the press-promoted legend of the gallantry and triumph of the retreat. The mood was very sombre. My blockhouses began to sag. We started seriously to prepare for a German invasion. Harold endured the Blitz in London, Ben in an anti-aircraft battery at Chatham and Vita at Sissinghurst, which would bear the brunt of a German assault, but I was sent to the coast of Lincolnshire, where no landing could conceivably occur. My battalion was held a few miles back, in mobile reserve. Buses were parked around our billets in Louth and surrounding farmhouses, ready to transport us to the point of attack, and I was given command of the motorcycle platoon, a scouting force. We would roar through the Lincolnshire countryside at dawn, waking the people and scaring their chickens but had little to report except mysterious lights and suspicious cuttings in the crops. Once Winston Churchill inspected us and in his honor we named our carriers (light-armoured vehicles) after his battleships. He was not impressed. "You've spelled *Indomitable* wrong," he said.

The most dramatic moment came in September 1940, when the codename "Cromwell" was telephoned to us, meaning "Invasion imminent," and I summoned my men for an Agincourt speech. "The enemy have landed. We don't yet know where, perhaps on this very coast. I know that you will do your duty." At dawn, after standing-to all night, we were told that it was a false alarm. My second speech, ordering them to stand-down, was less embarrassing than the first but more appreciated. For the first time I had seen fear in men's eyes.

My only experience of the fighting war came with my visits on leave to London when it was under air attack and to Sissinghurst, where we lunched out of doors to watch the fighter aircraft circling round each other like butter-flies. At night the searchlights melted through each other and occasion-ally caught a German bomber like a fly. Vita was writing her long poem, *The Garden:*

> Slow scissors walking up and down the black,
> Soundless collision of their closing blades.

I wrote to cheer her up:

> You do realise, don't you, that the Germans are very likely, if they in-vade, to use gas. Our intelligence reports say that the most probable types are Arsine (have you got the new respirator?), liquid blister gas, and Lewisite sprayed from the air, and pure acid. The safest way to avoid them is to stay indoors. Please do.

We remained at Louth for a whole year, then moved to different parts of Scotland—Pollock near Glasgow, Dalbeattie in Dumfriesshire, and finally Perth, where we stayed until sent overseas in November 1942. It seemed strange that for two and a half years after Dunkirk no employment could be found for our Brigade. Fresh troops were urgently needed in the Middle East, but there was too little shipping to take us there and supply us if we went. Lo-gistics stagnated us in Scotland and I began to feel ashamed to return yet again to Sissinghurst on leave without any action to report.

In fact, there was often the promise of action, but of so secret a nature that we could not tell our families, even Harold, who was a junior Minister in Churchill's Government. We were part of a force earmarked for emergency operations. Time after time we were alerted to land on some foreign shore and practiced for it in Highland lochs, but the junior officers were never told our destinations. As our battalion Intelligence Officer, Rex Whitworth, was privy to these secrets and given to talking in his sleep, we would bend over his bed in the hope of catching some indiscretion of which he would never have been guilty when awake. We learned nothing. So it was only after the war, when I was working on the Grenadier history, that I discovered that we were to have invaded northern Norway, Libya, the Azores, the Canary Islands and Sicily. Most of these projects originated in Churchill's restless brain, to impress the Americans and Russians that the British were still capable of operating on an oceanic and continental scale. They were squashed by Alan Brooke, the CIGS, for which he was rewarded by the Prime Minister with charges of timidity. But one project, the brainchild of Lord Mountbatten, was canceled only at the last moment—an attack on Alderney in the Channel Islands.

Alderney had been heavily fortified as an outpost of the German Atlantic Wall. In May 1942, the 1st Guards Brigade was ordered to capture it but not hold it for more than twelve hours. The sole purpose of the operation, it seems to me in retrospect, was to frighten the Germans and give the British public a treat. We were to do as much damage as we could, then withdraw, leaving the enemy to exult in our "defeat" and execute a number of their slave workers as tokens of it. We moved from Perth to the Isle of Wight to practice and prepare. My chief memory of those weeks is the extraordinary method by which we hoped to cross the wide moat that surrounded the strongest of the island forts. Our mortars would fire on to the battlements grappling irons attached to long ropes, by which we would swing ourselves across the moat and scale the wall, while a deluge of fire descended on our heads from the parapet forty feet above. My platoon was to be in the lead. We would not have survived it. The operation was canceled within twenty-four hours of zero-hour only because the Air Force insisted on bombing in darkness and the Navy on landing in daylight. Their plans were irreconcilable. When I announced the cancelation to my doomed platoon, there were loud cheers in which I joined.

On returning to Perth, I was made battalion Intelligence Officer in succession to Whitworth, a job that I had always coveted and to which I was far more suited than the command of a platoon. It would not carry the stigma of "staff-officer," for in so lowly a unit as a battalion every one of us would be exposed to danger. I had under me a sergeant and six men, whom I began to train in the interpretation of maps and air photographs, sand modeling, morse and semaphore, marking minefields, taping start lines, compass marches, interrogating prisoners, the organization and weapons of the German and Italian armies, writing messages and reports, and gathering information from civilians. We tried all this out on the uncomprehending, and incomprehensible, Highland population. In the absence of the Adjutant, John Buchanan, I acted for him.

Shortly before we embarked for North Africa, the battalion was inspected by King George VI. I described what happened in a letter to Vita:

The day before, I had been inoculated for typhoid, and felt like death. I hardly slept a wink, but decided next morning that this was an occasion that I must not miss. So I marched with the others to the North Inch, a lovely meadow on the banks of the Tay. We formed up in our companies, the officers three paces in front of the men. The King arrived at 10 A.M. There was a Royal Salute. The guardsmen presented arms, the drums rolled, and we stood stiffly to attention as he walked down the lines. I was presented. I let my head fall forward on my chest, as previously instructed, for one is not allowed to look directly into the eyes of Majesty, but I had the impression of a small man, beautifully dressed, with a bronzed face and astonishingly blue eyes.

It was after he passed me that I realised that I was about to faint. I had stood to attention in the blazing sun for about twenty minutes. The Tay bridge began to sway and swim. The ranks in front of me went all swizzly, then black. I could either wait till the King returned, and collapse at his feet; or do a bunk. I did a bunk, hoping that everyone would think that the Intelligence Officer had some special function connection with the King's security. I hid behind a cricket pavilion and buried my face in my hands, while three cheers rang out over the roof.

Three weeks later we sailed in convoy from Gourock. As I sat in the launch which was to take me out to the troopship, I held the tip of my walking stick against the harbor wall. When it separated, I thought a little prayer. I did not return home for nearly three years.

TUNISIA

The only remarkable event during the voyage was when I became godfather to a man five years older than myself, and black. He was a stoker from the Belgian Congo and was convinced that we would be torpedoed or sunk on the approaches to Algiers, and that he would die. He wished to die a Christian and appealed to the battalion padre to christen him. So there were sessions in the dining room each night, when I interpreted the basics of our religion into French. On the eve of our landing we christened him in a wine cooler. The padre asked our convert by what name he wished to be known. "Tallulah," he said firmly. We said that that was a girl's name. He must choose another. So he chose "Georges, *après le roi d'Angleterre.*" So Georges Tallulah he became. I gave him my Bible as a christening present. I have never seen him since.

He need not have feared disaster. We landed peacefully at the quays of Algiers, which had already been secured by the Allies, and camped outside the city. Ten days later we were called forward to drive five hundred miles into Tunisia. Dusky little children, with large eyes as brown and nervous as a young fawn's, and for clothing wearing nothing more than a patchwork of rags, swarmed round our lorries whenever we halted, holding up two fingers in the V-sign and begging for the biscuits that had already become a form of international currency.

We had little information about what lay ahead, except that it was grave. The Germans had landed a large force at Tunis and had already decimated a British battalion which attempted to capture it. Once we had crossed the Tunisian frontier, we continued the journey by night. There was great urgency. The British line was dangerously thin. At Béja a staff officer thrust his head through the window of our car to say, "Thank goodness you've arrived," and told us to cross the River Medjerda into Medjez-el-Bab, and defend the line of hills just beyond it. "He who holds Medjez," said the French, "holds Tunisia." So we dug in on the hills. Later that morning we saw our first Germans.

I observed four or five black shapes crawling like beetles over the plain in front of us, about fifty yards apart. When they spotted us, they opened fire, wheeling from side to side to shoot out sudden tongues of flame. It was little more than a reconnaissance in force, to which we replied not with tanks or artillery, for we had none, but with puny machine guns and a mortar. Our mortar officer was killed. I was extremely frightened, not knowing at this first encounter with the enemy that earth and space are a man's best protection in battle, earth to hide behind or in, and space because there is a great deal more of it than the bit you occupy yourself. Ninety-five percent of bullets or splinters are wasted in thin air.

This is not the place to give a detailed account of our role in the Tunisian campaign. It is enough to say that we occupied those hills for the next two months, calling them Grenadier Hill, and our battalion headquarters was in a cave. It was not then that I was in greatest danger, but forty-five years later. In 1988 I returned to Tunisia and hired a car to visit our old battlefield. I found the cave, parked the car beside it and walked a mile to discover whether there was any vestige of the trenches which we had dug on the crest. Remembering exactly where to look, I found a swelling in the ground as faint as the relics of a Roman marching camp and took a pace backwards to photograph it. I felt my foot give slightly. I turned to find behind me an open well, its mouth half concealed by bracken. If I had taken another step, I would certainly have fallen in. I tested the depth with a dropped stone—about sixty feet. How terrible a death it would have been. If I had not been killed instantly by the fall, I might have lain there for days, broken-limbed. The hills are uncultivated, seldom visited. Crying for help would have been as useless as appealing to a bird flying across the small circle of light far above me. Eventually they would have found my car. But would they ever have found me?

It was dull country round Medjez. There were no olive groves or orchards and the soil, though fertile, was scratched by primitive ploughs, allowed to lie fallow for several years, then rescratched. The spindly stalks of corn were the same color as the earth from which they sprang. The mountains were gray and bare. On this perennial background—the same Tunisia which Hannibal and Scipío Africanus had known—our invading armies remained locked together. Finding few buildings to shelter us, little native food to supplement our rations and a scanty and mostly uncomprehending population, we impinged far less on the civilian life of Tunisia than we later did in Italy. The targets for the artillery of both sides were barren hilltops and desiccated watercourses. Our tanks maneuvered over stony plateaux for which man had never previously found a use.

We were well armed and well fed. The more miserable the conditions, the healthier we became. At first we regarded the Germans as superior to our army in training and morale, thinking still of May–June 1940. Then we began to capture prisoners, and it was my task to interrogate them. My Göttingen German came in useful. I treated them with sympathy, made them sit down, gave them cigarettes, pretended to know their home town, asked about their families and gradually worked the conversation round to the immediate situation. What was their regiment? How long had they been in that position? What are the rations like and at what time do they reach the front line? So good was the intelligence fed to me by higher headquarters that often I was able to astonish a prisoner by asking whether Feldwebel Kranach's foot had yet healed. Most of them succumbed to this seductive treatment and I was able to add my small portion of new information to the thickening files. Sometimes I would accompany one of our patrols across the wide no-man's-land and experience the dangers that they faced every night. However carefully we trod, we could not avoid alerting the enemy sentries to our approach, but we would know of their presence only when they opened fire, blindly into the night, and the Schmeisser bullets fell around us, pattering like hailstones on crisp leaves:

I wrote to Vita:

How can I convey to you without indiscretion the atmosphere of the Tunisian scene? The trouble is that it is a military, not a Tunisian, atmosphere. What startles me most is not the strangeness of a foreign country, but the novelty of war. The French colonists and the native Arabs are no longer inhabitants, but spectators, tourists in the new world that we have created in their land. We have imposed a monstrous new civilisation on their farms and villages. Very seldom are we involved in killing. Most of the time, we are regrouping, refitting, speculating, planning, moving, looking, or merely waiting.

This uneasy, inconclusive warfare continued for about three months, until February 1943 when the First Army began to feel the grasp of Montgomery's hand. Rommel turned away from him after the fall of Tripoli and made a lightning dash to cut our communications. That was when, at the Sbiba pass, I tried to impress Virginia Cowles with my marksmanship. It was also there that I witnessed an amazing encounter. From my higher viewpoint on the ridge I watched the British and German tanks crawling up opposite slopes, for the moment blind to each other's approach but certain to meet on the crest at "point-blank range. We had no means of warning them. Each side was using, for the first time in Africa, its heaviest weapon, the British Churchill tank, the German Tiger tank. As the latter mounted the bigger gun, there was little hope for ours. Two Churchills were knocked out after a very brief mêleé and our whole force withdrew under cover of smoke. The panzers did not take advantage of their success. It was often like that. We wondered why they did not realize our weakness; they must often have wondered why we did not realize theirs.

Our Brigade was never again so active than during the following weeks. We were known as "the plumbers," because we were rushed from place to place to stop the leaks. After Sbiba it was Thala, after Thala, Kasserine. It was then that we first met the Americans. Their war, in southern Tunisia, had seemed separate from ours, and now we saw them tragically in retreat, no match for Rommel's mobile columns. An isolated troop carrier approached our little convoy of lorries, bristling with weapons and crammed with GIs. "He's right behind us!" they shouted, and then, with that engaging humor of all American troops, "Between us and him there's nothing but genuine, Bedou-ine A-rabs." We went laughing on our way. The land was deserted. Rommel and the Arabs had disappeared. We gained the summit of the Kasserine pass to find only the corpses of the battle six days before.

After Kasserine, 1st Guards Brigade became the infantry element in 6th Armoured Division, with which we remained associated till the end of the war. I was promoted to Brigade Intelligence Officer, now Captain Nicolson, a role and rank I was never to surpass, although in Italy I was offered the senior Intelligence job in 5th Corps with the rank of major. I refused it out of affection for my friends and reluctance to withdraw from the fighting front. "No gentleman," Uncle Fred had cautioned me, "ever consents to serve in a headquarters beyond the range of a medium gun." In the Grenadier battalion I had been the constant aide of my beloved CO, Colonel Algy Heber-Percy. When I "deserted" him for Brigade headquarters, he would scarcely speak to me. Slowly I managed to regain his respect, because I was the main channel of communication between 6th Armoured and his battalion, and began to dictate daily situation reports (sitreps) which were distributed upwards and downwards, informing Division what was happening on the ground, and the battalions what was happening on each side of us and beyond, even in Russia. My sitreps were highly unorthodox, written in conversational English, but after some hesitation they were accepted as a valuable contribution to morale. No longer should soldiers go into battle without knowing the reason why. I also began to give short talks to small groups in the Brigade, not confining myself to the military situation but on the history of Tunisia, the Beveridge Report, and the career and character of our commander-in-chief, General Alexander.

There followed the most exciting phase of the campaign. Our tanks broke through the Fondouk pass and captured Kairouan, myself in safe pursuit. On my radio I picked up a report from the Derbyshire Yeomanry that their armored cars had met the advance guards of the Eighth Army. A few hours later I saw Montgomery drive past, waving us out of his way as if First Army was irrelevant to his victory. Later I saw him accepting the surrender of Sousse. He mounted a pile of rubble, summoned a crowd around him, including the mayor, and addressed them in contemptuous terms, saying how pleased they must be to be liberated by the famous Eighth Army, when all of them were in mourning for a death in every family and the almost total destruction of their city. I hated Monty from that moment.

With John Buchanan I drove across the steppe to visit the Grenadier 6th Battalion which had suffered appalling casualties in the Mareth Line. John's brother had been killed and he heard the news as I stood beside him. I was particularly anxious about the fate of Mark Bonham Carter, who was posted missing. His sergeant gave me a very pessimistic account, but in writing to his mother, Lady Violet, I suppressed the worst of it, fortunately, because on the day she received my letter, she heard through the Red Cross that he was a prisoner, unwounded. She always imagined that we were the closest of friends, but we were not. I found him formidable and aloof.

We moved back to Medjez for the final battle. There were some preliminary skirmishes, in which my former company commander, Meysey Clive, was killed, a loss that I felt more keenly than any other throughout the war. We then assembled just east of Medjez, and at 3 A.M. on 6 May 1943 launched an attack which broke through the German line. I watched from a low hill as the flashes of the guns lit up the landscape with a dancing yellow light, and the shells, tearing overhead at the rate of five or six hundred a minute, burst a few seconds later on the opposite side of the valley like the flowering of a field of ruby tulips. When dawn came we could see the infantry swarming over the broken ground and the Churchill tanks lurching up behind them. The attack was so successful that within twenty-four hours our armored cars were entering Tunis in the same hour that the Americans captured Bizerta. The German-Italian Army was split in two. Our Division was ordered to mop up the southern corps by forcing the gap at Hammam Lif, a town built on a narrow shelf of land between a high hill and the sea. The Germans were holding it in strength. I climbed the hill to look down on the town and saw our tanks heading directly for it, losing half their strength before they reached the outskirts. The survivors engaged in street-fighting house by house, but the position was turned by two troops which dashed along the beach and through the breaking surf to emerge at the far end, leaving the garrison at a hopeless disadvantage.

The way was now open to complete the encirclement of the Afrika Korps. They occupied a range of formidable hills facing the Eighth Army and we were advancing from Hammamet in the opposite direction. It was a strategic coup of which generals must dream, the capitulation of 250,000 men *en rase campagne*. I described it for Vita and Harold:

I was determined not to miss the closing scene. I jumped into a captured Volkswagen and drove to the front. I arrived behind our leading tanks at about 4 in the afternoon [of 12 May 1943] while the battle was still going on, and the terms of surrender (which on our side were unconditional) were still under discussion. Wave after wave of medium bombers loosed their loads on the ridge which the Germans were still occupying. The Grenadiers and Coldstream moved forward in a long line. The Germans surrendered, forming up in their companies and battalions. Their commander asked permission to address his men for the last time. 'You need feel no shame,' he said. 'You have not surrendered to the Americans, but to the senior battalion in the British Army.' (Algy had told him this. It was quite untrue.) 'I trust you will maintain your discipline in captivity as finely as you did as fighting soldiers.' There was a great shout of Rah, rah, rah, followed by *Sieg Heil*s, which I thought a little incongruous in such circumstances. Then they marched off the hill singing 'Lilli Marlene', as proudly as if on parade in the Potsdamer Platz. They are curiously unmoved by their defeat. They have a medieval concept of war. A fine surrender is as glorious as a great victory.

The culminating incident of that day brought me a great benefit in later life, my encounter, at the very moment of his triumph, with General Alexander, which I described in the foreword of the biography which I wrote of him thirty years later. I drove my Volkswagen along the coast road to the point where a demolished bridge delayed the final junction of First and Eighth Armies, a place named Bou Ficha. I was not the first to arrive there. Our engineers were already laying a Bailey bridge to span the gap, and as I waited to cross it, I noticed with pity blunted by familiarity the corpse of an Italian soldier lying beside the bridge abutment, the belt of his machine gun trailing like a serpent in the dust.

At that moment a staff car drew up behind me, and out stepped Alexander. I stood aside as he walked up to the lip of the *wadi* and stared at its sandy bottom. I wondered what could be passing through his mind at the moment when everything he had planned and done since arriving in Africa nine months before had reached this fulfilment, at the moment (as he must have known) when the whole free world was acclaiming him. Which was dominant—a sense of triumph, or a sense of relief? Then he did something that showed me what sort of man he was. He walked up to the Italian machine gun, put the toe of his polished field boot under the magazine and toppled it, with a sharp jerk, into the ditch. It was a gesture of finality, but it was something more. It expressed all his loathing for the wastage of war and his contempt for the adulation of which he was then the hero. He turned on his heel, without a word or even a glance in my direction and drove off.

THE INTERVAL BETWEEN TWO CAMPAIGNS

It seems strange that for the next nine months my Brigade was again unemployed. In the First War, formations were siphoned in and out of the line with intervals of only a few days to rest. In the Second War, we were held interminably in reserve. When my father asked a friend in the War Office whether 6th Armoured Division might now be given some leave, he received the reply, "Do you really imagine that we will allow that tested blade to remain in its scabbard?" But we missed Sicily, we missed Salerno and Anzio, and the capture of Naples. We were billeted for most of this time in the lovely Algerian town of Constantine, where I taught myself Italian and enjoyed extensive leaves exploring the Atlas mountains and the desert as far as the ruined Roman town of Timgad.

There were two diversions. In June 1943 the Coldstream Guards captured Lampedusa, a small Italian island between Tunis and Sicily, and having nothing better to do, I begged a lift from the Navy on the first supply ship to land there. It was a beautiful night. I lay on deck in my sleeping bag, watching the masthead turn slow circles round Orion, while the waves broke against the bow in phosphorescent drops. When dawn came and we drew near the island, I saw through my field glasses that the coastal batteries were still manned by Italians. Was there some mistake? But as we entered the harbor, nobody shot at us, and we saw the ignominious white flag fluttering from the end of the pier. Willing Italian hands caught the lines which we threw out. The little town had been terribly smashed by our bombardment. Dead mules, stinking horribly, lay in the roadway. Some soldiers were still engaged in wheeling bags of cement to unfinished blockhouses, and when I pointed out in my new Italian that there was no need for this, as the island had already surrendered, they replied that they had received no orders to cease work. There was no feeling of humiliation or bitterness. With all their elaborate defences, all their good discipline and training, they had fired no more than twenty rounds in self-defence. I toured the batteries, swiveled the barrel of a gun to draw a bead on one of our passing destroyers. "Look," I said to the sergeant. "After all those years of waiting, was it not a great moment when you could fire your gun on such a target?" He laughed, pointing to the dugout, "We were all down there! The bombing was much too terrible." There was no bomb crater nearer than a quarter of a mile. I exaggerated the extent of our air power. I told him that five hundred planes had conquered the tiny neighbouring island of Linosa. *"Cinquecento aeroplani sulla Linosa!"* he cried in admiration. His reaction was an indication of how fast Italian morale was ebbing. A month later the Allies invaded Sicily and Mussolini fell.

For Christmas 1943 I flew to Cairo to attend a course on gas warfare and it was on leave from there that I met my brother Ben. He had been in Syria, interpreting air photographs for the Ninth Army and we arranged to meet in the King David Hotel in Jerusalem. Reaching the hotel early, I went to the men's lavatory and, while washing my hands, saw in the mirror Ben entering the room behind me. I had not seen him for two years. I was overcome with delight. Analytical as always, and longing to communicate, each of us gave an account of the other to Vita and Harold. This is what I wrote:

Voice, mannerisms, walk, nothing of that is changed. He behaves towards other soldiers in a very gentle manner, without authority. He is still apt to be silent. He will never be forthcoming, but always charming, painstaking, interested, and with a great capacity for friendship.

But to show you that nobody's character is entirely predictable, let me tell you this story. Ben told me at dinner that he might be sent to India because he had just had a row with his commanding officer. When I asked him what the row was about, an expression of extreme amusement passed over his face, and he pulled out of his pocket two pieces of paper. The first was a copy of the Christmas card which he had sent to his Colonel in Heliopolis. It was elaborately drawn by Ben, with little sprigs of holly in the corners, and it wished everyone at Heliopolis 'a very boozy Christmas'. The second bit of paper was a personal note from the Colonel, thanking Ben for his good wishes, but suggesting that they might have been conveyed in more respectful language. 'Why "boozy" Ben?' I asked. 'Well, you see, he drinks like a fish.'

Years later, I discovered what Ben had written about me:

He is more like himself than I have ever known him. I doubt if anyone of his age, as an Army officer, could have put a 7-days leave to better use. He is eager for any scrap of information. He radiates health, vigour, knowledge and good sense. I was however irritated by his studied understatement about the war. He told me of some gruelling experience at Hammam Lif ('Have you ever heard of it?' says Niggs, as though he were sitting in an armchair in Kensington recounting his war-stories to his grandchildren), and ends up. 'Yes. I really was rather fightened,' when one knows that the whole time he was terrified out of his life. *Je me demandais toujours pourquoi il voulait tout s'évader de la réalité.* This modesty of his is a form of conceit that I found particularly tiresome.

So to me was Ben's ridiculous use of French, even if it was a familiar quotation from Alain-Fournier.

We drove together across the Negeb to Cairo, calling at Beersheba to lunch with Ben's Balliol friend, Julian Oxford, who was dispensing justice to the Arabs like some modern Procurator of Judea. Having spent two days in Egypt, where I raced to the top of the Great Pyramid, I flew back to Algiers.

A month later, in February 1944, my Brigade was at last ordered to Italy.

ITALY

It was disappointing to those of us who fought in the Mediterranean that during the fiftieth-anniversary celebrations of the war no tribute was paid to our Tunisian victory and there was scarcely a mention of the Italian campaign. It was regarded as a sideshow, an aberration, a waste of manpower and time. The public were allowed to forget that there were not two fronts in Europe at the end of the war but three, and the third, in Italy, played a significant part. Churchill wrote that "it will long stand out in history as one of the most famous victories in the Second World War." You would not have thought so in May 1995.

Let us remember that for a whole year before the invasion of Normandy it was the Italian campaign that kept the Alliance on its toes, turned Italy from an enemy into a co-belligerent, drew scores of German divisions away from Russia and the Channel coast, gained new air bases from which to attack German industry, relieved Malta, brought about the surrender of the Italian fleet, gave the Balkan partisans new hope and massive supplies, and ended with the capitulation on Italian soil of an entire German army group. Some sideshow!

It was not a soft option to fight in Italy. The grain of the country—its mountain ranges and rivers—ran counter to the line of our advance and it required a series of desperate battles to surmount them, rewarded by exhilarating spurts up the length of one of the most historic countries in the world to liberate cities known by name to every schoolchild. But that was not the Italy we found in February 1944. Disembarking at Naples's shattered quays, we moved directly into the line south of Cassino. The country was mountainous, wild and deep in snow. There was no shelter. Supply was by mule, and it would take three hours to evacuate a wounded man from the front line to the nearest point approachable on wheels. *"Kein Menschenleben,"* as a German prisoner remarked to me: no life for a man. For me it was the hardest month of the war and the most dangerous, for our skeleton Brigade headquarters was pitched on a mountainside within range of the German mortars and we slept on the sopping ground under intermittent bombardment. One day I went with our signals officer to lay a line to the forward companies and we were caught in the open by a deluge of mortar bombs. My friend was wounded in the inner part of his thigh. The pain was so great that he begged me to kill him, fumbling for his revolver. We managed to lift him on to a stretcher, but he died on his way down the mountain. Later that month I was ordered to identify the German regiment facing us. Normally this would be done by sending a fighting patrol to seize a prisoner, but the corpse of a German soldier lay on the ridge between our front lines which at that point were only fifty feet apart. The pioneers constructed for me a long hook or gaff, which I caught in the man's clothing, and I pulled him toward me. I searched his decomposing body and found the paybook which gave us the information we needed. It was a horrible experience.

In the spring, our Brigade moved into Cassino, which lay in ruins, having twice resisted capture, and blocked any further advance along the Liri valley toward Rome. High above it stood the great Benedictine monastery. It was at the very moment when we took over the town that Harold wrote an article for the *Spectator* about the destruction of works of art in Italy, declaring that he would rather that his son were killed than allow Cassino's monastery to be destroyed. His article aroused great controversy at home and hilarity in Cassino itself. In spite of Harold's sacrificial offer, the monastery was bombed, and the Germans, who had hitherto treated it as neutral and sacred ground (their Corps commander, General von Senger, was a devout Catholic), now had an excuse to occupy its ruins and turn it into the most impregnable fortress in Italy. It was never captured only bypassed.

Those weeks in Cassino were less arduous than the preceding weeks in the mountains. We neither attacked nor were attacked. Our battalions led a troglodyte existence in the cellars of the town, and each evening I would accompany the porters to bring them news and mail. The Grenadier and Coldstream headquarters occupied the crypt of a church, the Welsh Guards the town jail, where Willie Bell would sit, writing poetry, separated from the Germans only by the thickness of a wall.

At 10.45 P.M. on 11 May 1944, there was a sudden pause in the spasmodic bombardment. At 11 exactly seven hundred guns split the night with the greatest barrage fired in five years of war.

The Poles captured Cassino by a pincer movement over the shoulder of

Monastery Hill. We linked up with the Anzio bridgehead. And on 4 June the Americans entered Rome, two days before the Allies landed in Normandy. We pushed slowly up the Tiber valley against weak German rearguards. The civilians suffered more than us. While we brought with us all the resources needed for life and battle, the peasants had so little that often they would dig up our empty ration tins for scraps of food, and when they were wounded (being less experienced than us at judging the feathery shuffle of a falling mortar bomb), they crawled to our aid posts for our charity and skills. They were well disposed towards us, treating us more as liberators than conquerors, if only because our arrival meant for them the end of the war. Our men were confident, healthy and even rather languid, in contrast to the Germans, who were tired, sick and suffered from the psychological effect of constant retreat and air attack, and the hostility of the people which grew, as summer advanced, into open partisan warfare. The only advantage which they enjoyed over us was to leave booby traps in the villas which we were bound to occupy. You pulled a lavatory chain and the roof blew off. But not many of them, even in moments of greatest stress, took the final step of desertion. When taken prisoner, their attitude was one almost of gratitude. They had been told by their officers that the British murdered their prisoners, or handed them over to the Russians for execution. In fact, we treated them no more harshly than one of our own soldiers under arrest. They never knew us as we knew them. They never saw our billets as we saw theirs, or handled our family photographs or read our letters, as I read theirs. From one of them I quoted to Harold this pathetic phrase: *"Gott sei Dank, lieber Hans, dass du die harte Ostfront endlich verlassen hast, und jetzt im schönen Italien bist."* "Thank God, dear Hans, that you have at last left the terrible Russian front for lovely Italy." I had taken the letter from the breast pocket of his dead body.

PERUGIA, FLORENCE AND THE END OF THE WAR

The day when we captured Perugia was for me the most exhilarating of the whole war. I record it here in the words that I used in my letter home:

> We came one evening within sight of the town. [I suppressed its name in the interests of security.] Looking across a valley filled with olives

and vineyards, I could see its great grey walls supporting the piazzas, palazzos and campaniles. Our forward company had just established itself in a villa where the contessa was terribly distressed for her furniture and parquet floors over which our guardsmen were gently clumping in hobnailed boots. I talked to George Lascelles and watched him prepare all boyishlike for the patrol from which he never returned. [He was wounded, captured, but survived Colditz to return after the war and become Lord Harewood.]

Next morning we reached the first houses at the foot of the hill. I drove in my jeep to a place where the Germans had felled trees to block the road, and watched the local Italians, agog to do anything to help us, tugging at the branches with shouts and grunts. Getting bored of waiting, I took the jeep across country to a minor road which was clear. An Italian was gesticulating wildly to our platoon commander and pointing towards the town. He told us that the Germans had left it the night before, and there was no reason why we should not drive straight in.

We looked at each other. Our armoured cars should enter first. We should take sappers with us, in case the road was mined. The Italian might well be leading us into an ambush. We should get permission. But these opportunities do not often occur, and the officer with me, Joshua Rowley, is a man of vivacity and courage. So we piled a small force into four jeeps, and drove, the Italian guide sitting on the bonnet, up and up, round and round, into the centre of the town.

In the main square there were few people as we drove in. They stopped and stared, and then waved and cheered. This was the signal for all the doors and windows to be flung open, and a great crowd poured into the streets, young and old, rich and poor, converging on our dusty little caravan. We could make little progress through the press of people. I had the impression of hundreds of laughing faces swimming before my eyes, people stretching out their hands to be shaken or just to touch my grubby shorts, people throwing carnations and roses and lilac over us so that soon we came to look like a float in a *fête des fleurs*. Finally we came to a halt before the cathedral. They seemed unable to believe that Englishmen would look like other men. I have never seen such looks of wonder and genuine happiness, and indeed I can think of no other occasion when the mass rejoicing of a liberated city could be equalled.

So there we sat for half an hour, laughing and being laughed at, covered with flowers, and I reported back by wireless that the town was clear. When I could get a reasonable view, I looked up at the grey building of which Mummy and Ben had so often spoken, but which I had never seen before. The Mayor then came forward to greet us officially. We discussed parochial details. The Germans, before retreating, had blown up the water mains; we assured him that AMGOT [Allied Military Government Occupied Territories] would bring up fresh water within the hour. Were there any German wounded left in the hospitals? He would take us round himself. Would all the political prisoners be released immediately? And would the Carabinieri please clear the streets for the passage of our tanks? All this, he assured us, would be done.

A few weeks later I was back in Perugia, in that same hospital, with jaundice, and perhaps sickened by the wastage and carnage I had seen. I wrote home that I had been lying under a great tree, looking up into its branches, and decided then and there that after the war I would become a forester. This was a wholly romantic idea. I knew nothing of forestry but thought it would be wonderful to pace my growing woods with a dog beside me, a wife at home and a son riding a pony along the forest tracks. My proposal caused consternation at Sissinghurst. My father sent me a book on trees, gently reminding me that they would take one hundred fifty years to grow to maturity. How would I make my living in the meantime? This modest ambition did not last long. Returning to my Brigade, I became utterly absorbed in the preparation to end the war.

After Perugia, Arezzo, then a long haul up the Arno valley to Florence. I looked down upon the city before we had crossed the river. The Germans were holding the north bank, we the south, and the bridges between us, except the Ponte Vecchio which was blocked, had been blown up. I saw no movement in the streets, no smoke, no sound, no traffic. Nobody had hung out their washing, there were no children at the street corners, the windows were all shuttered. Then I saw one old woman on the far side waving her panties in our direction, *ripae ulterioris amore,* and encouraging us to cross. Within a few days we did so. I called on Bernard Berenson at I Tatti, and described to him the damage I had seen to works of art, and to my surprise he replied with a paradox so dear to him. "My dear boy, it doesn't much matter; they've all been so beautifully photographed." I made friends with the Corsini family who owned a great palazzo on the Lungarno. They invited me to lunch, adding a little shyly, "Could you bring some British Army rations with you, as we have nothing to offer you?" So we sat down to a lunch of bully beef served by footmen off ancestral silver, and it was there that I met, for the only time in my life, Diamante Capponi, a Florentine girl. I was not the only one to fall instantly in love with her.

North of Florence we encountered mountains and constant rain, and in November our advance was halted at Fontanelice, in the Santerno valley just short of Imola. On Christmas Eve, the Germans rang the church bells of their front-line village to send the carol *"Stille Nacht, Heilige Nacht"* floating toward us across the snow. The commander of our battery ordered his gunners to fire a salvo at the church to stop this nonsense. I was incensed. Interrogating German prisoners three times a week, I sensed a community of feeling between enemies in the front line, a mutual sympathy for our predicament, of which soldiers in the rear had but little conception. We should not spoil this fragile relationship by a display of animosity which few of us genuinely felt.

In the new year, 1945, we were taken out of the line and rested for the next few months at Fermo on the Adriatic. I drove further down the coast to Bari, hoping to see Ben, who had been badly injured by a passing lorry, but he was invalided home before I reached him. I continued to Naples, and then with Willie Bell to Rome, where we stayed in the Palazzo Barberini. Willie wrote in his diary, "As we watched them creeping with a candle through the vast cold rooms, we thought that we were witnessing the final chapter in the story of the Roman aristocracy."

We rejoined our Brigade shortly before the spring offensive. We crossed the Rubicon in the wake of the tanks, then the Po northwest of Ferrara, and raced northwest across the Veneto almost unopposed to link up with Tito's partisans at Cividale. Pushing into the Alps at Caporetto, we heard the news that the Germans in Italy had capitulated to Alexander. We entered Austria on VE Day, 8 May 1945. I was anxious to fraternize with the Austrians, but my brigadier, Gerald Verney, had other ideas. Here we were conquerors, not liberators. "Out of my way, you scum!" he yelled at the welcoming citizens of

1. Harold Nicolson. "He told us that there were many virtues, but only three sins— cruelty, untruthfulness and sloth."

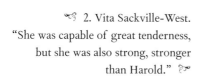

2. Vita Sackville-West. "She was capable of great tenderness, but she was also strong, stronger than Harold."

3. Ben and Nigel on the leaning tower of Pisa in 1930.

4. Vita with her sons at Long Barn in the late 1920s.

5. Virginia Woolf, photographed by Vita at Monk's House. "Why at the age of 44 did she embark without hesitation, apprehension or remorse upon a love affair with Vita?"

6. Nigel, Ben, and Virginia Woolf at Knole in 1928, when she was writing *Orlando*.

～ 7. At Long Barn in 1929. Ben, Harold, Nigel, and Vita. She hated being photographed. ～

～ 8. Sissinghurst in 1932. Vita had bought it two years earlier.
"She saw only the brick Elizabethan tower which rose above a battered compound." ～

9. A photograph taken in 1932 by Raymond Mortimer with his "delayed exposure" camera which allowed him time to include himself in the group. Left to right: Raymond, Edward Sackville-West, Harold, Nigel, Vita, Ben.

10. *The Shiant Islands, Outer Hebrides,* which Nigel bought as an undergraduate. The print is by William Daniell, 1819.

11. Nigel as a 2nd Lieutenant ("ensign")
in the Grenadier Guards, 1940.

12. Philippa in 1953, soon after our marriage. "Looking at this photograph, I wonder how I could ever have ceased to love her."

"*Lolita!*"

❧ 13. My two great controversies peaked simultaneously, *Lolita* and the Bournemouth ballot, and David Langdon linked them in a *Punch* cartoon of 18 February 1959. ❧

❧ 14. Lord Hailsham ("I always enjoy unusual situations.") announces the Bournemouth ballot on 24 January 1959, standing between Nigel and Major Grant, the Chairman of the Bournemouth East Conservative Association. ❧

Villach. But within days they came under our protection against Tito's threat to incorporate the southern province of Austria within Greater Yugoslavia, with its capital at Klagenfurt.

Those weeks on the lovely Wörther See, which should have been relaxing after so long a trial, were clouded by our betrayal to the Red Army of the Cossacks who had surrendered to us, and to Tito the Serbs to whom we had given asylum. This event was so shameful, and its consequences forty years later so grave, that I must describe them in a separate chapter. I refer to the famous Tolstoy–Aldington trial of 1989 in which I was the chief witness on Tolstoy's side.

How the war changed me

I said earlier that the war had little effect on my character and that I would have developed in much the same way had I spent those years in an office. It cured me of shyness, but not of undue reticence. I emerged still a virgin, for though I admired and desired women, I lacked the experience to make the first advance, for which there was ample opportunity in a country where we were temporarily the master race. I envied my closest Army friend, Dick Paget-Cooke, for his finesse with women, one of whom, an American Red Cross girl, he married in Florence before the war ended. Although I had a penpal, Sheila Graham, with whom I regularly corresponded from Africa and Italy, she could hardly be described as my girlfriend, since the term suggests a reciprocity of which she was innocently lacking. It was during those weeks in Austria that one evening I heard a brother officer call out from behind the air-mail *Times,* "Oh, David Bonsor's engaged." "Who to?" "Someone called Sheila Graham." Her letter arrived next day. It was no occasion for reproach, as I had never breathed or written to her a word of love, but it was a bitter moment.

I now realize that I treated not only women but soldiers, friendly and hostile, with exaggerated delicacy. In Lincolnshire I was known affectionately as "pink Nigel," because I thought that my platoon deserved to be taken into my confidence and I would discuss things with them when another man would simply give an order. The men sensed that you cannot discuss "things" in battle and that it was unwise to adopt the habit in our semi-peacetime manoeuvres. So I was made Intelligence Officer, at which I was adept, being fascinated by the conduct of the war on both sides, and speaking French, German and Italian with adequate fluency. My constant activity, the daily toing and froing between forward companies and rear headquarters, gave me a knowledge of the campaigns much greater than normal. I was able, being more or less a freelance, to join any part of our Brigade where there was likely to be some excitement, not in a spirit of bravado but curiosity, a desire to witness incidents that might become historic and to describe them. My presence was accepted since I was the reporter, upwards and downwards, of what they were doing and why they had to do it. I enjoyed my war because I had a taste for drama, was fortunate in avoiding wounds, capture, severe illness and disgrace, and because in the end we won. I was mentioned in despatches, like a subaltern at Salamanca, and was awarded the MBE, which some unkind person interpreted as Much Base Experience. It was a little more than that. That I was ashamed of enjoying my war appears from some of my letters home and to Enid Bagnold, to whom I once confessed that war degrades people, brutalizes them. But my mood was normally exultant. This may have been partly due to my father's replies. He urged me to practice writing, and the war was excellent copy. It was as if I was a war correspondent and he my editor. His wonderful letters, 2,000 words typed each week without fail, stimulated me to reply. Vita wrote to us, too, but dutifully, and it was only many years later, when I came to read her letters to Virginia Woolf, that I realised how seldom Ben or I provoked her to shed her reserve and write to us with the love and anxiety that we knew she felt. I was tactless in this respect. I would begin, "Another marvelous letter from Daddy," without any mention of hers, and she was hurt.

THE GRENADIER HISTORY

I returned to England, by air from Naples, on 17 July 1945. It was thrilling to see the English countryside again, a blessed plot, loved, prosperous, undamaged, calm. Even Croydon airport, where we landed, was like a cricket field, bounded by hedgerows. We went bounce, bounce, bounce on the grass, in brilliant sunshine. Then London, red buses again, bobbies, election posters on which some malcontent had scratched out Churchill's face. I rang Sissinghurst from my father's flat in the Temple.

'Daddy, it's Niggs.'

'Who?'

'Niggs. Nigel. Your son.'

'Oh.'

He feigned indifference, but I knew he was only pretending calm. 'Where are you?'

'In London.'

After a little more chat: 'Is it really you?'

'Yes. Can't you recognise my voice?'

'No. It's been three years.'

He then fetched Vita from the garden and she was in no doubt.

We reunited at Sissinghurst, Ben still in a plaster cast from his injury, and it was then that we gave our celebratory, but anticlimactic, party, when Vita mistook the lady from Hawkhurst for the lady from Biddenden.

I returned home ahead of the others because the Lieutenant-Colonel of my Regiment had invited me to write the wartime history of the Grenadiers. My periodic reports and copies of some of my letters must have attracted his attention and persuaded him that I had been sufficiently removed from the battle to grasp its broader purposes, yet sufficiently close to understand what battles are like. The history was to be in two volumes. I was to be the general editor and write the whole of volume II on the Mediterranean campaigns and the Dunkirk chapter of volume I. Patrick Forbes was to complete it by writing the story of the battalions in northwest Europe, from D Day to the German surrender. I was to have as my assistant Marmaduke Hussey, who had lost a leg at Anzio and been taken prisoner. There was to be a shorter, pamphlet, edition, published ahead of the two volumes.

Duke Hussey and I were allotted an office near Regimental Headquarters and later at Chelsea Barracks and immersed ourselves in the documents of all six battalions. We interviewed officers as they returned from leave, hospital, or prison camps, and slowly pieced together our narratives of the campaigns and battles, in some of which we had taken part. Others, like the 6th Battalion's battle on the Mareth Line, the most terrible fought by the Grenadier Guards in this war, we reconstructed from contemporary war diaries, maps, photographs and oral evidence.

To my disappointment I was deprived of my rank of Captain, and reduced to Lieutenant because the War Office did not recognize "historian" as a credible occupation. This demotion lost me not only pay but prestige. The Colonels and Brigadiers whom we interviewed took one glance at the solitary pips on my shoulders and were reluctant to take me seriously, apart from John Nelson, the bravest of the brave. I stayed a night with him and his wife, Jane, at Woking, and we sat up till 3 in the morning going over the 3rd Battalion's battles. The only blight on that happy occasion was when his small daughter Jennifer whispered to her mother, indicating me, "Mummy, is that man a German prisoner?"

I had two other problems with the history. Most of our informants were too modest to tell us how gallant they had been and a few had been insufficiently gallant. When we interviewed Bill Sidney, the future Lord De L'Isle, on his part in the Anzio battle where he won the VC, he understated his achievement to such an extent that I had to gild my account from other sources. But when the commanding officer of another battalion sought Dutch courage at the crisis of a battle, it was not something that I dared mention. I remembered the incident well, for I had reported it to my Brigadier: "The Colonel's drunk, sir." "Is he capable of command?" "Well, just." "Then let him carry on. He may have a stroke of genius." In the history, I described this episode with such discretion that it affects me still: I cannot bring myself to identify the officer or the battle. We lost both.

My history was elitist. Today I would not write it as I wrote it then. I would model it on Kipling's history of the Irish Guards in the First War. It was expected of me to give to the officers the precedence which they had enjoyed in action. Thus, while I listed every officer casualty in deatil—KA, W, PW and even WPWE (wounded, taken prisoner, escaped)—other Ranks were only named if they were killed or died of wounds, and there were over a thousand of them in the six battalions. Two thousand more were wounded, but their names went unrecorded. My readers might assume that it was an officers' war. As such it was well received by the officers and by our Colonel in Chief, the Princess Elizabeth, with whom I danced a ceremonial dance at Apsley House on the day of its publication, which happened to coincide with the announcement of her engagement to Prince Philip. Duke Hussey and I parted with mutual esteem, and when we next met he was Chairman of the Board of Governors of the BBC.

ALEX

I like to tell myself and others that my ambition to write the life of Field Marshal Alexander was implanted by the scene at Bou Ficha which I described earlier. I saw him quite often during the Italian campaign and was in his company once or twice, but only as an eavesdropper on his conversation. He represented all that I most admired in the English character: reticence, consideration for others, courage, resilience, diplomacy. Admiration for the man was supplemented by my continuing interest in military history. I heard that he had turned down many approaches from potential biographers, contenting himself with an unworthy memoir ghostwritten by John North, and unless I had powerful support he would politely refuse me too. So I turned to Harold Macmillan, his closest wartime friend, and he agreed to recommend me. What he wrote to Alexander I never knew, but it was enough to persuade him to make his papers available to me and to meet me in the autumn of 1969 for the first of many interviews. In June of that year, Alex died.

His widow honored his promise. She produced from the garage where he had stored them the files of his campaigns before entrusting them to the Public Records Office, and although she was unwilling to let me see his personal letters to her, she very readily submitted to my questions about his personality, tastes and married life. At intervals I stayed nights at Winkfield Lodge, the house on the edge of Windsor Great Park where he had lived in his retirement, and after dinner we would settle down with a tape recorder between us. Her memory was clear and her responses honest, but she was reticent. I asked her, for example, whether she thought Alex a handsome man when she first met him. After a pause for reflection, she replied, "Well, I've never really thought of that. I suppose he was," when everyone agreed that he was the best-looking officer in the British Army. She had furnished the house in Virginia Water taste. Woolly pads covered the seats of the lavatories and twin lights stood at each side of the dressing-table mirror. It was exactly what soldiers dream of when on night watch in the jungle or desert. The give-away were the books. The shelves carried many biographies and memoirs donated by their authors, but from their condition it seemed unlikely that Alex had opened any of them. He was a man without intellectual tastes except for painting, which he took seriously, encouraged by his friend Edward Seago. He was so fine and gentle a man that I began to wonder how he could have chosen so grisly a profession. Lady Alexander could throw no light on this paradox. She did not even consider it a paradox.

His senior colleagues were more forthcoming. I had interviews with two British Field Marshals, Templer and Harding, and both confirmed what I had suspected from Alan Brooke's diaries, that although Alex was a brave and charismatic soldier, he lacked Napoleonic qualities. He would submit to a man's stronger will, even if he was junior to him in rank, like Monty and Patton, and he did not have the perspective of a true strategist. He muddled the penultimate stages of the Tunisian campaign and failed to define the objectives of Anzio. It was not Alexander but Harding, who devised the offensive that ended with the capture of Rome. As Minister of Defence in Churchill's second Government, he was a flop. His Parliamentary Secretary, Nigel Birch, told me that Alex's one wish was to cause as little trouble as possible by interfering as little as possible. He wasn't really interested. He had no political feeling at all. But everyone loved him. Mountbatten put it to me like this:

He was essentially kind-hearted in every way. He was such a gentleman. He put up with insubordination. I never did. I fired senior officers and governors if they crossed me and I was convinced that they were wrong. I was far less popular than Alex. People knew I was ruthless. Alex was beloved by everybody because he had never harmed anybody.

Mountbatten also told me a story which on legal advice I omitted from the book because all three men involved were still alive. A group of senior colleagues gave a dinner for Montgomery for his seventieth birthday and Alex was in the chair. In replying to the toast in his honor, Monty said, "I owe my career to two people, both of whom are here—Alan Brooke and my chief of staff, Freddie de Guingand." Afterwards, Alexander said to him, uncharacteristically, "Monty, wasn't there someone else who did something to help you?" "No, nobody else, nobody else," he replied, and walked out.

I went to France and Sicily to visit battlefields with which I was unfamiliar, and to Canada and the United States to interview some of the generals who had served under him, but unlike Harding and Templer they were unwilling, I thought, to declare their true opinions. "He was a fine man" (Lemnitzer). "An officer's officer, the coolest of soldiers, the most civilised" (Bradley). When Mark Clark told me, "I never met a finer leader," I could not help pressing him.

"Do you think he had an original mind?"

"No question about it. In every case he was gentle and understanding."

"Was he sometimes too gentle?"

"No. He'd say what he wanted, and oftentimes that's the way we'd do it." "Oftentimes" was a significant word. I then asked him about the vexed question of the capture of Rome. Clark, in command at Anzio, had disregarded Alex's order to cut off the German retreat from Cassino in favour of a sudden dash for Rome, which he was determined to capture ahead of the British. Had he ignored Alexander's intention?

"No. I never violated his orders. I told him, and he agreed, that I would simultaneously advance on Rome and send a task force to Valmontone to cut the German communications. He never overruled me."

"He agreed to you doing both simultaneously?"

"That is correct."

"He had no comment to make upon the relative strengths of your two thrusts?"

"Yes, he did. But he left it to me. I told him exactly what I was going to do, and he acquiesced."

I knew this to be untrue. But who was I to dispute it further with one of America's most celebrated generals in his own study at Charleston, South Carolina? I needed only to state the facts, and his comments on them, and let the reader judge.

There were other problems of discretion. One concerned the evacuation of the British Expeditionary Force (BEF) from Dunkirk. The War Office files told a very different story from the official version published at the time. I found reports of British soldiers looting the drink shops and panic rushes to the quays. More awkward was the false legend that we had played fair with our French allies and evacuated them from Dunkirk in equal numbers with our own men in accordance with Churchill's promise to Reynaud, *"Bras dessus, bras dessous."* In fact fifty thousand Frenchmen held the perimeter while Alexander's Corps escaped. When I discussed this episode with General Sir William Morgan, who had been his Chief of Staff, he refused to believe it. We were sitting in the Garrick Club and he could not raise his voice to the pitch that he would have liked. "But I was there and you weren't!" he cried. Yes, but the eyewitness sees less of the battle than the historian. The French, German and British documents proved beyond doubt that the BEF owed its survival to French resistance, and I said so in my book.

Alex was published in 1973, the same year as *Portrait of a Marriage,* and both were serialized in the *Sunday Times.* I was pleased with the reviews by the two military historians whom I most admired, Michael Howard and John Keegan, and in general the book had a good reception. My severest critic was Lady Alexander. She had read the book in typescript, and asked me to take out only one half-sentence. ". . . lacking an easy smile or ready wit . . ." But on publication, she told people that she was hurt by the damage I had done to Alex's reputation, and she asked Harding to write a letter to *The Times* reembellishing it, little realizing that Harding himself had supplied me with much of my evidence. He persuaded her that such a letter would be most unwise. It was quite true that in his lifetime Alex had attracted nothing but praise. He had had a wonderfully successful career. His First War reputation was unequalled. He had saved his Corps at Dunkirk and his army in Burma. He had twice forced the capitulation of an army group, in Tunisia and Italy. He had been an excellent Governor-General in Canada. Churchill, Eisenhower and Macmillan loved him. Who was I to tarnish his fame? But the evidence was incontrovertible. I had come to like him more, but admire him less, as I made progress with the book, just as I liked Montgomery less and admired him more. Before he had even read my book, A. J. P. Taylor had told me that he thought Alex rather a dull man, and some of the reviews hinted that I had hero-worshipped someone who was not of the stuff that heroes are made of. I had incidental proof of this when Antonia Fraser and I spoke at a literary lunch at Farnham. She had just published her *Cromwell: Our Chief of Men,* and there was a long queue of customers for her signed copies. The queue for *Alex* was so short that the sales staff of Weidenfeld & Nicolson sympathetically tried to make up the numbers.

Still, it was my best book, or, as Vita said of *All Passion Spent,* "the book with which I am least displeased."

FIVE

THE WITNESS

❧ ❧

I isolate this incident because it involved me in a great double drama, of which the first part occurred in May 1945 and its sequel in October 1989. It raised once again a question of fundamental principle. To what extent are "superior orders" a legitimate defence for brutal behavior?

Let me summarize the events. At the end of the war in Europe, my Brigade was part of the British 5th Corps that occupied Carinthia, the southern province of Austria. We were ordered to hand over to the Red Army about forty thousand anti-Soviet Cossacks who had surrendered to us, and to Tito some thirty thousand Yugoslavs who had opposed him during the civil war and to whom we had granted asylum. The majority of these seventy thousand were murdered or died in captivity. Forty years later Count Nikolai Tolstoy, a collateral descendant of the great novelist but British born and bred, accused Lord Aldington, who had been a senior staff officer at the time, of callously organizing this betrayal. Aldington sued him for libel and in a famous trial the jury found in his favor, awarding him costs and £1.5 million in damages. I was Tolstoy's chief witness at the trial.

WHAT HAPPENED IN MAY 1945

Here I will record only what I knew then, refreshing my memory from my contemporary notes and reports. Fortuitously, I had kept them as a memento of the war, little thinking that one day they would form important evidence at a trial. They were in three sections. First there was the log book which we kept at the headquarters of 1st Guards Brigade. Some of it was in my own handwriting, but the bulk was written by other junior officers as they succeeded each other on duty throughout the twenty-four hours, like naval officers on watch. We would note in the log every message that reached us by radio, landline or liaison officer, but not written orders, which were filed separately. The second set of documents were my situation reports (sitreps) which I dictated each evening and distributed downwards to our battalions and upwards to the headquarters of our Division, 6th Armoured. No copies went directly to 5th Corps. Thirdly, I summarized our role in a document entitled. "Operations of 1st Guards Brigade in northern Italy and southern Austria. April–May 1945." It was distributed upwards and downwards in the same manner as the sitreps. On returning home in July 1945, I tossed the three documents into a tin box which I put in the attic, and forgot them for forty years.

I have no need to refer to them to re-create in my mind the excitement of those first few days in Austria. We crossed the frontier from Italy on the morning of VE Day, 8 May, and I have already described how the populations of the first Austrian towns which we entered, Villach and Klagenfurt, welcomed us more as liberators than conquerors. We were exultant. The war was over; we had won it and survived it. We were all young, and supremely healthy. We found ourselves in a part of Europe that was famously beautiful and relatively untouched by war. We had earned the right to occupy the loveliest of the castles and lakeside villas, commandeer the sailing boats, horses and cars of Austria's favorite holiday resort, and although fraternization was at first forbidden, it did not long survive the blandishments of a decorative population, and the evidence of British prisoners of war who had been put to work on Austrian farms and enjoyed themselves to such an extent that some of them were unwilling to return home.

It was against this background that we attempted to sort out a situation that might have proved chaotic. Carinthia was the sump of Europe, into which soldiers of several nationalities and thousands of refugee civilians had flooded to escape captivity or oppression by the Russians or Tito's partisans. They sought British protection from their enemies and from each other, and our task was relatively easy, because the martial law which we imposed was what they most desired. Our duty was to settle them in camps apart from each other, disarm them, feed them, compose their political differences as far as we could, before any thought could be given to their repatriation. They looked to us for security. For instance, one evening two officers appeared at the door of my caravan in Villach, one a German, the other Bulgarian, each representing a battalion of his army. The Bulgarians had been the prisoners of the Germans. Should the Germans now become the prisoners of the Bulgarians? Would we decide? We placed both battalions under British guard, but the Bulgarians, as our allies, would be entitled to regard themselves as free. Everyone accepted this ambiguous arrangement. We were also given responsibility for the entire Hungarian Corps for no other reason than that their general approached our Brigade headquarters before any other. We had to remind ourselves whether they were allies or ex-enemies. They were ex-enemies. We indicated on the map six areas where they should concentrate their men and gave them supplies from the food dumps, which were ample because Carinthia had been the major German supply base for the Italian campaign. There was no need to guard any of these "prisoners." They had no wish to escape. My Brigadier, Gerald Verney, told me to report our action to the chief staff officer of 5th Corps, Toby Low, who became Lord Aldington. It was the only occasion in the war that I reported to him direct. He was a brigadier; I a captain. I saluted; he nodded assent.

On our very first day in Austria we became aware of the threat to Carinthia by Tito's partisans. He claimed the province as part of Greater Yugoslavia, just as he claimed Venezia Giulia and Trieste from Italy, as legitimate rewards for his hard struggle. The partisans had anticipated us into Klagenfurt by a few hours, and posted up their proclamations on all the public buildings and in many villages nominally under our control. I still have a copy of the proclamation, which in translation from the German read ominously:

The Yugoslav army has entered Carinthia in order to clean the land once and for all time of Nazi criminals, and guarantee the Slovene and Austrian population a truly popular democracy, freedom and prosperity in the new, victorious and powerful Greater Yugoslavia. We hereby make known that throughout the whole of liberated Carinthia the military authority of the Yugoslav army has been established.

We tore down the posters and substituted our own, proclaiming Carinthia conquered but inviolate under British control. But Tito was our ally. He could not now be declared our enemy. It was a situation fraught with difficulty, but it was resolved with surprising ease, because our strength on the ground was so manifestly superior to Tito's and he could foresee as clearly as ourselves the inevitable result of an armed conflict. Although there was a large Slovenian minority in southern Carinthia, Villach and Klagenfurt were wholly German, and their resistance, backed by a British armored corps, would be insurmountable by what was largely a guerrilla force.

We were ordered to play it cool, to impede the partisans by every means short of shooting. All civilians threatened with rape or looting were to be taken into custody; we were to deny the roving bands of partisans access to petrol, food and transport; one of our tanks would "accidentally" break down on a vital bridge or across a railway line. Discourage, delay, check, obstruct—but nothing more. If the partisans insisted on passing our roadblocks, they must be allowed through. It was not at all easy to carry out these orders, and much depended on the good sense of the junior leaders, the platoon commanders and their sergeants. The men of equivalent rank in Tito's army were mostly uneducated, fiercy peasant boys, veterans of savage battles and determined to enjoy the fruits of their hard-won victory. We were left in no doubt what would be the fate of any enemy who fell into their hands. We had first encountered them in northern Italy on 7 May, when the log book recorded: "40 Italians are held prisoner by the partisans—almost certain to be shot." That was their reputation and our foreboding.

It was therefore with solicitude that we welcomed the anti-Tito refugees from Yugoslavia and gave them sanctuary in our small corner of Austria. On 12 May, 1st Guards Brigade was moved from Villach to guard the crossing over the River Drau at Ferlach and the railway that led from the frontier station at Rosenbach into Slovenia. Ours was the central sector of 5th Corps' front. Later that day we spotted a long column, which ultimately stretched ten miles, emerging from the mountains to the south of us and heading toward the bridge where the Grenadiers were waiting. I stood beside the Commanding Officer of the battalion, Peter Clifton, as the leader of the column came forward to meet us. He was a German, Oberst von Seeler. He told us that he had behind him a corps of ten thousand Germans, well disciplined, and a large group of disorganised refugees, some of them civilians fleeing from the partisans, but the majority, amounting to about twenty thousand, were soldiers,

Slovenes, Serbs, Croats and White Russians, who had fought against Tito, but were not under von Seeler's command.

If we had wished, it would have been simple to prevent them from crossing the river by taking up the decking of the bridge or stationing a single tank on it. But we let them pass. All that afternoon they streamed across, and on the near side of the bridge they threw their weapons on to dumps which we indicated. There were many women and children among them, utterly exhausted by their march over the mountains, and troops of horses. I remember seeing three camels in this endless cavalcade. All were intensely relieved to find themselves in the British zone and without complaint they staggered on another five miles to the makeshift camp where we established at Viktring, a few miles south of Klagenfurt. The Grenadiers patroled the perimeter of the camp to prevent the partisans following them. There was no need for the refugees to request, or for us to grant, asylum. Our actions were sufficient proof of it.

They settled into Viktring very quickly, relief overcoming their exhaustion, and within a few days organized parades, religious services, gymkhanas, concerts and schools. I strolled among them every day quite freely, and when the Germans and Russians were moved to other camps, I came to know the Serb, Slovene and Croat officers on terms approaching friendship. The British soldiers, with their endearing gift for simplification, recognized only two groups, Jugs and Tits. The Jugs were "our" Yugoslavs; the Tits were the partisans, enemies of the Jugs, but our allies. Everything was now calm. The partisans circled the camp in their stolen cars but made no attempt to penetrate it.

The Jugs relied wholly on us and trusted us. The day after we set up the Viktring camp, I wrote in my sitrep, "None of them can be repatriated except to almost certain death at the hands of Tito." That was only the first of my many warnings. We knew their probable fate if we did expel them, because of our previous experience of partisan behavior, and the Jugs told us so. They were not men who scared easily. They had just survived a terrifying war. Yet they were not ashamed to admit to us a terror that they had never shown in battle, the terror of being returned, without any means of self-defence, to a brutal enemy. All of them had fought against Tito and some of them, the Croatian Ustashi, had accepted German command and been guilty of appalling atrocities against the Serbs. But the great majority never accepted German leadership, and if sometimes compelled by the civil war to fight on the same side against Tito, they had been at most their co-belligerents, never their allies. They hoped for an Anglo-American victory in this war. Most of them were simple peasants in uniform. Their only crime was fear of Communism and their sole motivation for leaving their country was panic. Some of the women and children among them were camp followers and stayed with their men in the fields outside Viktring, but six thousand others had nothing to do with the soldiers. They were Slovenes who had fled from their farms and the poorer suburbs of Llubljana, and we lodged them separately in Viktring's vast monastery.

They had been there less than a week when we received from 6th Armoured Division the verbal warning that all anti-Tito Yugoslavs in our zone of Austria were to be surrendered to Tito. We could scarcely believe it. Someone must have blundered. But next day, 17 May, the order was confirmed in writing:

All Yugoslav nationals at present in the Corps area will be handed over to Tito forces as soon as possible. They will not be told of their destination.

This order was modified on the 18th by a supplementary order to the effect that for the moment the civilians need not be sent back unless they were camp followers, who would probably wish to accompany their men.

As we were not allowed to tell them where they were going, we had no alternative but to lie to them. We told them that we were sending them to other British camps in Italy, where it would be easier to guard and feed them, and where they could rejoin some of their compatriots who had surrendered to us earlier. I never knew who originated this lie. It may have been low down the chain of command, possibly in the Welsh Guards battalion, who were in charge at the stations. Whoever gave the original order did not have to confront, as we did, thousands of distraught men and women in the Viktring camp who would inevitably ask us, "Where are you sending us?" If we replied that we were forbidden to tell them, or that we did not know, they would immediately suspect the truth, and refuse to mount the trucks and trains. Even if we had been authorized to use force, how could we have compelled so vast a crowd by bayonet and bullet to obey us? There would have been an uncontrollable riot. So we lied to them and they departed from Viktring, confident that they had nothing to fear but a long, uncomfortable train journey to Italy.

The "repatriation" of the Jugs, as it was euphemistically called, lasted from 19 May to the end of the month, at the average rate of two trains a day, each carrying fifteen hundred people. They were ferried by road from Viktring to two rural stations, Maria Elend and Rosenbach, where they descended from the trucks and clambered aboard a train of old cattle-wagons. For the officers, women and children, two battered carriages were attached at the rear. I was present on most of these occasions, as a witness and reporter, not in command, but I was a party to the accepted lie. "Where are we going?" "You've already been told that you are going to Italy." One young Serbian officer who spoke good French had his suspicions. "Will you swear on your honor that we are going to Italy?" I replied, "I'll turn my back on you for half a minute and if you are still there when I turn round, you are going to Italy." He took the hint and in those thirty seconds disappeared into the forest.

Our guardsmen slid together the doors of the cattle trucks when they were full, and padlocked them. They also locked the carriage doors. When all was secure, they drew back from the train, and their places were immediately taken by Tito's partisans who had been hiding in the bushes and station buildings. The wagons were old and through cracks in the boarding the Jugs could see exactly what was happening. They began hammering on the inside of the wagon walls, shouting imprecations, not at the partisans, but at us, who had betrayed them, lied to them and sent at least the men among them to certain death. This scene was repeated day after day, twice a day. It was the most horrible experience of my life.

We did not have to wait months or years to discover the fate of these people. Two or three managed to escape the massacres and within a couple of days recrossed the frontier into Austria, where they told their compatriots at Viktring what had happened. They were not believed. The British were incapable of such perfidy. Then they told us. The trains had turned left for Slovenia after leaving the stations, instead of proceeding straight ahead for Italy (they could tell this by the motion of the wheels), and were unloaded at the provincial town of Kočevje, south of Ljubljana. There the prisoners were stripped, wired by their wrists in pairs and taken in trucks through a pine forest. After half an hour's journey they were marched along a track to the edge of a natural chasm, where they were shot in the neck and their bodies flung into the pit. Soon the mass grave was filled with thousands of naked corpses, the handful of living slowly suffocating and starving beneath the decomposing dead. After dark, three survivors managed to drag themselves out of the pit by a tree trunk dislodged by a stick of dynamite. The Yugoslav officer who organized this massacre, Simo Dubajic, who was later tracked down by Tolstoy, has given interviews to the press and television, admitting that he was dead drunk, but as a fanatical Communist he had no mercy. They were enemies of the people, he said, inhuman, and had to be destroyed.

Even before we heard these stories we protested against the inhumanity of what we had been ordered to do. It was endlessly discussed among us, and I expressed our common disgust in the last two sentences of the sitrep which I issued on 18 May, the day before the repatriations began. "The whole business," I wrote, "is most unsavory, and British troops have the utmost distaste in carrying out their orders. At the moment it is not known what higher policy lies behind the decision." For this I was severely reprimanded by General Murray, commanding 6th Armoured Division, not because he disagreed with my sentiments, but because I should never have uttered them in a semipublic document. He ordered me to "correct" the sitrep on the following day, and more or less dictated the relevant paragraph:

First impressions of the reception accorded to the Croats were definitely good. They were kindly and efficiently handled, and provided with light refreshments before continuing their journey by train to Yugoslavia. A Tito representative said that only the war criminals among them would be punished, and the remainder sent to work on their farms. We have every reason to believe that this policy, which accords with the previous practice of Tito's men, will be faithfully carried out.

There was not a word of truth in this statement, of which I still feel deeply ashamed. The only phrase that indicated my resentment was "light refreshments." There were, of course, no light refreshments on the trains and every man in our battalions knew it, recognizing my bitter comment for what it was. I believe that I was alone in expressing our collective indignation publicly, but others, in conversation and in their letters and diaries, spoke with equal anger. Anthony Crosland, the future Foreign Secretary in Jim Callaghan's Government, who was on the Intelligence staff of 6th Armoured, wrote at the time, "It was the most nauseating and cold-blooded act of war I have ever taken part in." Robin Rose Price, who commanded the Welsh Guards battalion, called it "an order of the most sinister duplicity," and his chaplain, the Rev. Malcolm Richards, gave evidence of the men's intense dislike for their unwholesome task. I refused to write further sitreps in Austria, as I would be forbidden to tell the truth, even about the survivors of the massacre, though their stories circulated by word of mouth throughout the Brigade.

Soldiers in a modern army cannot be prevented from reasoning why. We were well aware that so controversial an order could not have originated with 6th Armored or 5th Corps. For all we knew, it might have come down from the Chiefs of Staff in Washington, who were anxious to appease Tito. That he started to withdraw his partisans from Carinthia on the very day, 19 May, when the repatriations began, strengthened our suspicion that a deal had been struck at the highest level. In my summary of the campaign, written after the crisis was over, I said, "As all the world now knows, Tito agreed to withdraw his partisans . . . *As our contribution to the agreement* [my 1997 italics] it was decided to hand back to him all the Yugoslav prisoners in our hands." This was the explanation generally held at the time, but it was untrue. Toby Low (Lord Aldington), who conducted the negotiations with Tito's emissary on behalf of his general, made no such bargain. But few of us in May 1945 had heard of Toby Low.

I was little concerned with the Cossacks. A few thousand "White Russians," as we called them, were included in von Seeler's corps but within a few days they were moved to camps within another Division's sector, and were eventually returned to Italy. Another forty thousand were less fortunate. When they were surrendered to the Red Army in early June, the Welsh Guards were again allotted this unpleasant task, but I did not accompany them, as the battalion was temporarily detached from our Brigade. It is the Cossack story that has captured the headlines, possibly because the name has a cutlass ring about it which "dissident Yugoslavs" has not. But the Jug experience is the more significant in this account because Lord Aldington had more to do with it, and there was, in my opinion, less excuse for it. We were bound by no treaty obligation to return the Jugs, as we were by the Yalta Agreement to return most of the Cossacks.

At the higher levels of command there was some concern, specially after Alexander's visit to Austria on 4 June, that we might have treated the Yugoslavs too harshly and impetuously. Following the protest to him by a civilian officer, the six thousand refugees in the Viktring monastery were spared repatriation. When they were asked whether they wished to return to their native country, only one hundred and thirty volunteered. A report was called for from 6th Armoured Division and it was signed by General Murray on 25 June. He stated that "no members of the Slovene National Army or other Yugoslav forces hostile to the Allies have been handed over to the partisans," when thousands had been. He claimed that it had been "impossible" to prevent them from crossing the Drau, when there was no such difficulty. "Care was taken not to encourage or deny the rumor that their destination was Italy," when we deliberately propagated that rumor. Finally, "The Tito troops accepted them correctly, and this headquarters has no reliable evidence of their subsequent treatment in Yugoslavia." "Correctly" is an amazing euphemism for the treatment of which we had had clear evidence from the few survivors. In general the report justified our action by citing "superior orders." There was no expression of remorse.

A FORTY-YEAR INTERVAL

These events were not reported in the press at the time and, even among soldiers who had taken part in them, the memory slowly faded. From time to time, questions were asked in Parliament or from the Foreign Office, mostly concerning the fate of the Cossacks, and admissions of "error" began to creep into the replies, advancing to "a ghastly mistake" and "a serious blunder." The official hope was that the incident would not be too closely investigated by historians, but in 1974 Lord Bethell published *The Last Secret,* and in 1976 Nikolai Tolstoy followed it with his *Victims of Yalta,* both of which dealt mainly with the Cossacks. In the House of Lords in 1976, Lord Hankey, a senior Foreign Office official, expressed his "very deep regret that in the heat and utter turmoil of the summer of 1945, it was impossible for the military authorities to weed out individual cases. There were some sad mistakes." In the last volume of the official history of the Second World War, published in 1988, the repatriation of the Yugoslavs was summed up as "entirely satisfactory to the Allies," and when the author, General Sir William Jackson, was asked why he had not taken the opportunity to express some regret for what had occurred, he replied that it was a political decision, which the Army had to carry out.

Well, was it a political decision? Early in 1984, when I took part in a BBC *Timewatch* program which dealt with the repatriations, Nikolai Tolstoy wrote to *The Times* protesting that the program had given the false impression that Alexander was ultimately responsible for the massacres. As the author of the

Field Marshal's biography, I wrote to Tolstoy, whom I had never met, offering to show him the documents which I had rediscovered in my tin box. In his reply he told me of his intention to name Harold Macmillan as the chief culprit, since he had "set up a most elaborate deception tactic intended to pull the wool over the eyes both of Alexander and officers in the field." If this could be proved, it would indeed justify the military in calling it a political decision. Tolstoy developed his theory in *The Minister and the Massacres* (1986), where he made considerable use of my documents.

The book, which was a bestseller, was deeply researched in the British and American archives and told the story of the repatriations with great skill and vigor. It declared at the start that Harold Macmillan, while Resident Minister at Alexander's headquarters at Caserta and responsible for giving him political advice, had "largely engineered the whole affair" without informing him. Tolstoy ended the very last paragraph of the book by suggesting that the KGB may have had a hold on Macmillan throughout the remainder of his career as Minister of Defence, Foreign Secretary and Prime Minister. There was a strong hint of Russian blackmail in his enigmatic conclusion, "The KGB presumably had the best of reasons for knowing the whole of a story which in the West it has taken forty years to unravel."

This innuendo, coming at the very end of a brilliant exposé, caused an uproar. Tolstoy was denounced by the Conservative Party for casting a slur on the reputation of its most distinguished veteran. I, too, thought the conspiracy theory unjustified, and was led paradoxically to lay much of the blame on my own hero, Alexander, for his negligence in failing to understand the implications of the orders issued in his name, some of which were contradictory, and for delaying his visit to Austria until the repatriations were all but complete. I thought it inconceivable that Macmillan would deliberately conspire against the Field Marshal, the Commander-in-Chief, and by this time his closest military friend, on an issue which required their intimate co-operation. Nor did he have any motive for deceiving him. He felt no special animosity against the Cossacks or anti-Tito Yugoslavs. In fact, his instinct was to protect them. In 1984, he published his diary of the period, when another man might well have suppressed it, in which he acknowledged his misgivings about sending the Cossacks "to slavery, torture and probably death," but concluded that there was no alternative if we were to honor the pledge given by Churchill to Stalin at Yalta, and retrieve our liberated prisoners of war from the Red Army. As a civilian, Macmillan could not instruct 5th Corps to repatriate the Jugs when he visited Klagenfurt on 13 May, but he "concurred" with the fatal order issued by General Robertson in Alexander's name, and according to Alexander Kirk, his American opposite number on the Caserta staff, he "recommended" it. So strong was his influence that subordinate headquarters continued for weeks thereafter to refer to "Macmillan's advice" and even to his "verbal directive" in extenuation of their conduct.

My charge against Macmillan is not one of duplicity, but that he did not use his influence with his Commander to put a stop to what was undoubtedly an abominable crime, and that his indifference, combined with Alexander's indolence, were ultimately responsible for it. Macmillan never emphasized to the subordinate staffs the important distinction between Soviet and "White" Russians, the émigrés who had never lived in Soviet Russia and should not therefore have been handed over. There were some three thousand of them in Austria, including many senior generals, together with their German officers, and all of them were "repatriated" to a country of which they had never been citizens, to face immediate execution or a lingering death in Siberian camps. Nor did Macmillan investigate closely enough our inhuman treatment of the Jugs. He never returned to Austria. He never advised Churchill (with whom he spent two days at Chequers at the height of the crisis) to do everything possible to prevent the massacre. He defied the U.S. State Department's more humane policy. And he never seriously considered the alternatives. In the case of the Cossacks, he could have insisted on screening, to separate Whites from Reds, and supported Alexander's initiative to send them west to Eisenhower instead of east to Stalin. In the case of the Yugoslavs, he could have advised sending them to Italy in the returning supply lorries, or rearming them with the surrendered German weapons to fight Tito, if that was the only way to evict the partisans from Carinthia.

He did none of these things. In his biography of Harold Macmillan, Alistair Horne, who discussed the incident with him on no less than eight separate occasions, came to the conclusion that he was "far more tormented by it than he ever let on," but in public Macmillan remained unrepentant. Why? His negligence—I put it no more strongly—was something for which in his last years he could have apologized without loss of honor. Indeed, an apology would have satisfied honor.

Tolstoy has continued to insist that "it is virtually certain that Macmillan did deceive Alexander" (*Spectator*, 23 May 1992), repeating what he had alleged in his book *The Minister and the Massacres*. In June 1989, its publisher,

Century Hutchinson, on the advice of their counsel and without consulting the author, came to an agreement with Lord Aldington (Macmillan having died in 1986 without having taken legal action) that no further copies would be issued, and they paid him £30,000 in damages, though no court of law had pronounced it libelous. A year later, after the great trial had intervened, Aldington's solicitors wrote to all public libraries in England and Wales warning them that it would amount to a republication of the libels if they continued to loan the book. Most obeyed. The Bodleian told Ian Mitchell, a journalist favourable to Tolstoy, that the book "is in our Reserved Collection and we cannot make it available." The Cambridge University Library told him, "It is in a restricted class. I'm afraid we cannot let you see it." The London Library has continued to withhold the book from its members and, when I checked in the spring of 1997, not a single copy was available through any of Kent's public libraries. Presumably, no librarian had dared risk prosecution and there was no general protest against this unprecedented denial of free speech.

There was a second attempt at "damage limitation." A Brigadier, Anthony Cowgill, took it on himself to investigate the whole affair and published an Interim Report in September 1988. He and his colleagues, Christopher Booker, an able journalist, Lord Brimelow, a former high official in the Foreign Office, and Brigadier Tryon-Wilson, who had been the senior administrative officer in 5th Corps in 1945, claimed to have had no other motive than to "put the record straight." It was a private enquiry, undertaken at the authors' own expense, and without any official backing or assistance beyond what was available to any historian, including Tolstoy. These claims were widely questioned, as were the conclusions. The Preface stated: "Very grave charges have been levelled against a British Prime Minister [Macmillan] and the whole affair has appeared to reflect adversely on the reputation of the British Army." It surprised few people that the report concluded that there was no "Klagenfurt Conspiracy" (with which I agreed), that the action taken by 5th Corps, however regrettable, was authorized and due to "operational circumstances," and that Macmillan was in no way to blame.

When the Cowgill Interim Report was published, I wrote a long letter of criticism to Christopher Booker, and he invited me to meet him, Cowgill and Brimelow at lunch in the Carlton Club. Tryon-Wilson sent his apologies: he was tending his sheep in Cumbria. It was one of the least pleasing lunches I have ever eaten in a London club, but our discussion was amicable. Brimelow was the only one of the three who expressed personal hostility to Tolstoy: he would never consent to sit down in the same room with him, preferring arguments which are conducted on a "gentlemanly" level. Cowgill acknowledged that Tolstoy had done the State some service by discovering the documents on which his own report had been largely based, and there was no dispute between us that a great injustice had been committed. But it seemed to me that the more they exonerated Macmillan and the high command, the more they implicated 5th Corps, of which the commander was General Charles Keightley, and his Chief of Staff, Toby Low, later Lord Aldington.

Aldington was the only senior officer left alive who had been closely involved in the affair and Tolstoy was determined to prove his share of responsibility for what had happened. He has always denied that it was his intention to provoke Aldington to sue him, but in fact he did so, owing to a curious chain of circumstances.

A painter and property dealer in Tunbridge Wells called Nigel Watts had a long-standing grievance against Aldington, chairman of the insurance company, Sun Alliance, for refusing to allow his sister's case to go before the Insurance Ombudsman on the grounds that she had not appealed within the six-months permitted deadline. Watts came to hear of Tolstoy's parallel controversy with the peer and proposed to publish a damaging statement about Aldington's conduct in the Austrian affair. Tolstoy unwisely agreed, and when he received Watts's draft, it was so full of errors that he rewrote it himself. This was the document titled "War Crimes and the Wardenship of Winchester College." It was produced as a four-page typewritten leaflet, ill designed and awkward to handle, which came to be known as "the Winchester pamphlet." Ten thousand copies were run off and circulated to the Governors of Winchester College, of whom Aldington was Warden or Chairman, the parents of Winchester boys, all members of both Houses of Parliament, the press and Aldington's neighbors in Kent. Its purpose was to suggest that a man guilty of such appalling crimes was unworthy to be Warden of such a distinguished school.

When I first saw the pamphlet in 1987, I was appalled by certain passages in it. It began by summarizing fairly enough the narrative of the repatriations, then continued, "The man who issued every order and arranged every detail of the lying and brutality which resulted in these massacres was Brigadier Toby Low," and suggested that even if he was only obeying orders, "he would still stand arraigned of gross violation of the laws of war and humanity. . . . He arranged the perpetration of a major war-crime, in the full knowledge that the most barbarous and dishonorable aspects of his operation were throughout disapproved and unauthorized by the higher command, and in the full knowledge that a savage fate awaited those he was repatriating."

This was hot stuff. Worse was to follow: "Lord Aldington has been repeatedly charged in books and articles, by press and public, with being a major war-criminal, whose activities merit comparison with the worst butchers of Nazi Germany or Soviet Russia." There was no signature to the document and no mention of Watts's grievance. But Watts acknowledged his responsibility for it and Tolstoy its authorship. Aldington sued Watts for libel and, at his own request, Tolstoy was joined to him as co-defendant.

I was soon approached by Tolstoy's solicitors to give evidence at the trial and make my documents available to both sides. I made it clear that although I would support everything Tolstoy had written about the enormity of our action, I was unable to accept his allegations that Aldington had arranged every detail of it, and was as guilty as the major war criminals at Nuremberg. The most that I was prepared to say in court was that he did not expect the statements in the pamphlet to be taken literally, and that he had written them under strong emotional stress. Privately I considered that he had been intemperate. How could Aldington have arranged every detail, when details are left to subordinates, and he had left Austria a week before the Cossack repatriations began? To call him responsible was to imply that he was solely responsible, an impossibility in a tightly knit command structure. If he was a "war-criminal," so were all of us who had assisted in the execution of the plan. The central question was, Whose was the ultimate responsibility? But the trial could not be concerned with that. The jury could only be asked to decide whether Tolstoy's charges against Aldington were justified.

To refresh my memory before the trial began, I went with Nikolai to Austria in August 1988. I drove our hired car through the countryside of Carinthia, where fields as green and smooth as lawns, trailing forests, cuckoo-clock houses, pencil-pointed steeples and lakes with crinkled edges reminded me of the idyllic background to these atrocious events. I revisited the stations of Rosenbach and Maria Elend, drove to the Loibhl Pass which separated Austria from Yugoslavia, and toured the sites of the Viktring camp and the Ferlach bridge. We stayed two nights at Bleiburg, as guests of Graf Ariprand Thurn in his gaunt medieval castle, which had been the scene of the conference between a British Brigadier and a partisan captain, resulting in the massacre of thousands of Croats on 16 May. These events, the Count told us, were remembered by the old people: to the young they were as remote as the Black Death. Next day we drove to Judenberg, where the Cossacks were handed over to the Red Army at a bridge from which many of them threw themselves to an easier death. Returning to Klagenfurt I was joined by my daughter Rebecca, and I took her to the scene of my crimes. We won 250 schillings in the casino at Velden, and then drove over the mountains to Kitzbühel, where we spent four happy days. This was all before the storm.

THE TRIAL

I had never known Toby Aldington well, but we had been acquainted for many years, first in the Army as far as our disparate ranks allowed, then in the House of Commons, where he was Minister of State at the Board of Trade and Deputy Chairman of the Conservative Party, and latterly as neighbors in Kent where we very occasionally met at local events. But we had never been invited to each other's houses, until the summer of 1987 when he suggested that we might meet to discuss his impending suit against Tolstoy. This meeting never took place, because he could not agree to my conditions that a third person should be present (I suggested Lord Deedes, a friend of both of us), and that each would be free to repeat to our solicitors what the other said. I also told him that I was in a sense a hostile witness, as I intended to appear for Tolstoy, and considered the repatriation of the Jugs "disgraceful."

I did not see him again until we met in court. "Met" is an exaggeration, for although we sat on the same front bench throughout the trial, separated only by his young solicitor, Lindsay George, we never spoke until after I had given my evidence. Then I crossed the corridor to the men's lavatory to find one other person in it, Lord Aldington. The situation was awkward, as I had said some harsh things about him. So I muttered, "Well, Toby, I fear that all this must be rather a strain on you." He replied, "It has taken me ten hours to recover from being called a murderer." I started to remonstrate that I had said no such thing, nor even thought it, but by that time he was buttoning himself up, actually and metaphorically. I have not seen him since. He must regard me as an enemy, and in peacetime I am not used to having enemies. Once in 1994 when I invited another neighbor to lunch, she declined with the excuse, "You see, I'm a close friend of Toby Aldington." That, from her, hurt. Though her loyalty to Toby did her credit, I felt the snub undeserved. She must have imagined that I was doing everything to encourage Tolstoy to persecute him, when I was doing my utmost to restrain him.

Toby Aldington has had a distinguished career. In the war he won the DSO in action and became the second youngest Brigadier in the British Army. As a Minister he was well regarded and was one of Edward Heath's closest advisers. Harold Macmillan awarded him a peerage. In business he was Chairman or Director of many companies besides Sun Alliance, which helped him with his legal costs, and was Chairman of the Port of London Authority. But he never became a household name until the trial. He was not averse to publicity but did not seem to attract it. He was regarded as a high-level Establishment figure, a member of the Beefsteak and Carlton Clubs, high Tory, no more xenophobic than most members of his class, with a jolly, naval more than military, manner, yet emotional (he wept during the trial), family-loving and utterly unrepentant of his role in Austria.

I am sure that so civilized a man sympathized with the victims of the orders, but he did not show it during the trial. His main aim, understandably, was to exonerate himself. He claimed to have acted strictly in accordance with the orders he received, but if there was any ambiguity in those orders, he never gave the Jugs and Cossacks the benefit of the doubt. He could have said to General Keightley, "I suggest, sir, that we are being told to do something which is not only inhumane and contrary to the tradition of the Army, but unnecessary. Let me draft a signal to 8th Army proposing an alternative course, like sending the Jugs to the Tyrol or Italy, and screening the Cossacks." But he did not do this. Nor, to the best of my knowledge, did he ever visit the Viktring camp or the stations. In a BBC interview in 1985 he admitted that he would have advised his General differently if he had known that the Yugoslavs would be murdered, but he did not know. Nobody had told him.

So at the trial, an important part of the argument concerned his alleged ignorance of what their fate would be. It was Tolstoy's contention that if he genuinely believed Tito's emissary that they would be well treated, he was the only person in the Corps to do so. He must have known of the Bleiburg massacre and of Tito's indifference to the Geneva Convention. Even if my sitreps never reached him, he had many other sources of information and I wondered why our warnings never penetrated the barrier of 6th Armoured Division's headquarters, to whom I was reporting daily. I was prevented by rigid Army rules from approaching Toby Low or his General direct. Now I wish that I had done so.

I need not enter here into the complex arguments of the trial, which started in the High Court on 3 October 1989 and continued for seven weeks. Each day I commuted from Sissinghurst to London, and sat in court listening to the pleadings and evidence that I would later have to support or confute. Two eminent QCs were engaged, Richard Rampton for Tolstoy and Charles Gray for Aldington. It was my first experience of a major trial, and I was entranced by the skill of the advocates in mastering a subject hitherto totally unfamiliar to them, and by the dexterity and eloquence of their speeches. I was also impressed by the attention given to the evidence by the jury, twelve men and women who sat with us every day but whose anonymity remained inviolate to the end. I was less impressed by the Judge, Mr Justice Michael Davies, a homely old soul, who did not seem to react to the evidence with the sharpness of both Counsels, and appeared rather put out that most of the witnesses were older than himself. He left little doubt in our minds that if he had been a member of the jury he would have taken Aldington's side. This, I was told, is quite legitimate. A judge is not bound to appear completely impartial. It is, in fact, his duty to indicate which pan in the balance of argument carries, in his opinion, the greater weight. He does this by the familiar device of suggesting his own views indirectly ("You may think, members of the jury—but of course it is entirely for you to decide—that . . ."), and in his summing-up he can select from the opposing arguments those elements which emphasize one point of view rather than the other.

Lord Aldington was the first witness to be called. He adopted his Jolly Jack manner, but his attitude was not displeasing: he was the decent, courteous, reasonable, experienced war hero, politician and businessman. He told his familiar story: he had simply carried out his orders; he always reported to his superiors what he was about to do; he gained their consent; his motive was to "clear the decks" in case of a war with Tito; he never received any of my sitreps; he left Austria after giving minimal orders about the Cossacks. There was nothing of which he need feel ashamed.

Then it was Tolstoy's turn. His wife, Georgina, sat beside me and brought her two elder daughters, Alexandra and Anastasia, to support their dad and further their education. Nikolai Tolstoy started his evidence without the advantage of having Establishment opinion behind him. At London dinner parties, where the case was currently the only topic of conversation, it was thought "unfair" to persecute a man of seventy-five for something that he may or may not have done in his youth, and Tolstoy was unfortunate in his association with Nigel Watts, whose desire for revenge tarnished Tolstoy's more honorable motive. Nikolai thought that all would go well for him. I did not. He would have a problem in justifying the extreme language of the Winchester pamphlet. All depended on the impression he would make on the jury.

He entered the witness box on 25 October. That evening I wrote in my diary:

> He is dressed in a blue blazer with gold buttons and Simpson slacks, looks young, British, like a naval officer facing a court-martial which he expects to declare him innocent. His manner is articulate, calm, well-informed, very different from the crazy Cossack whom the jury had been told to expect. Rampton tries to get at his 'state of mind' when he wrote the pamphlet, excusing its intemperance by his 'natural anger at discovering the truth'. This is a clever, in fact the only possible, defence.

When Charles Gray began his cross-examination, Nikolai grew stronger and stronger. He said that if a German officer had been responsible for the fate of the seventy thousand, he would certainly have been charged with a war crime. Gray darted about, seeking an opening. What is a war criminal? Is he a person who participates in a policy which unexpectedly leads to a massacre? In that case, Churchill, Alexander, Macmillan, McCreery (commanding 8th Army) and Captain Nicolson (I was always referred to like this, for the first time in forty years) are also war criminals. Nikolai replied that Toby Low was one of the few people who could have stopped it. Then he tore to pieces General Murray's mendacious report. He ended the day with a splendid attack on Cowgill, who was sitting at the back of the court with Alistair Horne. I did not know that he had so much fire and eloquence in him and thought that I might have been wrong to advise him to play it cool. All the same, at the end of his evidence, I gave him only a 45/55 chance of winning.

The witnesses for the defence, apart from myself, were mostly Yugoslav refugees who had been brought to London at enormous expense from Canada, Tasmania, South America and the United States to give evidence of their ill-treatment by the British, Russians, Germans and partisans. But it had been agreed between the two sides that the hand-overs and the massacres *had* taken place, so their evidence was irrelevant. To their great disappointment they were not allowed to tell the stories which might have wrung the jury-men's hearts. The British witnesses were few, since most were dead. John Buchanan, the Brigade Major of 1st Guards Brigade, could remember nothing about the incident and had no letters or diary to remind him, and William Bell, who had shown me his letters expressing our common despair, was under-standably reluctant to give evidence against Aldington when it might appear to be in favor of Watts. We could have subpoenaed him, but I advised against it, since a reluctant witness makes a bad witness, and I believed that I could supply enough proof of what happened and how we felt.

On 13 November, the day after the Berlin Wall was breached, I took the stand. Spread over two days, my evidence took five hours. At first Richard Rampton led me through the events up to the formation of the Viktring camp and the order to repatriate the Jugs.

Q   On the receipt of the verbal order, the reaction in your Brigade was one of disbelief. Is that right?
A   Correct.
Q   When the written order arrived next day, what was the reaction then?
A   We considered it to be one of the most disgraceful operations that British troops have ever been ordered to undertake.

As I said that, I saw Lord Aldington, who was sitting just below me, bury his face in his hands, not from remorse, I surmised, but with astonishment that I could make so dreadful a charge.

Q   That seems a very strong reaction. Can you tell us the reason for it?
A   We were being ordered to hand over, to what we considered was almost certain death, thousands of people who had surrendered to us and come to trust us, and now we were to betray their trust and send them to their arch-enemies.

On the second day I was cross-examined by Charles Gray. Every witness has one advantage over the most skilful of Counsel, that he knows more about the subject than his interrogator and, if he has nothing to hide, he has nothing to fear. He asked me about high-level plans to evict Tito from Carinthia by force, and I was able to show that at our level we had no knowledge of them until the emergency was over. The repatriations began on the very day, 19 May, that Tito began to withdraw.

Then I was questioned about the sitrep in which I told the lie, on General Murray's orders, that we expected the Jugs to be well treated.

MR. GRAY If you had told the truth, you would not have been very popular.

A That is right.

THE JUDGE Would that have mattered really? You were not a career officer and the war was over.

A My Lord, I now feel that I should have disobeyed General Murray. I would probably have been court-martialled and might have gone to prison for a year. But I would have emerged with credit.

I finished my evidence without having to answer Gray's expected question: "Do you agree with Count Tolstoy that Lord Aldington arranged every detail which led to the massacres and that his behaviour was comparable to the worst excesses of the Nazis?" I had prepared my answer and warned Nikolai what it would be: "No, I do not agree. Count Tolstoy was indulging in a hyperbole which the facts do not justify. I do believe that what took place was a war-crime, but I do not consider Lord Aldington a war-criminal. Nonetheless he carried out his orders with alacrity and apparently without considering their purpose, consequences or alternatives." But I was not asked that question.

The closing addresses of the two QCs were more brilliant than equivalent speeches in Parliament, but the Judge's summing-up was more pedestrian. He was impeccably judicious in defining the law of libel, but when he came to examine the evidence, he did little to help Tolstoy's cause. As Rampton slyly remarked, one cannot expect the Judge to make a speech for the defence. Of me he said to the jury, "Whether you think Captain Nicolson was rather a wet, is a matter entirely for you"; and referring to one of Tolstoy's letters, he asked, "Is that the letter of a balanced historian, or the letter of a fanatic?" Later Nigel Watts shouted, "Your summing-up is a disgrace to the legal profession," and stormed out of court, never to reappear. To his credit, Judge Davies did not order his arrest for contempt.

The verdict came on 30 November 1989. To every question put to them, the jury found in favor of Aldington, and awarded him costs and £1.5 million in damages, treble the previous highest award in a libel case. The Judge then imposed an injunction on Watts and Tolstoy not to repeat the libel. Some newspapers reported that the award was received with gasps of astonishment, but my recollection is that there was dead silence for a few seconds, broken by a sob from Anastasia Tolstoy, aged fourteen. Her father put a consoling arm round her shoulders and led her away. Outside the court, Lord Aldington was declaring to the TV cameras, "I am absolutely delighted by the vindication of my reputation."

THE AFTERMATH

The press reaction was not quite so definite. Simon Jenkins in the *Sunday Times* summed up what many people were thinking: "Lord Aldington emerged as an unappetising figure. His basic explanation—'I was obeying orders'—was in essence that used by some of the Nuremberg defendants. It still echoes uncomfortably down the years. Orders can be just or unjust, and obedience to them likewise. 'We took the German officers out and shot them.'" But he continued: "Tolstoy went for Aldington obsessively, targeting him as a visible link in the chain of responsibility. This was unfair." It was true that Aldington attracted more than his proper share of blame because he was the only one left alive. I believed that the inquiry should be widened to discover who was really responsible. Cowgill had not done so. The trial was concerned with the responsibility of a single man. The official history of the war had evaded the issue. The chain of command had stretched from Churchill and Eden at Yalta to the Welsh guardsman who locked the last of the cattle trucks at Rosenbach. Should there not be an impartial inquiry, supported but not conducted by the Government? I put this suggestion to my MP, Sir Patrick Mayhew, who was then Attorney General. He referred it to Tom King, the Defence Secretary, and to Douglas Hurd, the Foreign Secretary. Both replied that it was now a matter for historians, not for the Government. It seemed that the case was closed.

Not quite. Tolstoy was determined to fight on. As he was bankrupted by his legal debts, he could not pay Aldington's costs or any part of the damages, which Aldington offered to reduce from £1.500 million to £300,000. Friends in Britain and abroad contributed to a Family Fund, of which Ludovic Kennedy, Bernard Braine MP and myself were the Trustees, so that the Tolstoys could still afford to live in their Abingdon house and educate their children. Meanwhile, Nikolai gathered evidence for an appeal.

He was emotionally engaged in the case to a greater extent than any of his British supporters. Half-Russian himself, though born in England and educated at Wellington College and Trinity College, Dublin, he felt deeply the injustice done to the Cossacks, specially the émigrés among them, and was determined to vindicate them. For the Yugoslavs he felt almost equally indignant. My own belief was that by his two books on the subject, and the publication of the evidence in the Cowgill Report and at the trial, he had amply made his point, and to pursue it further would only bore the public and the judiciary, and detract from his achievement. Ludovic Kennedy felt the same and together we tried to persuade him to abandon further litigation. In February 1991 I wrote to him:

> You insist on pursuing your case through the European Court and the British courts, putting yourself under great strain and incurring fresh expense, and writing Newsletters that are so slanted in your favour, so filled with venom against your opponents, so abusive of the British legal system, that even those who support you must question whether your obsession with this case has not rendered you crazy. . . . You won the moral victory; now you are in danger of throwing away that advantage by overstating your case.

It did no good. Nobody who has pursued an argument for so long, so valiantly, is likely to be deterred by the warnings of his friends. Georgina's support for her husband never wavered, and she dealt admirably with their precarious finances. With formidable resolution, Tolstoy pressed on with his crusade, appearing in person at successive court hearings, though often aided, without charge, by Richard Rampton. He had no lack of admirers. Like myself, they believed that in spite of his wilder charges, he had moral truth on his side. Men of distinction like Alexander Solzhenitsyn, Graham Greene and Hugh Thomas openly expressed their sympathy for him. Photographs of his attractive family appeared regularly in the illustrated magazines, and he lectured on the case in many foreign countries. His co-defendant, Nigel Watts, was less careful not to breach the injunction, and was sentenced to prison for eighteen months for referring to Aldington as "the most perfidious and treacherous war-criminal in Europe," and to the judiciary as corrupt.

Tolstoy appealed against the 1989 verdict and the size of the damages. His appeal was disallowed because he could not put down sufficient money as "security for costs" in case he lost again. He issued a writ for perjury against Aldington based on the claim that new evidence discovered in the Public Record Office indicated that he had lied to the court about the date of his departure from Austria. The writ was struck out *in camera*. The European Court of Human Rights at Strasbourg, in a rather muddled judgement, allowed that the award was excessive but did not pronounce on the merits of the case or the new evidence.

It always seemed to me that a deluge was about to engulf the Tolstoy household, but he managed to postpone from year to year the day when his house, library and other property would be sequestered by the Trustee in Bankruptcy. I had confidence that even if disaster struck, he would rise above the roar of the waters with his head held high. It was always an invigorating experience to visit the family at Abingdon, and to welcome them to Sissinghurst. I continued to plead with him to abandon his quest for a "smoking gun" that did not exist, and return to his lucrative profession as historian and novelist of the Dark Ages, but on this we disagreed.

There was one moment when I thought that the affair might be settled finally if not amicably. In 1991 the BBC broadcast a television documentary about these events under the title "A British Betrayal." It was admirably researched, and included much archive film, presenting the story with great fairness to both sides although Aldington refused the BBC's invitation to take part and Tolstoy was named as their "research assistant." Aldington issued a writ against the BBC, objecting particularly to the title. There had been no "British Betrayal." Hitherto he has not taken the BBC to court. A pity. If the fairness of the program could be decided without the two protagonists coming into direct confrontation with each other, both might at last be freed from the mutual recriminations that have dogged their lives for so long.

SIX

THE POLITICIAN

〜❦〜

The first time I entered the House of Commons was in November 1936, when I was aged nineteen. My father, the MP for West Leicester, had been nominated to Second the Address. Both those words demand capitals and therefore explanation. The Address is the strange method whereby Parliament thanks the Sovereign for her (in 1936, his, for the only time in Edward VIII's short reign) Gracious Speech, in which the Government's legislative program for the next session is outlined. Two back-bench MPs are chosen to Move and Second the Address before the serious debating begins. It is regarded as a great honor to be selected, for it is the only occasion when an unimportant member can be guaranteed a full house. Dame Florence Horsbrugh was the mover, my father the seconder. He was dressed, according to custom, in uniform, and the only uniform to which he was entitled (and that dubiously, because he had resigned from the Foreign Service in 1929) was that of the Diplomatic Corps. I was given a seat in the public gallery. I watched him anxiously.

Dame Florence spoke her piece beautifully and was warmly applauded. Harold then rose. By convention he was bound to mention his constituency, and the Leicester seat had been contested, unsuccessfully, both by Ramsay MacDonald, the former Labour Prime Minister, and by Winston Churchill. Thinking it a good opportunity to pay a compliment to both, Harold began, "My constituency, which, maybe in a moment of blindness, refrained from electing the Rt. Hon. Member for Epping [Churchill]," at which Churchill flashed out, "They also refrained from electing the Rt. Hon. Member for the Scottish Universities [MacDonald]." There were hoots of derision from the Labour members, with whom their former leader was in dire disgrace. Harold's speech was wrecked at its outset, and when he continued to heap on MacDonald's head the tributes which he had carefully prepared, the jeers redoubled. It was then that I realized that politics is the cruelest of professions.

After this near disaster, I lunched with my poor father, who had previously invited the very person whom he had inadvertently humiliated, Ramsay MacDonald. The old man was sweet to me. "It's vurry noice to see you following in your farrther's footsteps, my boy!" but, as I had been warned, he had only one subject of conversation, himself. He told us in detail how he had been sick at the Lord Mayor's banquet the night before. "A wave of hot sticky air hit me between the eyes and the next thing I knew was that I was being sick into a policeman's lap." He also told us what he was intending to wear on Armistice Day, how he was having his life mask taken that afternoon and how kind people had been to him in Canada. It was then that I learned my second political lesson: though modesty will get you nowhere, vanity is self-destructive.

LEICESTER AND FALMOUTH

In those prewar days I wasn't a politician at all. A single speech at the Oxford Union did not qualify me and my Newcastle experience fitted me more for the Civil Service than for politics. It taught me more about how to make unhappy people slightly less unhappy than the causes of unhappiness itself. But it undoubtedly bent me to the left, just as my German experience had tipped me temporarily to the right. I was born in the middle of the road. The war did little to divert me in one direction or another, but it did teach me how to speak and write. I became my Regiment's lecturer and historian.

I drifted into politics. When Harold lost West Leicester in the General Election of 1945, his Chairman, Bertie Jarvis, invited me to stand for the seat, on condition that I called myself Conservative, not National Labour, my father's label. So I found myself a Conservative, not with great conviction, and at successive Elections ladled out to the electorate a bowl of soup from the Party tureen. I was not alone in this. Few of us can claim that we joined our

Party after profound self-analysis. We join because of family tradition, or because our friends already belong, or because circumstances, like mine, steer us in that direction. Having joined, the average voter is reluctant to change and spends the rest of his life explaining why he could never have done anything else. The arguments, in fact, come after the decision. Political parties work on this foible. The Party vote is heavily weighted by electors who think it not only disloyal, but irresolute, to change their minds. The MP, on the other hand, discovers his true place in the political spectrum after some experience of Parliament itself. So, at least, it was with me.

The candidate, once selected, ignores the pejorative term "prospective" which belittles his status, and sees himself as halfway to Westminster. He is elated by the acclamation of his supporters at the adoption meeting, but it is not long before he realizes that few people are sufficiently interested in him to inquire his name. He must expect rebuffs outside the small circle where he is a hero, and strive, however humiliating the process, to make himself popular without displaying false fellowship. He must remember Edmund Burke's warning, "The very attempt towards pleasing everybody discovers a temper always flashy and insincere." He requires natural courtesy, an average capacity for concealing boredom, good humor and a gift for remembering names. It was in this latter quality that I was most deficient. Once I sat opposite a man in a train for two hours, reading the newspaper. I glanced at him; he glanced back at me. Later I heard that I had "cut dead" a leading Councillor of one of my wards. He was outraged. It never occurred to him that I had simply failed to recognize him.

The Leicester Election of 1950 was placid. My worst moment came when a woman asked me at a public meeting how much half a pound of butter cost. I had no idea and said so. She protested, "How can you stand there and ask us to send you to Parliament to represent us, when you don't even know the simplest facts that affect every family in the country?" It was the most effective heckle that I ever experienced. For other reasons, too, like mounting unemployment, I lost the Election to my Labour opponent, Barnett Janner, who had also defeated my father in 1945. To every question that I put to him from my platform, he replied, "Ask Dad," for Harold had stood as the Labour candidate at a Croydon by-election in 1948. But our apparent conflict did me more good than harm: the father represented old-fashioned Labour; the son modern Toryism. Or so my supporters said and I pretended not to hear.

Then came Falmouth and Camborne. I was adopted as the candidate for the seat because Cornishmen can seldom agree on a Cornishman, being too familiar with his personal history, and my uncle, Lord St. Levan, owned St. Michael's Mount. I nursed the seat with greater love than I ever nursed Leicester. Every Friday night I traveled by sleeper to Camborne, to be welcomed at breakfast by Donald Thomas, a solicitor and prominent benefactor of the National Trust, his wife, Viva, and their son Charles, who became a distinguished professor of archaeology. Or I would travel direct to Falmouth and stay with other friends, the Needhams, whose son Richard was to serve in the Thatcher Government.

The constituency stretched from coast to coast, the northern part bold and rugged, the southern (including the Fal estuary and the Helford River) almost tropical in its luxuriance. I walked the cliffs, the farms, the creeks, hoping that one day I might claim them as my fiefdom. I learned just enough about agriculture to impress the miners, and about tin mining to impress the farmers. At my first village fête, I faced disaster. There was a stall at which I was invited to guess the weight of a pig. My supporters crowded round me, urging me on, but not one had the wit to whisper a suggestion. I was at a total loss. Fortunately, in his excitement, the stall holder held out his list at an angle where I could just read the bids of previous contestants—47, 52, 60, 41—pounds, I guessed. I eyed the animal with an expert eye. "Fifty-six," I announced. "My God, you've won it!" It is by such underhand means that candidates for Parliament establish their credentials.

The Election campaign of 1951 was highly enjoyable, except for the result. I coped adequately with the friendly factory workers of Camborne and the hostile dockers at Falmouth, but I lost to Labour, owing to the last-minute intervention of a Liberal who had never been to Cornwall in his life. I called it a "frivolous candidature." I learned my third political lesson: never be bitter in defeat.

BOURNEMOUTH

Two electoral failures in succession do not, paradoxically, amount to an aborted political career. They stamp the rejected candidate as "experienced," just as a medieval squire qualified by lost battles to be dubbed a knight. I rose higher on the Central Office list of candidates, aided by my father's friendship with Jim Thomas, the Deputy Chairman of the Party in charge of candidate selection. It is in such ways that nepotism plays its hidden part. Jim put forward my name to the Conservative Association of Bournemouth East and Christchurch, a seat vacated by Brendan Bracken, who was made a peer soon after the 1951 Election. It was one of the safest seats in England, and I was told that there were four hundred other applicants for it. They were reduced by the Executive of the Association to a short list of six, of whom I was one.

I drove down to Bournemouth, feeling like a carpet-bagger. Thinking that the candidate must not appear before the Selection Committee completely penniless, I went to the Christchurch branch of my bank to cash a check and startled the cashier by introducing myself with the words. "I bark at Bankleys." I was exceedingly nervous and became more so when I discovered that my five rivals included Roy Harrod, the Oxford economist, and John Wyndham, Harold Macmillan's private secretary and boon companion, who arrived bearing a strong recommendation from his boss. Someone politically more astute than myself had advised me that my rivals were bound to emphasize their good points. My only chance was to emphasize my bad points, thereby gaining sympathy for my bashfulness and respect for my honesty.

I had four bad points, and with Machiavellian cunning deployed them one by one. I was not married—"yet," I added after a significant pause (there were many spinster daughters in Bournemouth). My father was a Socialist (excellent: the young generation has its head screwed on the right way). I was not well off: I had to earn my living (so do we all). And I could not promise always to do what I was told by them (who would expect him to?). In contrast, Roy Harrod lectured the Committee on the present state of the British economy which scared them, and when asked whether he would live in Bournemouth if elected, replied, "Good God, no!" John Wyndham flourished his letter from Macmillan, which made him appear an official nominee and therefore suspect.

The candidates withdrew to an upper room, all with wives except me, and for half an hour we made uneasy conversation. I do not have an acute aural memory, but the sound of the agent's footsteps mounting the uncarpeted stair will never leave me. He opened the door and spoke my name. "Good God!" said Roy Harrod again.

In a sense, of course, he was right. I may have been a plausible Member for Christchurch, but I was wrong for Bournemouth. The history of the two boroughs mirrored their different politics. Bournemouth did not exist, even as a fishing village, until 1810, and was a seaside resort and a place of retirement for people who had served in the civil, colonial and armed services, whilst

Christchurch had a history extending back to the Bronze Age, one of the loveliest priory churches in England and was more liberal in its attitudes. Among my future constituents there were three men of distinction: Sir Donald Bailey, who invented the military bridge named after him; Sir Horace Wilson, Neville Chamberlain's *éminence grise;* and Lord Quickswood, formerly Provost of Eton and now President of my Association. All supported me in my troubles. The Chairman was Major S. Grant, ex-Indian Army. He did not.

In those days, vast Conservative majorities on the south coast were cast-iron, even at by-elections. So I sailed through the preliminaries without a qualm, till polling day, 6 February 1952. Then something very dramatic happened. The King died. The news reached us in the middle of the morning and we panicked that our supporters might be too shocked to vote before the monarch was even cold in his bed, let alone in his grave. It was my mother who saved the day. She had come to Bournemouth to see her son elected. She telephoned friends in the BBC and persuaded them to broadcast a message that voting in the by-election was unaffected by this tragedy, and we supplemented it by loudspeaker announcements in the streets that Bournemouth and Christchurch had the honor of electing the first MP in the reign of Queen Elizabeth II. That did the trick. I had a majority of over fourteen thousand. Harold read the news on the tape at the Travellers Club and telegraphed his congratulations: "You have a safe seat for life."

HOUSE OF COMMONS

When the successful candidate at a by-election reaches Westminster, his arrival, unless the result has been very unexpected, is treated with disarming indifference. He is introduced at the end of Questions, flanked by two Members. Mine were Edward Heath, the Chief Whip, whom I had known at Balliol, and Anthony Nutting, whose constituency, Melton, was contiguous to Leicester. As I awaited the summons at the bar, a Labour Member, and previous Chancellor, Hugh Dalton, whispered in my ear, "In a few minutes you will walk behind the Speaker's chair into the obscurity from which you should never have emerged." It was meant kindly.

Later that day, Ted Heath took me to the smoking room to meet the Prime Minister. As we walked along the corridor, he said, "Remember, Winston simply hates small talk." I was already very alarmed by the forthcoming encounter, but now I panicked. What big talk could I possibly think up in the thirty seconds that remained? When we reached him, Churchill was reading the racing results. He had a horse running that day at Kempton Park. Heath introduced me: "This is Nicolson, sir. The new Member for Bournemouth East." He did not even look up. Heath then left us. I spoke my hastily prepared question: "Prime Minister, what do you consider the most important quality in a man?" At that he did look up and, over the rim of his spectacles and the rim of the newspaper, he spoke one word in reply: "Mettle." He then resumed his study of how his horse had done.

I never had another conversation with him, but twice I listened while he talked to others. Late one evening, again in the smoking room, he discussed with Aneurin Bevan, his most brilliant opponent, what permanent effect the Civil War had had on the British character. To me it was a revelation of both men's learning and mutual regard. The second occasion was disconcerting. A group of young Tories gathered round him to induce him to make some favourable reference to the Welfare State, with which Churchill was totally out of sympathy. Afterwards he said to an old friend, Sir Ralph Glyn, "Ralph, who were those young men talking to me just now? They're not members of our Party, surely? They're nothing but a bunch of pink pansies."

We were ardent for reform. We believed that the gap between rich and poor was too wide and should be narrowed, that the sick, unemployed and aged should be upheld by the hale and hearty, that the Trade Unions should be treated as allies not enemies, and that university entrance should be broadened to accept the underprivileged. The leaders of our truancy were R. A. Butler, Iain Macleod and Harold Macmillan, but it was Macmillan who delighted us most. He had been the candidates' favorite Minister, speaking to our small group as if we were already trusted colleagues. Once he produced from his pocket a rubber ball and a matchbox, rolling the ball over the table to represent Tory elasticity and love of compromise, slapping the box from face to face to illustrate Socialist rigidity. It wasn't intended as a fair comparison, but it was typical of his throw-away style. Here is another example, which I described to my wife in a letter after Macmillan became Prime Minister. We had invited him to address a small dining club of back-bench Members:

> After dinner he talked to us between puffs of a cigar and sips of brandy. 'I wonder,' he said, 'in what way we should design the future

of our country. What do the people want? Are they happier because they are richer? I don't think so. Were we happier when, fifty years ago, we had stables of horses and fifteen servants? Of course not. The horses were always going lame and the servants were always quarrelling. Even then, we would have been thankful to move into a service flat. But at least we could afford our servants and horses. Today the working people think they can afford their TV and cars, but of course they can't. We must manage to persuade them to work and save. They take prosperity for granted.

'It is the same with the Commonwealth. Tomorrow I have got to meet the Prime Ministers. They all expect me to say that we will invest £100 million in their countries. Four black faces, and six white faces, will look at me expectantly. What am I to tell them? Has it any meaning at all, this assembly of such different nations?'

Then I said to him, 'Prime Minister, when a new officer joined your staff at Eisenhower's headquarters in Algiers, you used to tell them: "We are the Greeks here, and the Americans are the Romans. We have the ideas, and do most of the work. They have the power. You mustn't mind this. It is the way that we exert our influence." Do you still believe that?' He replied, 'Yes, but the trouble is that our Party don't want to be Greeks. They want to be Romans. Toryism must change because our capacity has changed.'

That was the side of politics that I most enjoyed: association, if only tangentially, with men of humanity, wit and large experience, who had immense power in their hands. It was independent of Party. Once I was sitting in the tea room reading a newspaper when Clement Attlee, Leader of the Opposition, sat down opposite me. He saw the headline, upside down, "Dulles flays Attlee" (he had recently made a speech hostile to the U.S. Secretary of State, and this was Dulles's reply). "When, I wonder," he said, "will they ever write 'Attlee flays Dulles'?" He did not know who I was, except that I was not a member of his own Party. We were just fellow-MPs.

It struck me as sad—and still does—that the public never see the House of Commons in that guise. They are encouraged by televised combats to regard it as a bear garden, in which the only test of merit is the dexterity with which the champions handle their weapons. Because politicians treat each other with contempt, they are treated by the public with contempt. The electors urge them on. Although they consider the parliamentary charade unedifying, there would soon be complaints if politicians did not behave in this way. They would be accused of lacking guts and giving no leadership. Opinion polls always place politicians near the bottom of the popularity list. Asked to explain why, people will say that they consider them to be dishonest, unwilling to depart from the Party line or admit a mistake, lacking in humility, voting themselves higher salaries, and ignorant of the problems of ordinary men and women. The latter charge is the least deserved, because MPs through their postbags and surgeries gain a knowledge of ordinary people far greater than that of most ordinary people. The complaint that "they don't look after people like me" simply means that the voter's interests (usually financial) have not been satisfied to the extent that he hoped.

What is the reason for the public's distrust of their representatives? It can scarcely be due to suspicion that they are corrupt. The rarity of the occasions when an MP is found behaving dubiously is itself proof of honesty. There is far more chicanery in local government, and in most professions, than there is in Parliament. Is it then "broken promises"? This normally means that some policies are changed because circumstances turn out differently from those envisaged at the Election. Is it not creditable that Ministers can change their minds? It is often regarded as discreditable when they do not.

Our loss of faith in democracy has a deeper cause, in destructive cynicism. The theory that politics is a dirty business is fed by journalism that delights in disgrace and failure, and ignores originality, courage and success. Political ambition is regarded as faintly distasteful. Soliciting votes at Election time is a degrading necessity. It is called "self-seeking," when in every other profession self-seeking is normal practice, though conducted in more hidden ways. Politics is the most precarious and challenging of them all. There is no place except a battlefield that reveals a person's quality more rapidly and fairly than the House of Commons. It is an honorable profession, and if the elector disapproves of its staged animosities, the shouting, the intrigue, he should admit that he has stimulated it and that there is nothing that he enjoys more.

Most parliamentary debate involves no shouting. It can be sedate to the point of dullness, but the voter who derives his impression of Parliament from televised snippets of the dramatic occasions never sees this. Nor can he have any idea how formidable a place it is, how alarming it can be to address the House. Every word uttered is printed in *Hansard*, with no chance to retrieve an error of fact or taste. The back-bencher may have risen patiently for six hours in the hope of catching the Speaker's eye, hearing his "points" anticipated by others, and then he may not be called at all. If he is, he has an audience of perhaps a dozen, all of whom are urging him to sit down so that they can stand up, and who probably know more about the subject of debate than he does. He, feeling terribly amateur, is addressing a row of impatient professionals. He is not allowed to read his speech from a prepared text. His only support is the back of the bench in front of him, which reaches no higher than his knees. The shape of the Chamber obliges him to turn his back on his friends and confront his opponents. A parliamentary speech is so enervating an experience that even Lloyd George, the greatest orator of his times, said that he never rose to his feet at the despatch box without his knees knocking together.

There is also the problem of what the Member is to talk about. He must seek publicity for what he says, if only to gratify his constituents. So he searches the Order Paper for subjects which have a constituency angle, or of which he has some knowledge from his other profession, if he has one. I, for instance, could talk about publishing and censorship. But it was so rare a parliamentary topic that I found myself acquiring instant expertise in several others. My maiden speech was on emigration to the Commonwealth, a subject in which I showed no further interest. Or it might be local government finance, or the Heritage, or capital punishment. In all my seven years in the House I was never once called to speak on my major interest, foreign affairs.

Parliament teaches its Members that government is immensely complex and that a gift for administration is as important a qualification as strong political beliefs. The back-bench Member does not administer anything, but he investigates the work of people who do. To me, the Select Committees were the most enjoyable part of parliamentary life. I would be allotted by the Whips to one of them, whether I knew anything of the subject or not. Ignorance was called "a fresh mind." As a member of the Estimates Committee in the year when it was dealing with Defence, I spent happy days interrogating experts, visiting airfields and barracks, with colleagues of all three parties, and occasionally attention might be paid by Ministers to some aspects of the Committee's report.

THE EUROPEAN PARLIAMENT

In the 1950s it was known as the Consultative Assembly of the Council of Europe, and its members were nominated by governments from non-ministerial Members of their Parliaments. It was an opportunity for people like me, whose views on foreign affairs made little impact at Westminster, to shine with a fitful flame on the international stage, and it was an advantage if you could speak more than one foreign language. The disadvantages were that our constituents were not only ignorant of the Council's purpose but suspicious of it. To be a member of the British delegation added nothing to our local prestige: it was regarded as a distraction from our proper role, which was to defend our constituency's interests. Moreover, successive British Governments were lukewarm toward the Council. It was said that Ernest Bevin advocated Strasbourg as its headquarters (Amsterdam would have been much better) because everyone felt ill there, and the iller they felt, the less trouble they would cause.

But for the participants, Strasbourg was pure joy. It compensated for the humiliations of Westminster. The British in those early days were regarded with respect and even awe. It was a common delusion among us that we were founder members of a Brave New World. We were about to solve the problems of centuries, setting moral standards of international conduct that had never been adumbrated before. Once at a sub-committee meeting in Paris we spent a whole morning discussing the first line of the first clause of a European Charter of Human Rights: "Every man has the right to work." Each word of this doctrine was challenged: "every," "man," "right," "work." National philosophies were paraded at considerable length. The British were pragmatic, the French cynical, while the Greeks and Icelanders committed their Governments to social reforms which they had neither the will nor the cash to implement. The unspoken comment was that it mattered little what we decided: nobody outside Strasbourg would pay any attention. It was like one of those children's games that come in shiny boxes. This one was called "Foreign Secretaries."

We had a lovely time. Strasbourg is a beautiful city, its restaurants superb, and in the country the slopes of the Vosges were scarcely marred by the ruins of the Maginot Line, now huge slabs of concrete toppled sideways into the corn. We made frequent expeditions to this countryside, lunching at small inns with colleagues, members of the secretariat like Nicholas Sombart and visiting journalists like Frank Giles. Every evening there was some reception at which Alsatian wines and pâté de foie gras were consumed in quantity. We stole from the midnight hours time to catch up with the incessant paperwork.

There were also setbacks. In 1955 I, as *rapporteur* of the Council's cultural committee, wrote a paper proposing that we should extend a hand of friendship to countries behind the Iron Curtain by inviting them to send representatives to our committee as observers. After all, eastern Europe was as much the creator and inheritor of the European tradition as we were. I opened a debate on this theme and proposed a motion. Speaker after speaker, including members of my own delegation, denounced my plan, saying that it would create a dangerous precedent, "the thin edge of the wedge." The Communists would contaminate our democratic Assembly, and there would soon be a request to participate in our political and economic committees as well. As I found no support, I passed a note to the leader of our delegation, Hendrie Oakshott, offering to withdraw my motion. He nodded agreement, and looked at me with a mixture of relief, pity and contempt. Forty years later I still recall that look. I lacked the gift of persuading people to support ideas of which they initially disapprove—and that, after all, is the whole purpose of politics.

KÖNIGSWINTER

At Strasbourg we came to know our colleagues more intimately than was possible at Westminster. We were a small group of about a dozen, including some high-flyers like Florence Horsbrugh, Julian Amery and Robert Boothby, and by constant association at parties and in cabals we formed friendships that bore fruit on our return home. Still more valuable were the annual reunions at Königswinter on the Rhine, where the political apartheids between backbench and senior Members were temporarily eliminated. It was in this way that I came to know Hugh Gaitskell, Dick Crossman, Denis Healey, Roy Jenkins, John Strachey and other Labour leaders, and they inclined me more to the left than Bournemouth suspected, specially Healey, whose high spirits, gift for anecdote, mimicry and ballads, allied to his political shrewdness, entranced us all.

The originator and convener of the Königswinter Conference was Lilo Milchsack, the wife of an Anglophile, Nazi-hating ship owner of Düsseldorf. They had both survived the war by keeping their minds open but their mouths shut, and in 1947, with the support of Robert Birley, then in charge of German re-education in the British Zone, she founded the Deutsche–Englische Gesellschaft, which brought together British and German politicians, journalists, civil servants and academics to discuss subjects of mutual interest, like German reunification. The three-day conference was held in some discomfort in a Trade Union hostel opposite Godesberg, where Chamberlain had held his fatal meeting with Hitler in 1938.

The character of the conference was controversy laced with ribaldry and Moselle. There was boating on the Rhine, walking on the Drachenfeld, receptions in Bonn. Of one such reception, by Chancellor Adenauer, in April 1957, I wrote to my wife:

There were soldiers of the new Wehrmacht on either side of the entrance, and flunkies shepherding us along bright corridors towards an ante-room where we found this famous man with his flat, high-cheeked, yellow face, almost Mongoloid. He was wearing a badly cut blue suit and a waxen expression, but he stood remarkably upright for a man of eighty-three. I was told afterwards that he wasn't very pleased. He had a headache, and had just read the British Defence White Paper, which seemed to lower our commitment to NATO. I wandered into the garden with my champagne, and talked to Fritz Erler (who is almost certain to be a future German Prime Minister) and General von Senger, who was Kesselring's Corps Commander at Cassino. It is curious that these people should now represent half the wealth, power and dignity of Europe. In the more solemn moments of our Conference, the businessmen half boast, half warn us, that they are rapidly acquiring the whole commerce of the Far and Middle East, while their soldiers gently hint that if we cannot afford atomic rockets of our own, they can make them for us, free.

From Königswinter in that year some of us flew to Berlin, which was then under Russian blockade, and we were welcomed by Willy Brandt at the town hall. Looking around the table at the heads of his departments, I suddenly realized that half of them were maimed in some way or another—an empty sleeve, a hollow eye socket, three fingers missing from one hand, a face still pock-marked with powder burns—the scars of the most terrible war in history. Their victims were not the only sufferers. Afterwards, Birley took me to the old Ministry of War in the Bendlerstrasse and showed me the courtyard where Klaus von Stauffenberg and the other conspirators were shot on 20 July 1944, and then to the Harlem Art Gallery where he hurried me past the Canalettos and prettier Dutch to contemplate a single picture, a self-portrait by Rembrandt, which he described as "the supreme manifestation of the European genius." In such ways my education continued to make progress under the guidance of that wonderful man.

CAPITAL PUNISHMENT

Things had not gone too badly for me in Bournemouth. In the General Election of May 1955 I was reelected with an increased majority of 18,500 over Labour and Liberal opponents, and had only twice offended my supporters by my left-of-centre views. I had said in a public speech that Aneurin Bevan was not the monster that most Conservatives supposed: he was as good a patriot as I was. Two years later, I said that both major Parties stood for peace, prosperity and justice, and the only quarrel between us was about the means of attaining them. These trite observations created temporary consternation, but between them stretched months and years of peace and amity. In 1953 I married, to general acclaim, and bought a house near Christchurch. Juliet was born there in 1954 and Adam in 1957. I felt welcome wherever I went and, as my position strengthened, my confidence grew.

Then came capital punishment. It was a controversy in which I became deeply involved, largely because no other Tory back-bencher was willing to sponsor the abolitionist cause, knowing that it would split his constituency. I had voted for the abolition of the death penalty for murder before the 1955 Election and my attitude was well known in Bournemouth. At the time it aroused disagreement but little protest. In April 1956 the issue was again put before Parliament, and again I voted on a free vote in favor of abolition, declaring in my speech on the Second Reading of the Bill that I was doing so in the knowledge that a majority of my Conservative constituents disagreed with me. Far from alleviating criticism, this admission was considered outrageous. What then, I was asked, is the point of sending you to Westminster if you do the very opposite of what you know we want? I replied that a free vote in the

House meant that every Member was expected to vote according to his con-science, and while constituency opinion must weigh strongly with him it could not be decisive. I was driven to making this Burkean appeal, like every MP when he finds himself in trouble, because I truly believed that it was right. A Member must act in a manner which he considers to be in the interests of his constituents, even when they disagree with him. In this case, Bournemouth was the only constituency in the country whose majority view had been de-clared so openly to Parliament.

In theory, capital punishment was not a Party issue, but Socialists tended to support abolition and Conservatives to oppose it. The main burden of the parliamentary battle fell on Sydney Silverman, who was much disliked by Conservatives for his far-left opinions on other matters. His abolition Bill aroused exaggerated hostility among Conservatives in and out of Parliament. A correspondent to the *Daily Telegraph* wrote, "The nauseating drivel written by these MPs is enough to raise the gore and distend the stomach of an ox." I was one of the MPs whom he had particularly in mind, for I had seconded the Third Reading of Silverman's Bill, which was carried by 286 votes to 262 against Government advice, but the Lords reversed it. Two of my uncles made a rare trip to Westminster to vote, Sam St Levan to oppose the Bill, Eric Carnock to support it.

The arguments that convinced me were that mistakes could not be recti-fied if the condemned man was dead, that the experience of other countries showed that the death penalty was little deterrent to people intent on murder and that in a civilized country execution was almost as obscene as murder it-self. In any case, were suicide pacts, mercy killings, or *crimes passionels* much more abhorrent than robbery with violence against elderly people or the tor-ture of children, which were not punished by the ultimate penalty? Against this was the fear that abolition would place the public, the police and prison warders in danger of their lives. Spokesmen for the "retentionists" played on this fear. Lord Goddard, the Lord Chief Justice, told the House of Lords:

There was a dreadful case a few weeks ago of a little spinster, four feet nine inches in height, living on the edge of some mining village, and so afraid of being attacked that she had all the windows of her cottage screwed up. A young brute of about twenty-three broke into that house. He battered that poor little creature to death; all her ribs were broken and he cut her throat. All he got out of it was a small quantity of rather trivial jewellery. Are those people to be kept alive?

So murderers must be eliminated as an act of social hygiene. The notion of retribution entered the debate, the Old Testament against the New. The Bishop of Winchester, supporting the death penalty, referred to "the quasi-religious sense of awe" which an execution created, and the Bishop of Truro said that "'Whoso sheddeth man's blood, by man shall his blood be shed' has always appealed to mankind as an approximation of justice."

This was the view held by a majority of my constituents. But there were thousands of others, some of whom had voted for me and some not, who agreed with me and I became their spokesman. John Eden, MP for Bournemouth West, spoke for the majority. If I had succumbed to pressure, there would have been no local representative for abolition. The difference of opinion between John Eden and myself, I argued in a letter to the local paper, "simply represents the divisions of opinion in the Cabinet, the Church, Parliament, and almost any gathering of men and women. Why should Bournemouth pretend to a unanimity on this subject which certainly does not exist here or anywhere?" According to the polls, opinion was slowly swinging in favor of abolition, stimulated by the Home Secretary's refusal to reprieve Ruth Ellis, the last woman to be executed in Britain. If a Member tied himself strictly to what he conceived to be majority opinion, the time would surely come when he would feel obliged to vote in the opposite lobby for no better reason than that he guessed that a slight majority in his constituency now required him to do so. Was that not a foolish way of deciding a matter of principle? So throughout 1955 and the early part of 1956 I consistently voted abolitionist.

The Government was placed in an awkward position. On a free vote they had been knocked off their perch in the Commons, but reinstated by the Lords. The Bill was to return to Parliament in the autumn of 1956. We, the Conservative abolitionists, were in deep disgrace, and Peter Kirk and I, their spokesmen, in deepest disgrace of all. The Chief Whip, Edward Heath, didn't exactly summon me: he asked me to see him. I went. He told me that the Government had decided to introduce a Bill which would squash Silverman's but go halfway to meet it. Capital punishment would be abolished except for the most heinous crimes like the murder of police officers, and it would admit "diminished responsibility," or *crime passionel,* as a defence. I replied that I would vote for such a Bill, as it was better to approach total abolition in two steps with Government and public approval than in one step without it, and I hoped that it might appease Bournemouth. It didn't. One should not compromise if one wishes to be regarded as a leader of men. I lost the respect of both sides. Silverman was understandably furious and my constituents considered that I had forced the Government to introduce an unsatisfactory measure that wouldn't work. In fact it did. The Homicide Act, steered through Parliament by R. A. Butler, who showed considerable distaste for it, became law in March 1957 and there was no increase in the murder rate. In 1965 capital punishment was abolished absolutely for an experimental period of five years, and Parliament made this permanent in 1969. It was, in a sense, a victory, but I was no longer in a position to enjoy it. I had lost my seat owing to a far greater controversy, Suez.

THE SUEZ CRISIS

This was the most important incident in my life. I will describe what happened, not as an historical narrative, for the facts are well known, but as a personal experience.

I had always been pro-Israel. My father brought me up on the Balfour Declaration, which he had helped to draft in his Foreign Office years, and George Weidenfeld, who spent a year as assistant to Chaim Weizmann in Tel Aviv, confirmed what I had always believed, that the existence of Israel was payment of a moral debt and its survival a brilliant achievement. I had broadcast to Israel on the BBC's foreign service throughout 1955 and 1956, in alternate weeks with Dick Crossman, but I knew nothing of the country outside Jerusalem, where I had spent a few days in 1943.

It was therefore with delight that I accepted an invitation from the Israeli Government in April 1955, the month when Anthony Eden succeeded Churchill as Prime Minister. My companion was not Crossman but Patrick Gordon-Walker, who had been Secretary of State for Commonwealth Relations, and it was owing to his greater prestige that we were both accorded VIP status. We spent the first three days in the King David Hotel in Jerusalem, and then, separately, we toured the battlefields of the 1948 Israeli–Arab war, talked to Arab refugees in Jericho, drove to the Lebanese border and to the River Jordan, where Syrian guards yelled insults across the chasm, but I managed to collect a bottle of Jordan water for Juliet's christening. Then I went to Tel Aviv and Gaza, and bathed in the Dead Sea, visiting the antiquities whenever I had time. I spent a night in a kibbutz, Ramat Yoshanan, to experience something of the hardships and sense of common purpose that was building the State. There was no fighting at that moment, just watchfulness. I gained the impression that the Israelis were not too displeased by the tension. It gave their nation cohesion and drew blood money from the United States. The Arabs to whom I talked were committed to insoluble hostility toward the Jews. They sat by the Jordan moping for their lost farms and fearing Jewish economic penetration more than armed attack. "They captured the business and financial worlds of Paris, London, Berlin and New York," they said to me. "What will they do to us?" I had only to tour the Weizmann Institute at Rehovot and the vast technical college rising on the slopes of Mount Carmel to see what they meant. It was right against right, the twentieth century against the fifteenth.

I had tea with the Prime Minister, Moshe Sharett, a venerable patriarch. Several of his officials were present, but it was clear that they were not expected to say anything. I made some remark about the Turco–Iraqi Pact, which Britain had supported, and this prompted him to say how disappointed he was by the British attitude. "It was not a very friendly thing to do." "The Pact is directed against Russia," I said. "The Iraqis don't see it that way. It is obvious that their main enemy is Israel." "But she has no common frontier with you?" "With a modern air force, contiguity of frontiers is of little significance." Our interview was not going well.

I reminded him that Britain, France and the United States had signed the Tripartite Declaration in 1950 by which they were jointly bound to come to the aid of any country, Jewish or Arab, which was attacked by any other. Anthony Eden had told the House of Commons in 1954, "I know of few international instruments which carry as strong a commitment as that one does." It was the chief guarantee of peace in the Middle East. Sharett said that he had no confidence in it. The British Government had consistently refused to join in staff talks to work out the actual method by which help could be brought to Israel if she were attacked by any of her neighbours. I said that it was inconceivable that our Foreign Secretary, now Prime Minister, could give such an undertaking and then dishonor it. He was not convinced. I returned to London alarmed by the implications of what I had heard. The uncertainty of Allied intentions greatly increased the risk of war.

It seemed that even if we had the will to implement the Declaration, we lacked the means. While Harold Macmillan was still Foreign Secretary, in December 1955, he dined with a few back-bench MPs, and I asked him whether in fact we would go to the help of Jew or Arab if one attacked the other. "No," he replied. "All we have got is one Brigade in Cyprus, and we can't move that, because the Cypriots will rise if we do." "Then we can't keep our promise?" I asked. "No. But for heaven's sake, don't let us call our own bluff." That evening I wrote in my diary: "It's terrifying. If war breaks out in the Middle East, there will be a political crisis such as we have never known."

The whole world knew that the West could not afford to remain indifferent to an Arab–Israeli war. On 8 March 1956, Eden warned the 1922 Committee of back-bench Conservatives that he was not worried about our prestige but about oil. I wrote to my wife:

He painted a haunting picture of what would happen to our industry if the oil supply from the Arab states was cut off. Everything would just stop, and only when the mighty atom starts its work in ten years' time are we likely to be free of this terrible tie, which forces us to endure humiliations like sucking up to Nasser, neglecting the Jews ('our only real friends out there'), seeing our Foreign Secretary stoned at Bahrain, losing Glubb [Chief of Staff of the Arab Legion], toadying to the Iraqis—all for oil, oil, oil. He spat the words out. The meeting was sympathetic. I thought he looked tired and really worried. He kept on about 'that young king [Hussein of Jordan], only twenty. He doesn't know what he is doing. He'll let the Communists in if he thinks that will add to his popularity.' It was a grim, silent, crowded scene.

Then, on 26 July 1956, Colonel Abdul Nasser, at the end of a bitterly anti-Western speech in Alexandria, announced that at that moment his police were seizing the key installations of the Suez Canal Company. The anger aroused in Britain was violent and at first unanimous. Gaitskell, the Leader of the Opposition, said, "It's all very familiar. It is exactly the same that we encountered from Hitler and Mussolini," words which he came to regret, though he added that we should not act outside the United Nations. Few people noticed that although the act of nationalizing the Canal was condemned, it could not be legally challenged, because the 1888 Convention had said nothing about the ownership of the Canal, which ran through sovereign Egyptian territory. It said only that all nations would be guaranteed its free use, which Nasser had no intention of interrupting. He also agreed to compensate shareholders in the Suez Canal Company at the full market price.

These concessions in no way abated Conservative anger. I attended a meeting of the Foreign Affairs Committee on 31 July, at which Selwyn Lloyd, the Foreign Secretary, assured us that we must force Nasser to accept international control. Our plans included "certain military arrangements, one of which will be announced quite soon [calling up the reservists]. It will not be pleasant." There was a storm of cheering, but my impression was that Lloyd used such bellicose language because he felt his hold on the Party slipping. In answer to a question, he modified his previous statement by saying, "Members must not expect anything immediate. Our object is only to keep the waterway open. The nationalization doesn't particularly matter." Those were his exact words. They were ignored by the fire-eaters in the room, and a few of us moderates wrote to him that evening imploring him not to take the Suez Group, as we were beginning to call them, as representative of the whole Party.

From the start of the crisis, I believed that any attempt to solve it by military force would cause more trouble than it would cure. There were better ways of dealing with Nasser, better in the sense that they would be more effective, less costly, and command the support of the whole nation and all our allies. We should combine economic sanctions, sending our tankers round the Cape and laying new pipelines from the Gulf to the Mediterranean, with the threat of military action under the Tripartite Declaration if he attacked Israel. I advanced these ideas in a series of speeches which I made in my constituency during the late summer and early autumn of 1956. The reaction was almost unanimous: the use of military force to regain the Canal was unwise and unnecessary.

In early September I went to Oslo to attend a meeting of the Cultural Committee of the Council of Europe, and all the other delegates expressed to me their dismay at the bellicose noises emanating from Downing Street. Did we have the support of President Eisenhower in all this? Was Eden trying to prove himself a great war leader? On the 12th, Parliament was reconvened for a special session to discuss the crisis. Eden appeared to modify his attitude, saying at the very end of the debate, rather petulantly, that if Nasser turned down the proposal to form a Canal Users Association, which would run it, we would refer the whole dispute to the United Nations. We all knew that if the U.N. did nothing, the Suez Group would press for war. I warned my chairman, Major Grant, what my attitude would be:

I disagree with them for these reasons. It is folly to go to war if half your countrymen declare in advance that war is not justified. All European, American and Commonwealth opinion will be against us. War will not work, because the Canal will be blocked in retaliation, and the oil pipelines will be destroyed. And we cannot remain permanently in occupation of Egypt. We might be victorious, but weakened morally, physically and commercially.

If Nasser blocked the Canal, nobody would object if we invaded Egypt to unblock it. If he attacked Israel, we were bound to go to Israel's aid. But the Canal remained open and expertly managed by Egyptian pilots; and he did not attack Israel. On 29 October, Israel attacked him, and for the first time Nasser seemed to have some sort of legitimate grievance. When we and France joined in on Israel's side, he had a double grievance, and Russia and America were forced into an unnatural alliance to stop us, at the very moment when Russia, with equal callousness, invaded Hungary.

When Eden rose in the House of Commons on 30 October 1956, he spoke of the efforts which Britain had made to urge restraint on Israel and implied that her attack on Egypt had come to him as a complete surprise. We must put an immediate stop to the war to protect our people and the shipping in the Canal zone. He had therefore addressed to both Governments a twelve-hour ultimatum to cease fire and withdraw ten miles from the Canal. If either of them refused, we would intervene "to separate the combatants."

I remember that the House took this statement quietly, so great was our surprise, and it was only later that day, after an adjournment, that scepticism and suspicion surfaced, and grew during the succeeding week into the fiercest battle that Parliament had witnessed since the Munich crisis. Hugh Gaitskell accused the Government of abandoning the three principles that had guided British foreign policy since the Second World War: solidarity with the Commonwealth, the Anglo-American alliance and adherence to the Charter of the

United Nations. The whole world, he said, looked on our action as a transparent excuse to seize the Canal. But, he added, there was an even more serious charge, "that the whole business was a matter of collusion between the British and the French Governments and the Government of Israel."

If it were revealed that Britain and France had instigated the Israeli attack on Egypt and plotted with them to use it as a pretext for our intervention, Eden's Government would not have survived. Selwyn Lloyd firmly denied the charge: "It is quite wrong to state that Israel was incited to this action by Her Majesty's Government. There was no prior agreement between us about it," when he himself, at a meeting with the French and Israeli leaders outside Paris on 21 October, had negotiated in detail the timing and scope of the Israeli attack and our response to it.

I and many other MPs knew the outlines of this story within a day of the ultimatum. I wrote to my wife from the House of Commons on 31 October:

There was a rumour here last night that it is all a deep-laid plot. We would give the Israelis a free hand in Egypt provided that they did not attack Jordan. The ultimatum was all worked out beforehand. The Jews would accept, the Egyptians would refuse, and then we would have the excuse to attack Egypt, depose Nasser, and sail away, leaving a friendly Government in Cairo and Tel Aviv.

How did I know this? I was told it by William Clark, Eden's Press Secretary, who resigned in consequence. He said to me, "I don't mind supporting bad policies. That's my job. But what I won't stand is being told to tell lies in support of bad policies." When I repeated this to Robert Boothby, he could scarcely credit it. "Why," he said, "Eden is far too experienced to try such a trick, when he would certainly be found out. Then he would have either to lie to the House, or resign." He chose to lie. "There was no foreknowledge that Israel would attack Egypt." It may have started as a lie of state, but it was perpetuated as a lie of political convenience. When Anthony Nutting and Edward Boyle, both junior members of the Government, resigned their offices, the rumor gathered strength, to be slowly confirmed by private hints and guarded admissions. But it was not an argument that I or the other Suez rebels felt able to use in justification of our apostasy, either then or during the two years of my personal controversy with my electors. In the face of the Prime Minister's denial, it would not have been believed.

Meanwhile, during the week that intervened between the ultimatum and the Franco-British landings at Port Said on 5 November, the rebels said nothing in public for fear of demoralizing the men who were about to go into action. I put myself into the position of a grim-lipped paratrooper mounting his transport on a Cypriot airfield and hearing on the radio that a bunch of Tory back-benchers doubted the morality or wisdom of his mission. But at home the pressure to declare ourselves increased daily, particularly when the Russian attack on Hungary created a grotesque parallel to our own action. With the whole nation divided, irrespective of Party, should there not be some protest by Conservatives in Parliament? Lady Violet Bonham Carter buttonholed me in the lobby and, poking her gimlet nose into my face, demanded, "Is there not one of you with the courage to come out?" I murmured something about not letting down the troops. "Truce!" she cried. "What truce?" "I said 'troops,' Lady Violet, truly I did." "Oh troops," she snorted, unimpressed.

We did, however, make our views known in private. Our unofficial leader was neither Nutting nor Boyle, who kept aloof from us, but Sir Alec Spearman, in whose flat we met two or three times. The regular attenders were Walter Elliot, Robert Boothby, Lionel Heald, John Foster, David Price, Philip Bell, Jakie Astor, Keith Joseph and myself. We sat on Regency chairs, sipping whisky. A little mouse of a secretary sat in the corner taking notes, shocked by the terrible things that these men were saying about her Prime Minister. On 5 November we all signed a letter to him, regretting what had been done, and they agreed that I was free to make a stronger, and public, protest once the fighting had stopped.

I kept the Whips and Major Grant informed of what I intended to do, but when asked for my opinion by letter or at public meetings, I would hedge that the Prime Minister's policy was such-and-such, without committing myself. Then, on 6 November, only a day after the landings in Egypt, the Government announced a cease-fire, when our forces had reached barely a quarter of the way down the Canal, with the excuse that as the Israelis and Egyptians had stopped fighting our objective had been attained, an explanation that hoodwinked nobody. Harold Macmillan, Chancellor of the Exchequer, had advised the Cabinet that we faced financial ruin if we went on. Robert Skidelsky, the biographer of Keynes, has insisted that this excuse was quite without foundation. Nations do not go broke. They may stagger, but they always recover.

The true reason was that we lacked the ruthlessness to persist in an operation which had been condemned by the entire world and half our own people.

On 8 November there was to be a vote of confidence in the Government. I intended to abstain but would have little chance of catching the Speaker's eye to explain my reasons. So on the 7th I took advantage of an invitation to address the Bournemouth branch of the United Nations Association. It was exactly the platform I needed, at the moment when I most needed it. I would be speaking to an all-party organization of which Anthony Eden was himself President, and which stood for the principles which he had so often expounded. When I arrived at the hall I was handed a letter of bitter protest from Major Grant: "We would be ashamed and humiliated if the Member whom we elected so proudly only eighteen months ago should now add his voice to those raucous voices opposite who have only their miserable Party advantage in mind." I could not help respecting an intensity of feeling that matched my own.

I made the speech. If our nation had been wise, I asked, why had it not also been successful? If it had been just, why did our greatest friends condemn it? There were shouts of assent, but many of dissent. I was called a conceited traitor. Why did I think I knew better than the Prime Minister? I reminded them that in my autumn speeches I had warned them of what my likely attitude would be to the use of force and they had not disapproved. "But when action started," wrote Major Grant, "an entirely new situation arose. The die was cast. Unity and loyalty were the only things that mattered, and we looked to you for them in vain. What you did, in addition to being disloyal, seemed to me presumptuous, self-opinionated, mean and unworthy." That was the theme that he was to sustain for the next two years.

Next day, 8 November, I again saw Edward Heath. He asked me to support the Government in the vote that night. I said that I would do so if he could assure me that the purpose of our invasion was "to separate the combatants," as the Prime Minister claimed, and not to regain control of the Canal by a subterfuge. He held my gaze steadily and said nothing. I thanked him for his honesty, told him that I would abstain and left the room.

There can be few people who can identify the single most important moment in their lives. For me it was undoubtedly at 10 P.M. that evening when I sat in the House of Commons library as the division bells started to ring and Members trooped into the lobbies to vote. There were seven other Conservative abstainers: Sir Edward Boyle, Anthony Nutting, Sir Robert Boothby, J. J.

Astor, Sir Frank Medlicott, Colonel Banks and William Yates. The only one to survive politically was Robert Boothby. Our bigger guns, Elliot, Heald, Foster, Joseph and Spearman, decided at the last moment to vote with the Government. There was an absurd anti-climax. Robert Rhodes James, then a young division clerk, recorded by mistake that I had voted in the Government lobby, and that Godfrey Nicholson, MP for Farnham (who always referred to me as the Nicolson without an H to his name), had abstained. In fact, he had voted for the Government, and I had not voted at all. "This hideous error," as Rhodes James later described it in a footnote to his biography of Anthony Eden, was soon corrected, and was not apparently noticed by anyone except him, Godfrey and me.

A few days later Anthony Head, the Defence Minister, spoke to the Conservative Defence Committee, hoping to still back-bench pro-Suez criticism that the military operation had been bungled. He was at pains to explain why we didn't take the shortest route to Cairo by landing at Alexandria. That had been the original intention, he said, but as our "ostensible" reason was to separate the combatants, we were obliged to land nearer the point where the combatants would clash. If that was the ostensible reason, I asked, what was the real reason? No reply was given. The question was thought to be in poor taste. Everyone knew by this time that our sole purpose was to topple Nasser and regain the Canal, but these were motives that the Government consistently denied.

Anthony Eden went to Jamaica to recover his health, and on his return he met the 1922 Committee on 18 December. He was asked by Tom Iremonger to deny the rumor that we and the French had colluded with Israel. He gave an equivocal reply. I then spoke:

I am one of those who were disloyal to the Prime Minister. When I have had to explain to my constituents why I abstained in the vote of confidence, I have said that I thought the operation inexpedient. The reasons why we had to halt it prematurely were the same reasons which could and should have been foreseen in time to prevent us embarking on it at all.

But those were not my only reasons. I thought the operation not only inexpedient, but wrong in principle. It was undertaken in such a way as to oblige honourable men, including the Prime Minister himself, to make use of methods and arguments which were themselves dishonourable. I have been shocked by the series of half-truths which we have been obliged to tell.

There were shouts of "What?" "Which?" and other storm signals, but Eden said, "Let him go on." So I went on:

I will give some examples, Iremonger raised one of them just now— the charge of collusion. Why did the Prime Minister not give him a more direct denial? And why did we not tell the Americans what we were about to do? It has been said that there was no time. There was plenty of time. Then this legend that we 'helped' the UN, when we defied it, and cast our veto for the first time in its history. And what did the Prime Minister mean by saying just now that 'we did everything by warning' to stop the Israel–Arab war? Whom did we warn of what? Did we warn Israel not to attack Egypt? Why did we not invoke the Tripartite Declaration, which was devised for exactly this sort of emergency?

Eden replied that he would not accuse me, or those like me, of disloyalty. It had always been a matter of pride that Conservatives should be free to say exactly what they thought. "But surely you don't imagine that we enjoyed going behind the back of the UN and the Americans? What was the alternative? Let the war spread? As for 'half-truths,' if they existed at all, they were not serious or many in number, and are always necessary in this sort of operation that demands extreme secrecy. As for the Tripartite Declaration, I must look up your point. I haven't got it in my head."

I made a note of what had been said immediately after the meeting. That Eden took my criticisms so generously was typical of him. But he also said at the same meeting that if he had been dealt the same hand again, he would play it in exactly the same way. I was not the only one to think that illness had clouded his judgment.

He resigned on 9 January 1957. Back-benchers were not consulted about his successor. I would have supported Harold Macmillan in any case, as Butler had been ambivalent during the crisis. Having defended the Prime Minister at the despatch box, he would cheerfully tell his friends in the smoking room that the whole affair had been a disaster. So Macmillan became Prime Minister. Addressing the 1922 Committee after his election, he said that the great moments in our history had been not when we conquered, but when we led. "The broad stream of Conservative thought is fed by many tributaries which we should not allow to dissolve into a shapeless delta. We have always been a tolerant Party. We do not expel those who disagree with us. If we had, I would not be here myself." This was vintage Macmillan. I thought of Bournemouth.

DE-SELECTION

My abstention in the vote of confidence, the back-bencher's ultimate weapon, led to the biggest political upheaval that Bournemouth has ever known. I was determined not to succumb to demands for my resignation and regretted that Anthony Nutting had felt it necessary to resign his seat as well as his office. From my postbag I knew that I had many supporters among those who had voted for me in 1955 and even more among those who had not. There must be someone like me to argue the case for the MP's right to disagree. But I already had an inkling of the difficulty I faced in presenting the trite distinction between a representative and a delegate which Burke had enunciated nearly two centuries before. Burke was not widely read in Bournemouth and there was undoubted confusion in people's minds. The Chairman of one of my Association's branches wrote to me as early as 10 November to register his strong disapproval of my behavior, and continued, "We appreciate that you are entitled to your own opinion, but feel it is your duty to support the Government in a national crisis." I replied that if we are always bound to vote for a policy which we consider fundamentally wrong, it seemed to me that democracy would become entirely meaningless.

But opinion in the branches was so strongly critical of me that the Executive, having sent a telegram to Downing Street repudiating their Member and pledging loyalty to the Government, drew up a Resolution to be debated at a special meeting on 5 December, deploring my UNA speech, and "instructing the Executive Committee to take such action as may be deemed necessary." I knew what that meant. It meant severing relations with me and adopting a new candidate to take my place.

I was allowed to address that meeting, which was packed. The police did their best to quiet an angry crowd against whom the doors had been shut. I said that to blame me would be like blaming the lamb for the arrangements inside the slaughterhouse, but I assured them that if I were asked for my resignation I would refuse, and would hold other meetings to which they could all come.

Inside the hall, I spoke for forty minutes, dividing the speech into two halves—why I thought as I did and why I spoke as I thought—and ended by playing my trump card. The President of my Association, Lord Quickswood, had written a letter which he permitted me to read out:

No one complains of Mr Nicolson's personal fitness for Parliament. The complaint seems to be that he has voted according to his conscience but against his Party, and I have no hesitation whatever in saying that he has done quite rightly in so voting.

It did no good. The bulk of the audience had come armed with Resolutions passed by their branch committees, all of which were hostile to me. I was asked to leave at the end of my speech, but reports in the local papers, and friends like Dr. E. W. Deane, told me what happened next. A Conservative Councillor mounted the platform and said, "You have listened to a long and skilful torrent of words. Your attention has been diverted from the issue. Are you going to be represented by a loyal Conservative or not? Do you want Nicolson or Eden? [Cries of Eden! Eden!] Whom do you want, a Conservative or a piebald politician?" A motion of no-confidence was put to the meeting, and the Executive was instructed to seek a new candidate. It was carried by 298 votes to 92.

A small group of my supporters, headed by Brigadier J. S. Windsor, was formed for the purpose of organizing meetings where I could state my case, but I was barred from the Association's offices and all contact with their branches. When the Young Conservatives invited me to address them they were immediately disbanded. The Association's agent, Arthur Cowley, was placed in a difficult position, for he and I were still on excellent terms. I told him that his duty lay with his Executive and he honorably performed it, but he cannot have enjoyed implementing their next move, a proposal that applicants for membership of the Association would be required to sign a pledge that they would support the new candidate and not me.

The new candidate was Major James Friend, an ex-Army officer who managed his stepson's estates in Staffordshire. He immediately imposed his personality on the constituency. At his first press conference he declared that his minor success in a previous political contest "was chiefly due to local leadership which I learnt as a regimental officer in the hills of Palestine and in the desert." On colonial policy he said, "We must have the moral fibre to maintain law and order in our possessions, without which we face extinction by younger nations." On Edward Boyle's readmission to Macmillan's Government he commented, "As he is obviously very young and inexperienced, they are giving him a second chance." At his adoption meeting, he replied to the inevitable question, "An MP should do as his Party wants on major issues of policy. Whatever his personal views are, he should support the Government."

I was delighted that the Association had chosen someone so different from myself, but to keep on reasonably amicable terms with him I wrote to him on 1 April 1957 explaining my future plans and asking him not to let rumor embitter our relationship. He replied, *in toto*, "I have read the letter which you sent to me from the House of Common on April Fool's Day."

I put my case before a wider public in a book called *People and Parliament* (1958). It discussed what Burke's doctrine actually meant in modern practice and asked the question, What is an MP for? I took capital punishment and the Suez crisis as examples of the MP's dilemma, and described what had happened to me. The tone of the book was conciliatory. I admitted that a constituency had every right to replace their MP if he displeased them but pleaded that they should exercise that right with caution, lest they undermine the purpose of Parliament itself. I argued that the debate within the political parties was as important to our democracy as the debate between them. I took care to be generous to individuals like Major Grant, stating their point of view as fully as my own. The only complaint which I received was from a prominent opponent, Mrs. Openshaw, that I had not mentioned her at all. In the wider world the book was well received. Bernard Levin said that I had done the State some service, but when I discussed it on radio with Herbert Morrison, the Labour Leader, he asked me if another constituency would not suit me better. "But I *love* Bournemouth," I replied. My mother telephoned me afterwards to complain that I was always being so beastly fair to my opponents. She did not understand that I wished to create the impression that in this controversy I was the gentleman and Friend the intruder. I was not wholly without guile.

Brian Meade, editor of the *Christchurch Times*, gave me unwavering support, and our dispute now became one of more than local interest. With the exception of *Express* newspapers, I was given credit for defending a major principle. Everyone had held their views on Suez so strongly that they were unlikely to change in a hurry, and I tried to switch the argument away from its rights and wrongs. I held several meetings in my two boroughs to debate the democratic issues and was supported at one of them by four fellow Conservative Members who on Suez had taken a view opposite to mine. They were Joan Vickers, Sir Hugh Lucas-Tooth, John Peyton and the Prime Minister's son, Maurice Macmillan. The Financial Secretary to the Treasury, J. E. S. Simon, who at the last moment was unable to join them as arranged, sent a friendly message to be read out at the meeting. But I could not persuade the Party Leaders to make any significant gesture in my support. The Prime Minister, when asked his opinion, said that it was a good convention that the Conservative Leader never interfered between a Member and his Association, and he trusted Bournemouth to act in the interests of the Party "locally and nationally," a phrase which I and my opponents interpreted in opposite ways. Meanwhile I used the local press to publicize my parliamentary activities on behalf of Bournemouth's crumbling cliffs, impoverished old people, famous Symphony Orchestra and excellent hotels. I was once foolish enough to joke that my only achievement during my seven years in Parliament was to persuade the Home Office to extend the work permits of Spanish waiters from three months to six. Forty years later Sue Lawley quoted this remark when interviewing me for *Desert Island Discs*, but with the kindly supplementary, "I suspect that wasn't quite true?" No, it wasn't.

Then something wonderful happened. Major Friend made a fool of himself and was obliged to resign. I had acquired a valuable ally in Anthony Howard, then only twenty-four, whose first job in his distinguished career was as political correspondent to *Reynolds News*. I do not think that he considered me a very effective politician—for instance, I was bad at recognizing people, including, at first, himself—but he was amused by my predicament and contemptuous of my opponents. He noticed that Friend had denied any connection with the League of Empire Loyalists, a far-right organization that had disgraced itself at the recent Conservative Conference by calling Macmillan a traitor. He decided to investigate further, and discovered that Friend had not only addressed the inaugural meeting of the League's Bournemouth branch but had subscribed to its funds, entertained its national chairman to lunch, encouraged its members to join my Association and supplied them with the dates of my Bournemouth meetings where they could cause trouble to "Master Nigel." Friend said, "I am not a member or supporter of the League, and approve neither its objects nor its methods, and I take this opportunity of publicly dissociating myself from it." The League was infuriated by this brush-off and gave Tony Howard letters which implicated Friend still further.

This development caused such excitement that Lord Hailsham, Chairman of the Conservative Party, felt obliged to interview both Friend and me. I do not know what he said to Friend, but it remains my suspicion that he did the political equivalent of leaving him alone in a locked room with a bottle of whisky and a loaded revolver, telling him to do the decent thing. Friend resigned his Bournemouth candidature. Major Grant said that I should resign too. I saw now reason why I should be made the victim for my rival's errors and refused. That did not prevent a clutch of potential candidates from offering themselves for the seat, among them Randolph Churchill, who declared that as he wished to reenter Parliament as a Conservative, it seemed sensible to apply for a constituency where there were a great many Conservative voters.

I was greatly helped by his clownish intervention. It introduced a note of comedy into the drama and made me seem almost respectable in comparison. Randolph planted his standard in the Bath Hotel in Bournemouth, and between daily press conferences he invited selected constituents to lunch. He was nice about me and my wife ("an extremely pretty girl"), but to his guests and potential supporters he showed no mercy: "Poor dears, they have no idea what politics are about." The hotel servants were loud in their complaints of his rudeness.

When I saw Lord Hailsham in the House of Lords on 21 January 1959, his manner was sympathetic, a touch impish. I did not know what his attitude to Suez had been (he was First Lord of the Admiralty at the time) and only learned many years later from his book *The Door Wherein I Went* (1975) that in the Government he was "the odd man out, having been doubtful, or worse, about going in, and even more doubtful about stopping when we did." There was no point in discussing that affair, but he said that the Bournemouth controversy was damaging the Party nationally and must be ended. How? He would descend on Bournemouth in person and speak to my Executive. I could be present too. He would first propose that they should take me back and, if they refused, as they probably would, he would suggest that they hold a postal ballot of the whole Association to decide whether they wished me to stand as their candidate at the next General Election. There could be no question of adopting a new candidate until they had declared that they did not want me. I was delighted by this suggestion and refrained from reminding him that I had myself proposed it two years before (see *The Times*, 15 February 1957), and had repeated it many times since. Major Grant had dismissed it as "airy-fairy nonsense" and "wholly unconstitutional." With his great authority, Hailsham might persuade the Executive to reverse that judgment. Before leaving him, I assured him that there was no truth whatever in the rumor that Randolph and I were in collusion. He said, "I don't think we need spend a moment's thought on Randolph."

Three days later he came to Bournemouth with an escort of Central Office officials, and met the Executive at the Association's headquarters. As I walked toward it, there were boos and cheers from a large crowd, supplemented by the Empire Loyalists' loudspeaker van yelling, "Traitor Nigel!" Cowley met me at the door and took me upstairs, where I found Lord Hailsham and forty members of the Executive. There was dead silence as I entered the room. I was invited to speak. By a fortunate chance, the *News Chronicle* had published an opinion poll that morning showing that forty-seven percent of Conservatives in Bournemouth supported me. How was it that the Executive, which claimed to represent all Conservatives in the constituency, did not include a single member who was on my side? But I did not want to provoke them. We were there to settle our dispute. ("Traitor Nigel" floated through the windows.) If the Executive could not agree to take me back, could we not refer the question to the membership as a whole? After answering a few questions, all hostile, I left them to deliberate.

An hour later I was asked to return. Hailsham told me that the Executive had refused to take me back but had agreed to a postal ballot. Voters would be asked the single question, "Do you want Mr Nicolson as your official candidate at the next Election?" It would be organized by the Wessex Area of the Party and paid for from Central Office funds. Would I abide by the result of the ballot? I said I would. Then came the critical question, "It is proposed that no new members should be admitted to the Association until the ballot is over." I objected strongly. It would throw doubt on the whole procedure if the existing membership was frozen. Genuine Conservatives, who were not already members, must be allowed to qualify for a vote. Hailsham asked me, "What is the minimum time that you would regard as reasonable to let new members join?" "A month," I replied. There was a shout of disapproval, but he persuaded them to let him be the arbiter. I agreed, but if he decided to freeze the membership forthwith, I would claim the right to appeal to the Prime Minister, as Leader of the Party. There were further cries of outrage, but Hailsham said, "I don't think that you will find that necessary." In the event, he ruled that a fortnight would suffice.

We then went to the Carlton Hotel for a press conference. By chance he and I found ourselves standing side by side in the men's lavatory. "You seem to have enjoyed that," I said. "I always enjoy unusual situations," he replied. Then he, Major Grant and I sat at a table in the ballroom and he announced our agreement. He said that the postal ballot was without precedence in British politics. It showed that neither Burke nor his successors were wholly right: an MP is not a delegate, but his constituency is not wedded to him whatever he says or does. I thanked him for his help and publicly promised to abide by the result of the ballot, even if I lost it by a single vote. Major Grant said that he was grateful to the Chairman but didn't look it.

So began Bournemouth's primary Election. There was time enough for us to hold rival meetings in all parts of the constituency, and 1,600 new members joined the Association in time to vote. The *Lolita* controversy (see next chapter) reached its peak at the very moment when I was trying to sell myself as sea-green incorruptible. On 18 February, the day when the ballot papers were delivered to the voters, *Punch* published a cartoon by David Langdon of a woman shouting "Lolita!" at her errant child, while a group of Bournemouth residents, huddled under a promenade shelter, looked on with extreme disapproval. I was handicapped in other ways too. I was denied the right to speak to the Association's clubs and branches, and refused the names and addresses of its members, so my appeal could only be made by door-to-door canvassing and at public meetings, one of which was chaired for me by Sir Horace Wilson. By the Hailsham rules a written statement by both sides was included with the ballot papers. The Executive's said:

Nothing has occurred to alter the Conservative view of his acceptance of Mr Gaitskell's invitation to desert Sir Anthony Eden at the critical time of Suez, also of his general outlook—so often in accord with that of the Socialists, especially in deploring the hanging of murderers.

Mine was more modest and better expressed. "Examine my record in the constituency and at Westminster. I do not ask you to agree with everything I have said or done. I only ask you to agree that it was my duty to say what I truly believed." On the front cover there was a photograph of me looking statesmanlike, and on the back favorable comments on my performance by right-wing newspapers and individuals, including one from Sir Toby Low (Lord Aldington), who had said, "I am proud to know Nigel Nicolson, because I know him to be a man of extreme moral courage."

The result of the ballot was announced on 26 February 1959. I waited by the telephone in my father's rooms in Albany, Piccadilly. A number of reporters were grouped behind me, including Anthony Howard, who was now writing for the *Manchester Guardian*. The telephone rang. I scribbled down the figures as they were read out to me from Central Office: for me, 3,671; against, 3,762. I had lost by ninety-one. Was Lolita, that *ragazzina pericolosa*, as the *Corriere della Sera* called her, responsible for that ninety-one?

Everyone was most kind. My father gave me a silver vase, which still stands on my writing table, with an inscription engraved round the rim, "N.N. from H.N. Nov 7 1956–March 25 1957 *Aliis licet, tibi non licet*" (let others do what you must never do). Edward Heath said that I had behaved honorably, Hailsham that I was "still in good standing with the Party," and *The Times* in a leader next day expressed the hope that "so useful a Member of Parliament will now find a more congenial constituency." The implication was deserved. I was not suited to Bournemouth. I was distrusted there. If I had won by ninety-one votes, my position would have been very difficult. Half the Association would have resented my candidature at the Election. They nominated a country gentleman, and a member of the Church Assembly, called John Cordle, who said of Suez, "It was the British thing to do," and he remained their MP for the next eighteen years.

UNITED NATIONS

There were still five months to go before Parliament was dissolved and I served out my time with a certain feeling of liberation. I had escaped with my skin, but not with my clothes. Two Liberal constituencies invited me to stand, but I was damaged goods, unsaleable, and I spent the General Election in the Outer Hebrides writing a book about Lord Leverhulme.

I wondered how to shape the rest of my life. I was forty-two. I needed to earn more than my publishing firm could pay me. My parliamentary salary had been £1,750, which I had supplemented by writing weekly book reviews for a Manchester paper and by a directorship in a small independent airline called Falcon Airways. Now all three sources of income dried up simultaneously: I lost my seat, the newspaper folded and one of Falcon's three aircraft crashed. I applied for a job in the United Nations, supported by letters from Hugh Foot (Lord Caradon) and Sir Gladwyn Jebb (Lord Gladwyn), both luminaries of the UN, but I never received even an acknowledgement. So I returned to publishing.

My United Nations links did have one result. I was already a member of UNA's Executive and now they invited me to be their chairman. My six-year chairmanship coincided with the period when the U.N. was in disgrace with the British public, and I often felt like the leader of a supporters' club whose team were regularly losing their matches. "We, the people," for whose benefit the UN had been founded, had little influence on governments. Our UNA was not professional enough to impress the Foreign Office or to combat public apathy. Our membership was composed mainly of survivors of the League of Nations Union, and although some of our six hundred branches (virtually one per parliamentary constituency) could rally some four hundred members or more, it was depressing to visit a place like Huddersfield and find a dozen elderly people gathered to hear me, including the poor mayor, who had been persuaded that it was his duty to attend. I believed that UNA should cease to aim for a national membership. It lacked dynamism and there was insufficient popular support for a pro-U.N. crusade. It should alter its entire character, I thought, become a specialized study group like Chatham House, the Institute for Strategic Studies or the David Davies Memorial Institute. It should be a fount of expert knowledge about the U.N., organize lectures and issue publications at a high level. Prejudice and misunderstanding about the United Nations could be dispelled by informed argument better than by emotional appeals. I did not press these ideas very strongly, and never in public, because there was too great a commitment to the branches, the regional officers, the youth movement and the education program to suggest their abolition. Our younger members urged me to adopt more dramatic methods to gain attention. It was the period when the Campaign for Nuclear Disarmament was organizing demonstrations in Whitehall, with Bertrand Russell at the hub of their sit-down circles. Could we not do the same? I replied that if we sat down outside the Foreign Office we would not be invited to sit down inside. Foreign Secretaries would listen patiently as we explained the Resolutions passed at our annual conference. I remember one such session with Sir Alec Douglas-Home, who clearly had little sympathy with the U.N., and I caught the eye of his private secretary, who was taking notes.

There were meetings of the World Federation of UNAs in places like Delhi, Warsaw and Monrovia, where we echoed the cold-war debates of our ambassadors in New York. I took much pleasure in these verbal contests with the Soviet delegates, though the Director of our UNA, Charles Judd, begged me to modify my attitude for the sake of amity. I twice led groups to New York itself to witness the U.N. in action, and as our UNA was the largest in the world, successive Secretary Generals paid us flattering attention, particularly U Thant, who once took me to the window of his office on the top floor of the U.N. building to contrast the brilliance of Manhattan on one side with the "decent traffic of mankind" up the East River on the other. There was no doubt which he preferred.

In September 1963, I wrote to my father from New York:

Patrick Dean [our permanent representative at the UN] tells me that the Secretary General is 150 per cent pro-British, and is saddened that our Government should alternatively blow hot and cold. I explained to U Thant that people like the Warden [John Sparrow] were nervous of surrendering British sovereignty to black, yellow and even coffee-coloured nations. The only way for the UN to become popular in Britain is for it to do brave things successfully. Could he not take the initiative in suggesting operations that only the UN could undertake, like taking over all the communications to and from divided Berlin? One of our troubles is that in England we never see any branch of the UN in action—it is something remote. Let us have in London a symbol of its presence, for instance by concentrating all its British offices in a tower building on the south bank opposite the Houses of Parliament [where UNA's own office was], and site in the United Kingdom the proposed UN University. He quite liked all this, but the Indian beside him [Chakravarthi Narashiman, *Chef de Cabinet* to the Secretary General] glowered, no doubt thinking that there was something a good deal more sinister behind what I was saying.

When U Thant came to London, it was our duty to arrange a public luncheon in his honor. We gave it at the Dorchester on 28 April 1966, and the three Party Leaders, who were also our Presidents, the Prime Minister (Harold Wilson), Edward Heath and Jo Grimond were the supporting speakers. During the lunch, I was warned that members of the League of Empire Loyalists were present, and intended to make trouble when U Thant rose to speak, since they considered that our membership of the United Nations was inconsistent with loyalty to the Queen. I suggested to Harold Wilson that I should announce their presence during my short introductory speech and invite them, if they had come to shout something, to shout it at me instead of at our guest of honor. "Well," said Wilson, amused, "You can try it on. It's very risky. But it might work." So I tried it. I allowed them one minute for their demonstration. They were taken aback, since they had come prepared to interrupt, not to orate, and their slogans were expended after thirty seconds. "Come on! Come on!" shouted the happy audience. The Loyalists slunk out and U Thant spoke without interruption.

The most effective contribution that UNA made to policy in my time was the publication of a book on disarmament, financed by Philip Noel-Baker—who donated to UNA a large part of his Nobel Peace Prize—and written by Hugh Thomas before he disappeared to Spain to write his great work on the Civil War. Our contribution to Third World development was less successful. There was our cheese factory in Igoumenitsa in Epirus and our bee farm in Crete, which I opened with the help of the local archimandrite, but I do not believe that either of them survived as the co-operatives which we intended. Too much of the money subscribed to causes like the Freedom from Hunger Campaign disappeared into undeserving pockets. It should not have been the responsibility of private charities, but of governments, and governments were hampered by the taxpayer's lack of enthusiasm. I remember Barbara Castle's frustration, when she was Minister of Overseas Development, at her inability to respond more generously to our appeals.

Such was UNA. The days that I spent chairing committees or attending WFUNA conferences were highly enjoyable, but I realized that I was helping to keep alive an organization that was increasingly ineffectual. Far from being top heavy, UNA was not top heavy enough. It lacked substance. I wanted to move the WFUNA staff from Geneva to New York, where they would be in daily contact with the delegations and might exert more influence. But like my proposal to slim and sharpen our own Association, it was not to be. Our Res-

olutions, beginning "Considering," "Regretting," "Strongly believing" or
"Anxious," fell too often on deaf ears, or on no ears at all. I remember how
Christopher Chataway and I once spoke on U.N. Day from the plinth of Nelson's Column to a gathering of thirty people in Trafalgar Square. It was from
this same platform that Aneurin Bevan had addressed a crowd of thousands at
the height of the Suez affair. It took a crisis to stimulate love or hatred of the
U.N. The great achievements of its specialized agencies were ignored because
they were remote and unspectacular, and whenever the U.N. intervened politically, as in Cyprus or the Congo, it seemed to falter, if not to fail. To me it was
a bitter recollection that its finest hour, in 1956, had been at the expense of my
own country. That incident had not endeared the U.N. to our people, nor our
Government to the U.N. At a London reception for Dag Hammarskjöld, Selwyn Lloyd, still Foreign Secretary under Macmillan, had introduced me to
him with the joke. "This is Nicolson, Secretary General, who had the effron-
tery to say that we were wrong about Suez." I shall not forget the expression
on Hammarskjöld's face. It was one of bleak contempt that the Foreign Secretary could make so poor a joke.

EUROPE

Two experiences influenced me strongly to support Britain's role in the European Community. One was my membership for two years of the Council of
Europe at Strasbourg; the second was when in the summer of 1967 I drove
through ten countries of Western Europe, and three behind the Iron Curtain,
to write *Great Houses of the Western World*, and realized, as if for the first time,
its homogeneity. It was therefore with much pleasure that I accepted an invitation to play a small part in the Referendum of June 1975 which was to decide
whether Britain was to remain a member of the Community. For years we had
struggled to get in; and once in, we often gave the impression that we were
struggling to get out. A poll in 1974 resulted in an astonishing seventy-five
percent of "Don't Knows," which meant that we didn't much care.

My role was as President of an all-party Committee formed in Tunbridge
Wells to drum up support for a Yes vote in the Referendum. The sitting mem-
ber for the constituency, Patrick Mayhew, and two local representatives of the
Labour and Liberal Parties, sunk their differences for two months for this sin-

gle purpose, and I was considered sufficiently neutral (I had twice voted Liberal since 1959) to act as coachman to their troika.

It was equivalent to an Election campaign, with no candidates. At first we aroused little enthusiasm. At one early meeting, in Southborough, only one person turned up, an elderly woman who came armed with quotations from Deuteronomy to prove that political controversy was evil. But soon we gathered an energetic team to hold meetings and distribute leaflets throughout the constituency. We argued that the Referendum was particularly important for Kent, since we were the main corridor for continental trade and traffic and had experienced more than any other county the impact of two world wars. A strong European union would prevent a third. Tunbridge Wells was populated by a high proportion of business and professional people: they knew what a divorce from Europe would mean. As for the farmers, if we failed to take advantage of the Common Agricultural Policy, we would be reduced to growing the only crop that we could grow more cheaply than any other country— grass. I hoped not to be questioned on this assertion. Nor on this: "A nation which has founded two Empires should not be timid to join forces with our natural allies across the Channel!" But propagandists are not on oath.

The arguments of the No lobby were less convincing and their local organization was not a patch on ours. We formed Committees in every parish, opened a shop and information center in the Pantiles, Tunbridge Wells, and on the eve of the poll staged a mass meeting in the Town Hall addressed by Christopher Chataway. On polling day, 5 June, our vans broadcast a stream of exhortation down every village street, and met the commuter trains as they disgorged their passengers at Staplehurst and Paddock Wood. The result was very satisfactory. In Kent, sixty-seven percent of the electorate cast their votes, two out of three in favour of remaining in the Community. The national poll was just as favourable, only the Hebrides and the Shetlands returning a majority for No.

That was my last performance in politics. It brought me another bonus: it gained me the friendship of Patrick Mayhew, who remained our MP until his retirement at the General Election of 1997, having held the offices of Solicitor General, Attorney General and Secretary of State for Northern Ireland. I met him and his wife Jean no more than once a year, sometimes at dinner in each other's houses, sometimes by chance in trains, sometimes in the Beefsteak Club, and I cannot claim to have known him intimately. My affection for him grew in proportion to my admiration. Holding the most challenging post in the Cabinet, which he had strongly solicited from Margaret Thatcher (unsuccessfully) and from John Major (successfully), he conducted the Irish negotiations with a patience undiminished by his disappointments. He tolerated with wry amusement the security precautions that his job made essential, and in the House of Commons he was the only Minister to escape the insults of the Opposition, because by his tact and calm he had made a controversial issue a common problem.

Patrick was a main cause of my rejoining the Conservative Party in 1996. Another was respect for John Major's resilience, political skill and attitude to Europe. I had been attracted by Mrs. Thatcher's speech at Bruges in 1988, when she denounced federation but advocated community, and it bore fruit in Major's cautious approach to the Maastricht Treaty in 1991. Politically, I have returned to the fold which I joined with so little thought in 1946, but I am a back number. "You are well out of it," a friend said to me sympathetically. "No," I replied, "just out of it."

SEVEN

THE PUBLISHER

I did not become a publisher until I was demobilized from the Army early
in 1947. Most temporary officers served out their time in Germany, Palestine or the Far East. I was more fortunate in being commissioned to write
the war history of the Grenadier Guards while I nursed the Leicester seat as its
parliamentary candidate. Duke Hussey and I established our office next to the
tailor's shop in Chelsea Barracks, where I lodged until in 1946 I moved to 10
Neville Terrace, South Kensington, a house which I shared with my father and
my brother Ben. We were fed our breakfast but little more by Stanley Parrot,
who had been my soldier-servant throughout the war. Now he was married,
with a baby, and they occupied the basement rooms, while we were sand-
wiched, one above the other, to the full height of the house.

It lacked elegance. James Pope-Hennessy said that it was like a boarding
house for bombed-out Indian students. Nor was our cohabitation an ideal
arrangement. I was twenty-nine and Ben thirty-two, and our paths were di-
verging. Late one winter's night Harold returned to find an inebriated Philip
Toynbee stretched out on his sofa. "Well," said Ben, "he had nowhere else to
go. You can hardly expect him to sleep on the Embankment on a night like
this." There were four for breakfast next morning. It was a very silent meal. It
was not long afterwards that Ben left us to set up in a flat of his own, and his
rooms at Neville Terrace ("Devil Terrace," Harold called it) were taken by
my uncle Fred, 2nd Lord Carnock. That, too, was an unsatisfactory plan.

Having nothing else to do, he drank. There was a pub, the Anglesea Arms, immediately opposite our house, and night after night the other customers would help the elderly and enormously stout peer across the street to be put to bed by Parrot.

Reading my diary of this period, I am puzzled that I was able to afford the life style that it records. On a lieutenant's pay, supplemented to some small extent by the interest on my grandmother's legacy, I managed to dress to the sartorial standards demanded by the Brigade of Guards in and out of uniform, pay my share of the rent and Parrot's wages, travel weekly to Leicester, eat expensively in the Guards Club and Soho restaurants, buy a small car and wedding presents for my friends, and spend three nights in Paris, and two weeks (with Shirley Morgan and Fred Warner) on Lake Garda. Yet there is no mention in my diary of economy or penury. My life was enjoyably social. I traveled to distant parts of the country for parties and dances, to Aldershot and Catterick to interview key witnesses for my history, to Sissinghurst for most weekends, and in London I was entertaining or being entertained every night. It was the period when my generation were pairing off. Everyone was marrying, or trying to marry, someone else. Frank Giles married my cousin, Kitty Sackville; Willie Bell married Belinda Dawson; John Buchanan married Janet Pennycuick; Rex Whitworth married June Edwards; and I was trying to marry Shirley Morgan. There were other girls who enlivened our set, like Laurian Jones (Enid Bagnold's daughter), Rosemary Lyttelton, Virginia Forbes-Adam, Iris Peake (the loveliest) and Vivien Mosley (the merriest), some of whom drifted out of my life, or more often I drifted out of theirs. We were constructing the social life that the war had denied us but to which the war had indirectly contributed. As I was still an officer, I was delegated by the Adjutant to escort Miss Attlee to a Buckingham Palace ball (she hated it), and there were occasions like this:

29 April 1946. Dine with Iain Moncreiffe on guard [at St. James's Palace]. It was a male party of fifteen, all in evening dress, and the table was laid with candelabra and plate. Iain had brought down from Easter Moncreiffe his own eighteenth-century table-cloths and a set of glasses with his monogram which he had had made in Venice. I sat next to Jean Babilée, the star of the new French ballet, said to be the new Nijinsky. He is only twenty-three. He tells me about his time

with the Resistance south of Tours. He speaks very little English, so I explain to him in French exactly what the King's Guard is. Then the Scots Guard pipers circle round the table playing the lament of the Moncreiffes and God knows what else. At the end Iain gives the chief piper a tot of whisky and they toast the King in Gaelic. Babilée is much impressed. He asks me, '*C'est toujours comme ça?*' Well, not always, I reply, but the Captain is an eccentric and a very romantic man.

That was one side of my life. Another was provided by my father in whose name I was adopted from time to time by the London hostesses, Emerald Cunard and Sibyl Colefax. They were in undeclared competition. I once heard Lady Cunard pause in mid-flow to say, "I'm talking too much, like Lady Colefax," a comparison which was quite unjustified, for Sibyl was the less talkative of the two, and kinder to the young. On another occasion, Lady Cunard called to me down the length of her dining-room table, "Nigel, tell us about your girl-friends," and twelve pairs of experienced eyes turned toward me. Sibyl would never have done that. She was herself accident-prone. I took her to the cinema to watch on the Movietone News the departure of Louis and Edwina Mountbatten from Delhi at the end of his Viceroyalty. She muttered to me: "What they didn't show was Edwina kissing goodbye to Nehru at the airport. That deeply shocked Indian opinion and undid all the good that Dickie had done." The woman in the seat in front of us turned round: "Hullo, Sibyl. I thought I recognized your voice." It was Edwina Mountbatten, and her husband was beside her. When the lights went down for the feature film, I whispered to Sibyl, "Would you like to leave?" She agreed, but later that evening, when I escorted her to a ball at the Belgian Embassy, we found ourselves standing in line just behind the Mountbattens. They were among her closest friends.

My life provided me with occupation but not a profession. The Grenadier history would soon be finished, and it was very doubtful that I would win northwest Leicester at the Election. What was I to do? I toyed with the idea of making peasant-type pottery at the Frittenden brickworks near Sissinghurst, for the Wealden clay was perfect raw material and lay in quantity beneath our farmlands. Our tenant farmer, Oswald Beale, was less enthused by my project, and when I invited Dick Paget-Cooke to join me as a partner in this doomed enterprise, he declined, distrusting both my financial acumen and my skill with pots. Then, at breakfast on 26 July 1946, Ben said that he had been lunching with George Weidenfeld, the editor of the new book-magazine *Contact*, who had asked him if he knew of any young man who would take on the job of assistant editor. Ben replied that he had a younger brother who might suit him admirably.

CONTACT

That was how it began. Before I even met George, I asked my father's opinion. He was then broadcasting twice weekly from Paris about the Peace Conference, and as time was short, I suggested to him by letter that if he approved of the idea, he was to use the word "approval" at the start of his next talk; if not, "disapproval"; and if doubtful, "ambiguous." Vita, Ben and I then sat by the radio, listening. "I very much approve of Mr. Bevin's policy," Harold began. Not "approval." Had the code misfired? We decided that the coincidence would be unlikely, and that he was encouraging me to go ahead.

George Weidenfeld and I met for the first time two days later, at lunch with Ben at the White Tower restaurant in Soho. For half an hour we did not mention *Contact* at all, and when we did, it was without any reference to the main purpose of the lunch. George always approaches any decision with caution and a certain shyness. "He is not at all bossy" was my first impression. "He has great enthusiasm and a multitude of bright ideas." He explained that *Contact* was an illustrated monthly, upper-middle-brow and left of center in character, which dealt with politics, international relations, literature and the arts. All this I already knew, because the first issue had been published. "But what about me?" I eventually asked. "Would a future Tory MP be suitable as assistant editor of a left-wing magazine?" George waved this objection aside. I would give it "balance," he said. I would be "earthy." I would pilot every issue through the presses and would have much to do with the foreign editions (there were none). I would travel a lot in Europe and to the United States. It sounded more than I deserved or was equipped for. There was I, without any qualifications whatever, not soliciting a job in high-class journalism, but being pressed to accept one. I was to be paid £750 a year, which I described to Shirley as "very generous," but at a subsequent meeting it was reduced to £500, "until we find our feet."

That was the trouble. As George has written in his autobiography, "The company was fraught with financial worries and veered from one crisis to the next. We were forever teetering on the verge of bankruptcy." I invested some of my capital, and persuaded Vita, Ben and a family friend, Richard Rumbold, to invest more. All of them eventually recovered their investments, but I lost mine when the company was reorganized in 1956. I do not nurse any grievance against George. Being innumerate, I contributed little to the solution of our business problems, although for the only time in my life I lay awake at nights worrying about them. George was the person who saved the firm time after time by finding a new backer or winning a new contract. My role was editorial. I commissioned articles, vetted them, and wrote others myself. We employed a staff of fifteen in a three room office in Manchester Square. We pretended, as young firms are often obliged to do, to a competence and solvency which were not justified by the facts.

Looking back, I realize that *Contact* could never had succeeded. The formula was wrong. It was neither book nor magazine. Owing to regulations that forbade the publication of new journals while paper was still in short supply, we pretended that *Contact* was a book, giving each issue a separate title like *The Public's Progress*, or *Grand Perspective*, and binding it in hard covers. But it had a magazine's format, appeared at regular intervals and carried advertisements. The contributors were eminent; Bertrand Russell, Reinhold Niebuhr, Arnold Toynbee, Harold Macmillan, V. S. Pritchett, Elizabeth Bowen, Ernst Gombrich, Clive Bell, Richard Crossman and Rose Macaulay. My father gave us his diary of the Nuremberg trials and Vita wrote an article about traveling. But their articles were ill presented. An acre of unrelieved type faced an acre of colored diagrams and drawings. The serious reader was put off by the gaudy display; the popular reader, who might have enjoyed the novelties, was deterred by the profundities of the prose. All found the "books" expensive and of a size that would not fit easily into their shelves. Was it a publication to keep or throw away? What was its audience? It had a certain *succès d'estime*, but in other quarters it was ridiculed. Its reputation was fixed in some people's imaginations by the cover picture of the first issue: a huge photograph of Ernest Bevin's left eye and a considerable portion of his nose.

My first task, it seemed to me, was to give *Contact* a more sober look. My taste and nature were fastidious; George's were adventurous. There was a difference of temperament. When I took up my duties in January 1947, I used tough language. I said that the magazine should dress like a lady, not as a tart, and that it must have an attitude of its own, not rest content with providing a forum for other people's ideas. George did not disagree, but found it difficult to alter course in mid-stream. Our art editor, Henrion (he had initials, F. H. K., but to us he was never anything but Henrion), insisted that he was an innovator in magazine design and refused to change his style. It became a tussle between us and, on the day when I was demobilized at Aldershot ('Good luck, sir. Mind your step in civvy street!'), Henrion resigned. Under the new art editor, Vivian Ridler, *Contact* became less bizarre, but its other disadvantages remained. Sales dropped from ten thousand copies per issue to four thousand, losing us £2,000 every time. Within six weeks of my arrival in Manchester Square we faced ruin. George had set himself standards so high that I found that we had paid for forty articles, including one by George Orwell, which he had rejected as unworthy. "Why?" asked Vita when I reported this to her with pride. "He's a great name." "But his article was not one of his best." "Well, what does that matter? Nobody reads that sort of thing in any case." It dawned on me that she might be right.

George Weidenfeld had a remarkable capacity for survival. He and I spent hours together in a Danish teashop, for our office was too small to allow sufficient privacy for strategical discussion, debating how to raise fresh capital, or at least fresh income. I had exhausted the family resources on which I could decently draw, and my one appeal to City friends drew a blank. At the eleventh hour, George produced three lifebelts to keep us afloat. One was a young fox-hunting man, George Lowther, who had an interest in publishing and an inherited fortune. He was persuaded to invest £10,000. The second was a contract to publish for Unilever a sumptuous quarterly called *Progress*. The third was by far the most important, to publish children's books for Marks & Spencer. George already had a slight connection with the firm through his friendship with Flora Solomon, who ran its staff-welfare department, and later he formed a closer link by his marriage to Jane Sieff, daughter of Edward Sieff and niece of Israel (later Lord) Sieff, who was joint managing director with Simon Marks. One day, shortly before Christmas 1947, Israel invited George to lunch. The scene is well described in George's memoirs:

He came to the point very quickly. 'Young man, I like your handwriting. *Contact* is original, but you'll never make any money. You'd better turn to other things as well. I've an idea for you.' Without further ado, he motioned me out of the room. We drove to the Marble Arch store where crowds of people were milling around buying Christmas presents. We made our way to a counter covered with garishly presented children's classics which had been imported from America. 'They're selling like hot cakes,' Sieff explained. . . . 'Why don't you do books like that for us?'

That was the salvation of our company. It put six feet of water under our keel. We were given an order for fifty thousand copies of each of six children's classics in a special M & S edition called Heirloom and the contract was renewed in subsequent years. The titles included *Treasure Island, Grimm's Fairy Tales, Heidi* and *Alice in Wonderland,* and were illustrated by Edward Ardizzone, the Zinkeissen sisters, Philip Gough and other artists who were happy with so enjoyable a commission. George gave them only two instructions: when the text says that the heroine is wearing a green pinafore, the picture must show it green, not blue; and the children in the drawings must have sweet faces. When we needed a text for *King Arthur,* Malory's being too austere, and *Robin Hood,* of which no classic version existed, we gave a young editor in our office a few weeks off to rewrite them. She was then known as Antonia Pakenham, later Fraser, later Pinter. These were her first books and they are still in print.

Though the *Heirloom* series saved our bacon, its benefits would not be apparent until we produced the books and 1948 was a dreadful year. Our funds were running perilously low, as *Contact* continued to lose money. Scheme after scheme fell through, as hard-headed accountants warned their clients against romantic adventures like ours. We never hid the true facts from them, but we did make the most of our prospects. I quote from my diary an interview in December 1948:

At 10 P.M. I went by appointment to see Lord Barrington and his nephew and heir, Patrick, who was in a terrible state, crouching by the fire and all but sobbing. When he went out of the room, Lord B. said that he was highly neurotic and had been much worried by our proposal [to invest £10,000 in *Contact*]. Then he asked me some penetrating questions about our business, which I answered, apparently to his satisfaction. When Patrick returned, his uncle said that he had better pay the £10,000, as he thinks the business is sound, but he warned me not to undertake jobs which we could not fulfil. Patrick rose from the carpet, and walked silently to the writing table, where on a dirty bit of paper he penned this note to his accountant: 'Please pay the £10,000 into the account of Contact Publications Ltd,' and signed it. He gave the note to me to read, and put it in an envelope for me to post. Claret was brought up cold from the cellar, and we drank a little gloomily to the success of our venture. Patrick was to be given a job in our office at £600 a year. It was not a dishonest procedure, but to me it was unpleasant. I then left, posted the letter, and rang up George to say that he could sleep sound. He said that *Contact* was now between him and me as equal partners.

Of course we were not equal partners. As the generator of most of our income, as I was of the capital, he was the managing director and was rightly paid more. He had greater resilience than me, an acuter mind, more daring. His character had been forged in a hotter furnace. I often asked myself what I would be doing if, like him, I had been born an Austrian, forced at the age of eighteen into exile, arriving in London penniless and almost friendless on the eve of war with his own country. He made his way through the monitoring service of the BBC, broadcasting to Germany, Italy and occasionally to France when he was still in theory an enemy alien. When I first met him, he was only twenty-six, and had formed a circle of friends in intellectual and aristocratic England far wider than my own. Yet he was without conceit or snobbishness. He enjoyed the company of stimulating people of any nationality or class. He loved England, although I came to think that his spiritual home was Israel or the United States, but Conrad Black was right to call him the personification of European civilization. I still have to think which nation he is referring to when he ways "we."

Once when we were walking to our next engagement after giving lunch to some Trade Unionists, a lunch which we could ill afford and which bore no fruit, he suddenly swung me into an office in Sackville Street, saying that he had an appointment to be naturalized British, and would I be his witness and sponsor? In a grimy back room, filled with men bent over ledgers, George embraced his new country, swearing on a greasy Bible allegiance to the King. As we walked out into the street and he resumed our previous conversation, I asked him whether it was not an emotional moment for him. Did he feel no pang of farewell to Austria, no surge of welcome from Great Britain? "No," he replied. "That conflict is over. This is merely the consummation of a fact." He hailed a taxi. I said that we could not afford taxis. We should go by bus. He said that the two partners in a flourishing business could not arrive at their next appointment by bus. We took a taxi.

He had a sweetness of nature, a gift for persuasion both in business and in friendship. *In extremis* he was a great fighter. He held our firm together with a minimum of deviousness, and a maximum of courage and resource. Only once did I see him lose his temper, and then it was not with me, but on my behalf. I had been invited to lunch by the editor of a rival magazine, *Fortune*, who suggested that I should join his staff. I told George of this offer, as a joke. He seized the telephone and upbraided his rival in scorching terms of which I had hitherto not thought him capable. There was no possibility of my accepting the offer. I had hitched my wagon to George's star and felt no regrets. I was more than a respectable front to his ambitions. He trusted me to manage the firm when for the greater part of a year, 1950, he went to Israel as President Weizmann's *Chef de Cabinet*, and returned partly out of loyalty to me, and partly, I believe, because he felt that he would never be wholly acceptable as an Israeli, speaking only rudimentary Hebrew and lacking the experience of a kibbutz or Israel's wars. Emotionally he wanted to stay with Weizmann but felt morally committed to me and the other investors, and to his parents, who had followed him to London. His return was an act of loyalty, not one of self-sacrifice. He has made a career for himself as a British citizen which far exceeded what he could have achieved in Israel, where he might have risen high in the diplomatic service but could not happily have engaged in the hurly-burly of Israeli politics.

WEIDENFELD & NICOLSON

Contact died in 1950. It was a bitter blow to George, whose first child it was, but he agreed with me that its prestige was not enough to justify its losses. We had already decided in principle to turn to general publishing under a new imprint, Weidenfeld & Nicolson. *Contact* had published a few books apart from the magazine, of which the first, on the coal industry, was by the young Labour MP, Harold Wilson. Now we launched our first real list, with the memoirs or biographies of Mussolini, Schacht, Tito, Gorki and Charlotte

Haldane, a curious selection for a refugee from Nazi oppression but solid enough to justify a major party at Brown's Hotel on 10 November 1949, the date which should be commemorated as the founding of the firm. It was typical of our penury and ambition that we gave the guests the cheapest possible brand of champagne, but enough of it was drunk (109 bottles by 150 people) to render the party a success. The guest list mirrored our past and future, the friends whom we had made and the authors whose work we hoped to publish. Among the former were Peter Quennell, Alan Pryce-Jones, Peter Ustinov, Moura Budberg, Simon Marks, Nicholas and Olga Davenport, John Sparrow, Richard Crossman and James Pope-Hennessy. Among the prospects were Compton Mackenzie, Cyril Joad, Somerset Maugham and Rose Macaulay. Charlotte Haldane was the only person who looked indignant, because she had imagined that the party was being given for her, and few people paid her much attention. George asked my father afterwards whether he considered the party a milestone in our progress, or another nail in our coffin. "A golden nail," he replied. We dragged the survivors to the Gargoyle, the night club which had become almost an annexe to our office, and there we stayed till 2 A.M.

A month later George left for Israel.

During the next two years I fought three parliamentary Elections— Leicester, Falmouth and Bournemouth—and was elected for the third. At the same time I managed to keep the firm going on the Heirloom library and the legacy of commissioned books which George had left me. Slowly we clambered out of the abyss. We had a gifted staff. When Clarissa Churchill left us to marry Anthony Eden she was succeeded by Antonia Pakenham, who brought with her a fellow-student, Vanessa Jebb, Gladwyn's daughter, who later married Hugh Thomas. Another recruit was Sonia Orwell. We formed a congenial team.

A year after his return from Israel, George married Jane Sieff. I was best man at their wedding in a Bayswater synagogue and there was a reception at the Dorchester. The couple were well established in a house in Chester Square which Edward Sieff bought for them, next door to the house which George's parents already occupied. It was there that he began to acquire a reputation as London's supreme host, but Jane was not the ideal hostess. She was very young, brought up in the clannish world of the Marks–Sieff family, and was unused to the intellectual and sometimes raffish society to which George introduced her. I would see her sitting nervously silent at one end of a long dining-room table, with Cyril Connolly, perhaps, on one side of her and the

American Ambassador on the other, while from the far end George signaled to her with anxious looks to do the duty for which she felt so inadequate. He now reproaches himself for failing to understand her needs, and for what he calls his "casual infidelities," but it came as a shock to him when she suddenly walked out only two years after their wedding to marry a French student with whom she had fallen in love. There is one treasured relict of his first marriage, his only child, Laura, whom I meet in his company once every few years, and always with delight. She is now married, with children, and retains the freshness, delicacy and beauty of her youth. I have seldom been more moved than by her impromptu speech at her father's seventieth birthday party, when with a composure that she cannot have inherited from him, she expressed the affection that we all felt.

George Weidenfeld is a very affectionate man. He has suffered more abuse and prejudice, some of it anti-Semitic, than most people, but he possesses the gift of healing to a rare degree. He bears few resentments. His dinner parties are full of ex-adversaries. At first I complained loudly of his lavish hospitality. We could not afford it. But gradually it grew on me that it was excellent business as well. His conviviality brought together people of his different worlds in circumstances that warmed them to their host. The people whom he attracted to his table were often potential authors, once we had lost the need for potential investors, and they were as much beneficiaries as benefactors, for he excelled at marrying authors to subjects, seeding ideas which might die or germinate. His eloquence was seductive. He has never lost his strong Viennese accent, but he speaks the English language (and French and Italian) with a fluency rarely acquired by natives, and possesses a deep mental reservoir of remembered reading. His attention sometimes wandered. I would say to him, "George, you haven't been listening to a word I've been saying." "Oh yes I have." "Well, tell me what I've said." Then he would repeat verbatim my last two sentences, but not their context. On the other hand, when his interest *is* wholly engaged, his intelligence is captivating. I have seen him talking to a small group of intellectuals or politicians about some subject like Bosnia, on which he was not an acknowledged expert, and one by one they fall silent while he pours out a cornucopia of facts and ideas, never dominating, never unctuous, but provocative, stimulating, responsive.

If he was a failed editor, he was a great publisher. We embarked on our venture with little experience and had almost no help from fellow-publishers, who disapproved of the hybrid *Contact* and of selling books through chain stores. We sought advice from two of the most eminent. One was Jonathan Cape. George recollects that he gave us lunch at Claridge's, but I am convinced that we gave him lunch, and while warning us that a publisher's profits come from his economies, he ordered for himself the most expensive food and wine on offer. The other was Sir Stanley Unwin, who said, "I can only give you one piece of advice. No book on South America will ever sell. Any book on Mary Queen of Scots will always sell. If you understand that, you are publishers." He was forgetting Peter Fleming's *Brazilian Adventure*, one of the bestsellers of all time. But he was right in his prediction. Antonia Fraser's *Mary Queen of Scots* was one of our greatest successes.

It was the companionableness of publishing that I most enjoyed, the collaboration of a dozen likeable people for a common end, and the diversity of our publications in fact and fiction. It is true that a publisher is only a midwife, not a parent. He turns other people's manuscripts into saleable books. It is not possible to be bored, but it is possible to despair. We were blamed by reviewers for misspellings and errors of date or fact which I always regarded as the author's responsibility. There were authors who telephoned daily to inquire how many copies of their book had sold and to complain that they saw no copy on sale at W. H. Smith in Godalming. The most successful authors were the least troublesome. I am proud to have had a hand in Rose Macaulay's *Pleasures of Ruins*, Maurice Bowra's *The Greek Experience* and Saul Bellow's *The Adventures of Augie March*. There is no more pleasurable occupation than to work closely with a talented author, have him or her accept improvements to phrase or plot, find the perfect illustration for the jacket, and "integrate" a book so that a picture appears alongside the relevant text. The editor's role is a humble one, but it is as deeply satisfying to him as to the author when he sees "his" book filling Hatchards' front window.

I spent much time, even after I was elected to Parliament, on these occupations, but I will describe only one of them, for it was dramatic in its incidence and had a major influence on the firm's fortunes and reputation, and on mine. I speak of *Lolita*.

LOLITA

It was here that my political and publishing lives converged. The book made the name of Weidenfeld & Nicolson familiar to press and publishers worldwide, and contributed to the loss of my seat in Parliament. In his memoirs, George Weidenfeld gives an account of the affair which is overgenerous to me. He suggests that I gave him full support throughout. In fact, I was dubious about the book at the start and later tried to minimize the damage which its publication would do to my political career.

Lolita, the girl, was the creation of Vladimir Nabokov, the Professor of Russian Literature at Cornell University, U.S.A. She was a flirtatious twelve-year-old, a sex kitten, an embryonic Bardot, with whom a middle-aged man, Humbert Humbert, falls in love. He marries Lolita's mother, who is then killed in a car crash. Humbert and Lolita travel through America, motel to motel, until inevitably Lolita falls for a younger man. The novel ends in despair. Lolita dies in childbirth, and Humbert of a heart attack. Its critics maintained that it depicted all that was most squalid in human conduct. It was corrupting. Girls of Lolita's age would read the book and begin to think that they possessed powers of attraction which they had not hitherto suspected. Men of Humbert's age would look at little girls with a new eye. When once they patted them affectionately on the hair, they would now pat them lustfully on the bottom. The delightful innocence of childhood would be tarnished. No man would trust his young daughter with his closest friend. The book must be banned.

If that was the general opinion, no decent publisher would take a second look at the novel. If it was written without art, with the intention to titillate and the hope of gain (what lawyers call the *mens rea*), it would be pornography. But *Lolita* did not fit this definition. Its sexual incidents were suggested more than described. A child would not understand the passages to which greatest objection was taken and an adult who hoped to find food for his lust would be disappointed. Moreover, the novel ridiculed its two main characters. Lolita is sentimental, conceited and selfish; Humbert is a self-confessed pervert, whose only merit is that he despises himself. Their life together, apart from a few moments of ecstasy on the man's part, and indifferent surrender on the girl's, is a slow degradation. Four lives are ruined by his guilty passion. How, then, could any reader imagine Humbert's experience to be worth imitating? Nabokov had no need to point the moral. His book is an implicit condemnation of what it describes. It is not corrupting. It is more likely to have the opposite effect, to lower the sexual appetite. It is a function of literature to explore the ramifications of sexual desire and this book is a work of great originality, an aggressive book, an explosion of anger against the imperfection of mankind. That was the defence.

My own opinion wavered between these two extremes. *Lolita* emerged as the most controversial book of the decade at the very moment when Parliament was reconsidering the law of obscene publications. A Select Committee, of which I was a member, was attempting to replace the century-old definition that a publication is obscene if it has a tendency to "deprave or corrupt" its readers, a definition which was thought to be too vague. Who was to say that a person had been "corrupted" by reading a book or looking at a picture? Was it likely that a young woman would confess, "I was a good girl till I read *Love Lies Bleeding*"? And if censorship is necessary, why confine it to sexual matters? Is a murder story an incitement to murder? Are books that describe the delights of gambling, drunkenness, drugs or gluttony not equally corrupting?

Many witnesses appeared before our Committee to suggest a new definition, but they were as much at a loss as we were. A. P. Herbert, who had just published a draft Bill on the subject, told us that in his opinion a book should be banned if it provoked "libidinous thoughts." "But," I suggested to him, "any novel that deals with love between men and women could provoke libidinous thoughts. So, for that matter, could an advertisement for women's underwear." "Well," Herbert replied, "let us say improper libidinous thoughts, thoughts that are contrary to a sense of public decency." I described another sitting of the Committee in a letter to Vita of 17 December 1957:

We had evidence yesterday from the Public Morality Council, for which the charming Lady Cynthia Colville was the chief witness. From her little bag she fished out some revolting postcards as examples of the sort of thing that we ought to make illegal. We passed them quickly from hand to hand, lest it be thought that we had more than an academic interest in them. Then Lady Cynthia got into a terrible muddle. I asked her, 'Would you ban *La Vie Parisienne*?' 'Certainly not.' 'But people buy it for its erotic stimulus?' 'That's their own affair.' 'At that rate, everything could be said to be a person's own affair. We should leave everything to individual taste and judgement.' 'Oh no, we mustn't do that.'

I tried to persuade Roy Jenkins, whose Bill emerged from the Select Committee's Report, that we should add to the notion of corruption the concept of "shocking": a work is obscene if it "grossly offends a reasonable man." I moved to an amendment to that effect, but it was rejected, fortunately, I thought later, because it might have trapped *Lolita*. The Report retained "deprave or corrupt," but admitted literary merit as a palliative, a definition which was passed into law in July 1959 and saved *Lolita*.

The book had already been published in Paris by a firm called the Olympia Press, and by Putnam's in America, but when a copy of the Olympia edition was imported into England in September 1958, a magistrate's court fined the bookseller £20. It was, in effect, banned. So we took a great risk in signing a contract with Nabokov to publish a British edition. The *Sunday Express* had already denounced it as "sheer unrestrained pornography," and our side replied with a letter to *The Times* signed by leading members of the literary establishment, including A. Alvarez, Isaiah Berlin, Maurice Bowra, Allen Lane, Compton Mackenzie, Iris Murdoch, William Plomer, Stephen Spender and Angus Wilson. But there were others closer to me who opposed publication. Raymond Mortimer advised delay: the public was not yet ready for it. My father hated the book and begged me to avoid becoming involved. Vita saw no literary merit in it at all, and was "horrified and appalled" by the thought that we might publish it. I replied that we were now committed to it, and if we abandoned publication we would be accused of cowardice and betraying a great principle. The controversy coincided with the passage of Jenkins's Bill through its many stages. It was quoted as a "test case" and, as I was known to be the potential publisher, I found it difficult to avoid criticism, both in Parliament and in my constituency.

I did not conceal from George my misgivings. I had not read the book before the contract was signed, and when I did I was shocked by it. It seemed to me saturated in lust. I implored him, and his two new partners, Nicolas Thompson and Anthony Marreco, to test legal opinion by some form of token publication, and to say publicly that if the authorities made it clear that they would prosecute us, we would abandon the idea completely. Our solicitor, Peter Carter-Ruck, and our Counsel, John Foster, advised us that prosecution was unlikely, but if it happened we would probably win. They approved my idea of a token publication, either by importing a single copy and inviting a test trial of it, or by prosecuting a public library like Tunbridge Wells's which had been circulating their copy of the book for years.

On 16 December 1958 the House of Commons debated the Select Committee's Report. The Home Secretary, R. A. Butler, said that the Government accepted its main recommendations, which was not surprising, since they were non-inflammatory. In his reply, Roy Jenkins threw the name *Lolita* across the floor, and defended it against shouts that the book was obscene. I was called last in the debate. I could not express my reservations without disloyalty to my partners, but I did say that I regretted that there was no method by which a publisher could consult the authorities before publication, as they could in the theater and film industries. Rab turned round from the front bench and muttered, "Censorship!" I replied that I would rather be subject to his censorship before publication than to a jury's afterwards. "Publish and be damned" is very bad advice," I concluded. "I do not in the very least wish to be damned." Butler asked me to see him in private after the debate, and told me that *Lolita* would stand a better chance after the Jenkins Bill had become law. That was some encouragement, but it was not the consensus of the Cabinet.

The very next evening the Attorney General, Sir Reginald Manningham-Buller (we called him Bullying Manner), accosted me in the lobby and, jabbing his finger at me in the presence of several witnesses, said, "If you publish *Lolita* you will be in the dock." "Even after the Bill has become law?" I asked. "That won't make any difference. The book is thoroughly obscene. I'm giving you a clear warning."

This made me all the more anxious to expose the book to the trial of a single copy. It would amount to asking permission to publish it. It would show our good faith and save us the expense of printing an entire edition which we might later be ordered to destroy. I could not persuade my partners to announce this as our intention, and when I was questioned about it on television by Ludovic Kennedy, I could only reply that I thought the book a remarkable work of literature, and that we hoped to publish it in the near future. I was committed to defend a novel in which I did not wholly believe and which might do me infinite harm. George was distressed on my behalf, but Nicolas Thompson would not budge an inch to help me, although this was at the height of the Friend-Hailsham crisis in Bournemouth, where my strongest card was a reputation for probity. Now I was in danger of losing it. The vicar of Christchurch warned me that the publication of *Lolita* would do me irreparable damage. I still believed that the test-case method would exonerate me, and on Christmas Eve 1958 I told George that I would resign as a director of Weidenfeld & Nicolson if he did not adopt it and allow me to explain my reasons publicly. "If I have to choose between *Lolita* and my career," I wrote to him, "I will choose my career. But the test case obviates the choice." Although by this time I held only a handful of shares in the firm, my resignation would do it much harm. So at a board meeting on 1 January 1959, the test case was agreed. If it went against us, we would cancel publication. George and Nicolas accepted this policy reluctantly. I could understand why. It seemed illogical to invite prosecution of a book for which we had signed a contract with the author. I do not believe that Nabokov was ever informed of the ploy.

On that same day Ted Heath, still Chief Whip, sent for me for another distressing but amicable interview. He begged me to cancel publication, for otherwise the Bill would become a *Lolita* Bill. Conservatives would vote against it, the Socialists in favor, and unanimity between the parties would be wrecked. I asked him if he had read the book. He had. He had found it "rather boring." "Well, if it is boring, it cannot be corrupting." But I did not pursue that argument. I asked him what he thought of the test case, and he replied that this was a matter for us, not for the Government. So I returned to the Attorney General. He said that even if a jury pronounced in favor of the book, that would not deter the Director of Public Prosecutions from bringing his own case against us. I asked. "How certain is he to prosecute us?" "Ninety-nine-point-nine percent certain," he replied. Nevertheless, I announced the test case in a speech in Bournemouth on 1 February, in the middle of the postal ballot that was to decide my political future. The announcement received wide publicity and support. It was a novel idea and seemed fair.

For a time, the favored method for bringing about the test case was to sue the Tunbridge Wells library for circulating the Olympia Press edition. Then our new Counsel, Gerald Gardiner QC, who became Lord Chancellor in the Wilson Government, advised us to print a small edition, sell one or two copies to friends, and send another to the DPP, Sir Theobald Matthew, telling him what we had done and inviting him "to consider the matter." We wrote that we believed that the book had great literary merit, but we did not wish to break the law. It was implicit in our letter that we were prepared to defend the novel in court. We received an acknowledgment, but no decision. We printed twenty thousand copies and held our breath. When the time limit which we had given Sir Theobald was about to expire, we invited Vladimir Nabokov to London and sent our friends an invitation to launch *Lolita* at a party in the Ritz Hotel on 5 November 1959.

George and I met Nabokov and his wife at the St James's Hotel, I for the first time. I liked him very much. He had none of the petulance or arrogance that I expected. He was rather shy. For the first half hour of our discussion,

Lolita's name was not mentioned, as if we were all instinctively hesitating to light the fuse. Then Nabokov described to us how a French friend of his had introduced to him his newest mistress. "She was a very young girl," he said. "In fact, she was Lolita." The spell was broken. I had half an hour with him alone as we drove to a dinner party which we had arranged in his honor. I wrote to my wife:

> I asked him, 'You don't like people saying that *Lolita* is a cautionary tale, do you?' 'Well,' he answered, 'it is to this extent: that in the end Humbert feels remorse for having destroyed a child. What people fail to realize is that the point of the book is contained in the last thirty pages, when Humbert discovers that he loves this creature for whom he had previously felt only a perverted form of passion.' 'So the novel is about love?' 'Yes, it is. He only discovers that he loves Lolita when she is faithless, scrounging, pregnant and hideous. I don't in the least object to the argument that his peculiar perversion leads to great unhappiness and remorse. I did not write it as a cautionary tale, but as a slice of life. It is, if you like, a tragedy.'

The dinner party was given in the White Tower restaurant where I had first met George. I placed Nabokov between Roy Jenkins and Victor Pritchett, two of his greatest supporters. Others, almost equally eminent, were furious at not being invited.

The Ritz party followed four days later. The invitation was discreetly worded: "Mr. George Weidenfeld requests the pleasure of your company to meet Mr. and Mrs. Vladimir Nabokov." There was no mention of *Lolita*, but everyone knew that the party was intended to celebrate the publication of the book next day and that we were still in doubt whether the DPP intended to prosecute us. The expectation was that he would not, for during the summer the mood had changed. Jenkins's Bill had passed successfully into law; *Lolita* had ben published without trouble by leading firms in France, Germany and Italy; the General Election of October 1959 had returned Macmillan (himself a liberal publisher) with an increased majority; and our test-case proposal had created a favorable impression. But Manningham Buller was still Attorney General and the stern warning that he had given me was by now public knowledge. Would he retreat? Fortunately, the decision rested not with him but with Sir Theobald. In the middle of the party George was called to the telephone and an anonymous voice, possibly from the DPP's office, or from an even higher source, told him, "This is highly irregular, but I am a great supporter of your cause. You can go ahead. The DPP has decided not to prosecute." I announced the news to the assembled company, which included the cream of literary and political London. The cheers could have been heard as far as Hyde Park Corner. It was headline news next day and within a month *Lolita* had sold over one hundred thousand copies.

It was a triumph for George. His nerve had held in face of much discouragement including my own. His defence of *Lolita* had liberalized the law of obscene publications a whole year before the trial of *Lady Chatterley's Lover*. The row had certainly jeopardized my chances of success in the Bournemouth ballot, because my two great controversies peaked simultaneously. I was hurt that among the many letters of commiseration that I received, not one came from the Weidenfeld office. But I was consoled that my device of the "trial of a token copy" was a contributing factor to our success and a useful precedent for other publishers. I was amused to read some months later that when Butler, still Home Secretary, was asked why an official of his department had given us advance notice that we could publish the book without fear of prosecution, he could truthfully reply that none of his officials had told us any such thing. He did not need to add, such are the limits of *suppressio veri* allowed to governments, that this information was leaked to us by another department.

WEIDENFELD WITHOUT NICOLSON

I was weakened in the *Lolita* controversy by the fact that I was only a minority shareholder in the company and, although still a director, I had little influence on my partners. Weidenfeld & Nicolson had published many prestigious books during my seven years in Parliament, but its finances were again precarious owing to the termination of the M & S contract in 1956, although they had sold two hundred fifty thousand of our Heirloom books every year for eight years. It was less of a blow to our fortunes than it would have been a few years earlier, but George begged me to make one last effort to recapture the prize, imagining that an appeal from a House of Commons man might be more persuasive than if he went himself. It was the most painful interview of my life. I waited in Marcus Sieff's outer office with four other suppliants, each of us holding his sample, my neighbor a golliwog, I a dummy of *Black Beauty*, and one by one we were admitted. The golliwog man came out shaking his head sadly. I went in next. I thought, most unwisely, that if I pulled a little rank I might have more success. I asked Mr. Sieff (as he then was) if by chance he had read my recent speech in the Commons in strong support of Israel. He had not read it. Nor could he recall ever having read *Black Beauty*. The interview lasted three minutes. I was refused. The next hopeful (in men's underwear) was summoned. It was not a brutal process, but it gave me a taste of commercial competition to which I was not temperamentally suited.

Things came to a head in August of that year. The Board of our Company decided that in order to save it from liquidation fresh capital must be injected, and this would only be possible if the existing shares were scrapped. Nicolas Thompson and Tony Marreco loaned us sufficient money to carry on, but in the process I lost my investment, retaining, in place of my loans, twenty-five hundred shares which George bought from me in succeeding years. At any other time my loss might have seemed catastrophic, for I had no other capital, but I did not particularly care, since my mind was wholly occupied by the Suez crisis, and as my investment had never borne any dividends it seemed to make little difference whether the capital was intact or not.

George Weidenfeld remained the controlling partner. He had just married his second wife, Barbara, ex-wife of Cyril Connolly. The wedding reception was a miserable occasion. Barbara stood in one corner acting the happy bride, while George glowered in the other, his face as black as thunder. He had intended little more than an affair. Now he was trapped into a marriage. As is well known, for both have published their accounts of it, it ended in disaster. Barbara, having left Cyril for George, now left George to rejoin Cyril. Within a few months they were divorced.

For four years, 1960–63, I worked full time for the firm, reconciled to being Spencer to George's Marks. These years were not unenjoyable. I took charge of the illustrated co-edition books, a role in which Ed Victor later succeeded me. It was one of George's major achievements to persuade foreign publishers to collaborate with us in producing books of common interest to be published simultaneously in different languages and with shared illustrations. Our financial risks were minimal, because each book was sold internationally before a word of it had been written. Our first co-edition series was the History of Civilisation, of which Bowra's *The Greek Experience* and Michael

Grant's *The World of Rome* were the first two volumes. My series was less prestigious. They were coffee-table books, highly illustrated, intended for a mass market, with such titles as *The Past We Share* (Anglo–American), *The March of the Cross* (Christianity) and *Ships and Seamen*. My father gave us his last book, *Monarchy*. Then came the "Greats," *Great Private Collections*, *Great Palaces*, *Great Military Battles*, *Great Rivers* (I wrote the chapter on the Thames) and *Great Houses* by Sacheverell Sitwell, which was our blue-ribbon book.

It was lavishly produced to the designs of Mark Boxer, and I went to Italy to supervise the printing at the Istituto Italiano d'Arti Grafiche of Bergamo. I spent many hours building up the book's dummy by pasting in the text and pictures as fast as the presses provided them. The compositors hustled in and out of my room with questions about "il paste-up" and the "secondo colore." When the dummy was finished, I took it to Mondadori in Milan to turn it into finished books. Then I went to Garzanti, also in Milan, to oversee the printing of Lady Hesketh's book on tartans. I bent over an old compositor who was tapping out on his monotype machine "The McNab of McNab was hitching up his trews" and asked him what he thought of Highland dress. He stared at me uncomprehending. He did not understand a word of what he was setting, but followed the copy letter by letter with amazing accuracy. The books were beautifully produced, and I carried back to London the first bound copy of *Great Houses* and showed it to Mark Boxer with pride. He flicked through the pages with mounting impatience, noting that this caption was crooked, that sky too blue, and ended by throwing the book aside with disappointment and reproach. He was a formidable perfectionist.

Thus was I occupied for four years, alternating with my Chairmanship of the United Nations Association and frequent journeys abroad to lead the British UNA delegation to New York and other conferences of the World Federation. It was not a satisfactory life. In 1963 I was forty-six, and wondered whether I was destined to spend the rest of my working days turning other people's manuscripts into books and pasting in their illustrations. Nicolas Thompson could not conceal from me his reasonable hope that I might move on, leaving him as George's effective partner and chief of staff, a role to which he was better suited than myself.

We had words about it and the upshot was that I resigned in January 1964, remaining an outside director of the firm until it was sold to Anthony Cheetham in 1992, but playing an increasingly sleepy part in its affairs. Instead, I wrote books which the firm published and contributed more to its success by writing than I had by editing. In one year, 1973, *Alex* and *Portrait of a Marriage* were serialized by the *Sunday Times* and were at the top of the best-seller lists, and in 1977 *Mary Curzon* won the Whitbread Prize for biography. My father's three volumes of *Letters* and *Diary* were committed by him to Collins, and Virginia Woolf's letters by Quentin Bell to the Hogarth Press. Otherwise I remained linked to my old firm by books and friendship. When Nicolas left (he later became Managing Director of Heinemann), he was succeeded as Managing Director by Christopher Falkus, who for ten years rented with his wife Gila the South Cottage at Sissinghurst, where he was followed in his tenancy by Ed Victor.

George's major successes came after I had ceased to play an active part in the firm, but I kept in touch and watched with vicarious pleasure its expanding reputation. To this day, I glow with pride when I see on the bestseller list a title published by "Weidenfeld & Nicolson" with which I had nothing whatever to do. By 1974 the Company and its subsidiaries were publishing some 175 new books a year, concentrating on biographies, up-market fiction and art books. Its turnover in that year was £2.4 million and its net profit £150,000. It was accepted as one of the leading British publishing houses, and George as Crown Prince of the annual Frankfurt Book Fair. His social life, and his political activities, expanded in pace with his publishing success. His flat in Chelsea Embankment became the venue for scintillating parties, and from time to time I was invited to join them, witnessing some strange scenes, like the dinner party at which the stars were the Prime Minister (Harold Wilson), Laurence Olivier, Henry Kissinger, and Princess Michael of Kent, and the ageing Olivier, unsteady on his feet, collapsed on a tray of drinks, from which he was rescued by Edna O'Brien.

Recently George and I have not met more than twice a year. I have lived more and more in the country, and although he has three times been to Sissinghurst, his pleasure in gardens and the countryside extends little beyond satisfaction that they exist. I have never known a more urban man. His apogee was his fourth wedding. Long after his third marriage, to Sandra Payson, collapsed, he told me that he was thinking of marrying again. "No, George," I said, "you are not a marriageable man." How wrong I was. He had met Annabelle Whitestone. If you are being married for the fourth time at the age of seventy-two, even if your bride has never been married before, you might arrange a quiet lunch for a few friends and a discreet honeymoon in Bournemouth. That is not George's style. When he married Annabelle in July 1992 he gave, or was given, several parties to celebrate it. There was the stag party on the wedding eve at the Garrick Club, followed next day by a lunch party given by Drue Heinz for fifty guests, in the evening a gathering of several hundred friends at the National Portrait Gallery and, to round off the day, a dinner party for intimates. Part of the honeymoon was spent on Ann Getty's yacht berthed off Barcelona during the Olympic Games, and five months later there was a religious marriage in Jerusalem, at which the canopy was held at its four corners by Teddy Kollek (Mayor of Jerusalem), Shimon Peres, Isaiah Berlin and Michael Sella (former head of the Weizmann Institute). For George, this grandeur was not excessive. He enjoys display. He is also the most companionable of men. When he published his autobiography in 1994, he called it *Remembering My Good Friends*. At Conrad Black's party to launch it at the Hyde Park Hotel, the tablecloths were overprinted with pages of the book, and I lifted my plate to read between fork and spoon that I had been too timid in my love life. I considered this statement as the speeches rolled over my head and came to the conclusion that he was right.

When Harold Wilson, in his resignation honors, elevated George from a knighthood to a peerage as Baron Weidenfeld of Chelsea, I wrote to him:

My dear George,

It moves me very much, when I look back on the struggles that you have endured, to see you enter a harbour from which you will sail out again and again on new voyages of exploration, but a harbour to which you can always return, where you will feel welcomed, secure, honoured and loved. Dear George, you have deserved this more than any of the other honorands, for you started with the least advantages, and by courage, hard work, intelligence and enterprise, you have created something of enduring value. Today I share the happiness which you must feel, and send you not only my congratulations but my thanks.

Yours affectionately,
Nigel.

I would say the same today.

EIGHT

THE COUNTRYMAN

I am not a true countryman. I have owned land, but never farmed it. I have never hunted. I have fished in the sea, but never in the lakes or rivers. I once shot a stag in Scotland and swore never to do so again after gazing into its dying eyes. I have never shot birds. My ignorance of country matters is shameful. I could not tell you the gestation period of a cow, distinguish between a fir and spruce. Nor explain why during a prolonged drought the water sucked up by evaporation does not immediately return in a deluge of rain. I was taught to ride in Hanover by a Nazi *Rittmeister*, but have never been astride a horse since. Does a badger squeak? A goat sleep? I shall never know.

My countrymanship is enjoyment of the countryside, its peace, its fecundity, its beauty (from a distance, for in close-up it can be horrid). I like living alongside animals, tamed and wild. There is the proximity of every convenience, but none of that neighbor-closeness that can be so offensive in towns. Although a squirrel can gnaw through my electric wiring, a dead rat block a drain or the snow congest our lane, these disadvantages are outweighed by the freedom of country living. There are no problems with guarding one's privacy. Children can play outside all day. Cars can be parked anywhere. The night sky is untarnished by urban lights. Best of all, there is room to make a garden.

SISSINGHURST

It was on a wet day in 1930 that we first saw the place. I was thirteen. Vita was brought there by a land agent, Donald Beale, whose brother Oswald was the owner-farmer of the neighboring Bettenham. She was searching for an old house where she could make a new garden, now that a chicken farmer threatened to develop the fields round Long Barn. She found Sissinghurst. It was almost derelict. The large farmhouse, built in 1855, was sturdy enough, but Vita was uninterested in Victorian improvements. She saw only the brick Elizabethan tower which rose above a battered compound and the isolated fragments of a once-splendid manor house which could be reclaimed from the farm animals that occupied many of them. The walls and two arms of an ancient moat were fixed points round which she and Harold could create a garden. It became their joint enterprise until their deaths, and their memorial afterwards.

The rain teemed down as we picked our way through the accumulated rubbish of several centuries. There was no garden: only a few rows of cabbages. For a few moments, the rain ceased, the clouds parted and the sun lit up the gable-end of the long Tudor building, drawing from the bricks the sunlight that they had absorbed. It was at that moment, I believe, that Vita made up her mind. She turned to me and said simply, "I think we shall be very happy here."

With the indifference of most teenagers to potential happiness—we demand instant gratification—I exclaimed, thinking of our comfortable cottage at Long Barn, "But we haven't got to live here, have we? There's nowhere to live." There was no electricity, no drainage except for sump-pits, no water apart from wells and rain-butts and not a single habitable room except in the farmhouse and two cottages occupied by laborers. We took possession of one of them when Vita bought the place, with the farm of four hundred acres, for £12,375, within three weeks of first seeing it. She made it quite clear that Sissinghurst belonged to her, not Harold, not even jointly. The initials V. S–W were indelibly branded into the woodwork of the farmcarts and garden tools.

The place was so decrepit that we remained at Long Barn for two years, visiting Sissinghurst at weekends in great discomfort. My parents described the experience with different degrees of enthusiasm, Vita in her poem "Sissinghurst," dramatizing it:

Here, tall and damask as a summer flower.
Rise the brick gable and the springing tower,

and in her novel, *Family History* (1932), where it became the romantic retreat of her hero Miles Vane-Merrick. Harold was more candid about its drawbacks. In a broadcast in November 1930 he described their first meal in the South Cottage:

I am not an exacting man, but there are four things that I hate. One is soup from tablets; another is sardines; a third, tongue; and the fourth is cheese in wedges. All these four objects had been selected by Edith [Vita] for my evening meal. I ate it sparingly. She then said that we must wash up. Now, much as I dislike sardines when they are whole. I dislike them even more when they are remains. It is a difficult thing to do neatly, specially by the light of one candle and in cold water. "Isn't this delicious?" said Edith. I agreed it was.

He was not born to be a pioneer's husband, but they were both young in 1930 (Harold forty-four, and Vita thirty-eight), and it strikes me now, as it never did at the time, how audacious it was to buy a ruin, restore it and make a six-acre garden within it, when Harold had just abandoned one profession which he loved, diplomacy, for another which he hated, journalism, and had no money except what he earned, and as fast as he earned it, spent it. He warmed to Sissinghurst because he could organize its redemption, make the lakes, modernize, to some extent, the buildings, and plan the garden, having a talent for these enterprises that Vita lacked. If the buildings were shabby, their structure was so sound that the great gale of October 1987 shook the long buildings and the tower like jellies but did no damage, while it tore off a complete gable from the farmhouse. There were sufficient relics of the old manor to create a village house, where different members of the family could live apart from each other and meet communally for meals. Sissinghurst exemplified Vita's notion of domesticity. She was fond of quoting some lines from *The Prophet* by Khalil Gibran:

Let there be spaces in your togetherness.
Love one another, but make not a bond of love . . .
Fill each other's cup, but drink not from one cup . . .

There were spaces enough. In one cottage Harold and Vita had their bedrooms, and he his writing room. On the first floor of the tower she made a
sanctum which was so private that I entered it only two or three times in the
thirty-two years that she occupied it. Ben and I slept in the Priest's House,
which also contained the dining room and kitchen. Our cook, Mrs. Staples,
lived with her family in one half of the long building, and Jack Copper,
chauffeur-handyman, with his family in the other half.

Surprisingly, it is not a haunted house. It should be. I spent the first two
months after retiring from Weidenfeld writing its history, and discovered in
the Maidstone archives that it had been the scene of much suffering. The most
distinguished, and most brutal, member of the family who built it, Sir John
Baker, was a persecutor of Catholics under Henry VIII and of Puritans under
Queen Mary, trimming his sails to the prevailing wind, and amassed a fortune.
He was known locally as Bloody Baker. Vita admired him, particularly when
she discovered that his daughter, Cecilie, married Sir Thomas Sackville and
became chatelaine of Knole. His son, Richard, entertained Queen Elizabeth
here for three nights in 1573, but that was the summit of Sissinghurst's glory.
The Bakers backed the wrong side in the Civil War, and failed ultimately to
produce an heir. The house became a prison for French sailors captured during the Seven Years War (1756–63), and they did so much damage that in about
1800 the courtyard containing the grandest rooms was demolished for the sake
of its building materials and the rest became the parish poorhouse. If Vita had
not bought it in 1930, the sixteenth-century house would probably not now exist.

We all worked hard, Vita and Harold by inclination, Ben and I because we
had nothing else to do. The daily routine was monastic. Breakfast at 8:30, read
and write till lunch time, work in the garden or the woods till tea, two more
studious hours from 5 till 7, dinner at 8, bed at 10. A few guests came for meals,
but none to stay the night. There were occasional expeditions, as when we
skated round the moat of Bodiam Castle on Christmas Eve, or drove to Rodmell to visit the Woolfs. We were not bored or lonely. There was activity all

around us, on the farm, on the restorations and in the making of the garden. Ben and I were the laborers, Harold the designer, Vita the plantswoman.

The garden, in effect, is a portrait of their marriage. It combines classical symmetry (Harold) with overflowing romanticism (Vita). Just as they furnished the house with dark oak and fading tapestries, so they banished from the garden anything flash, smart or self-consciously modern. They must be surrounded by evidence of passing time, the slow thickening of a yew hedge or a fraying tassel. As I pace the garden that they created I remember how it came to look like this. How Harold took me into the field outside the garden wall and planted a stake at the spot which he had carefully calculated on paper, joining it with string to a second stake with which I walked in a circle using it like a compass, scoring the grass to sketch the future position of the yew hedge which we call the Rondel. On another day I stood above the moat with a bamboo cane to which I tied a handkerchief and, following my father's hand signals from the tower steps, moved right or left until he was satisfied that he had found the exact spot for the statue of Dionysus which stands there to this day.

It is a garden that invites exploration, a succession of privacies, as Harold described it, formal in outline, with a controlled abandon in its planting. When the central path to the Lime Walk had been laid, he fetched Vita to look at it. "What do you think?" "It's just like Platform 5 at Charing Cross," she replied. She thought it rigid, with classical statues gesticulating to each other from either end and Tuscan pots standing at carefully measured intervals. She preferred the extension to the yew walk which kinks beyond the rose garden wall because in 1930 I planted my bamboo slightly out of line. (I have heard visitors say that this is proof of Harold's genius as a garden designer. "Anyone else would have made it straight.") Although Vita liked to see hedges tonsured to perfection, lawns as smooth as billiard tables and tall plants staked against ungainly flopping, she allowed wild flowers to invade the garden, and if roses strayed over a path she would not cut them back: the visitor must duck. She was ruthless in uprooting her failures, always experimenting with new varieties and different groupings, carrying around a single flower to try its color against others before planting it. She was a painter in flowers. But a garden, she would insist, is not like a painting, which is inanimate, ruined by alteration, but a living, growing, changing work of art. Plants die; new ones are introduced. The soil welcomes or rejects. Drought, frost, tempest, disease, birds, insects and old age do acceptable damage. A garden is eternally moribund, eternally renascent. Its annual cycle is like a play, with acts and scenes, each lasting a few days or weeks.

All this is well described, and with greater horticultural knowledge than I possess, in Anne Scott-James's *Sissinghurst: The Making of the Garden* (1975), Jane Brown's two books *Vita's Other World* (1985) and *Sissinghurst: Portrait of a Garden* (1990), and Tony Lord's *Gardening at Sissinghurst* (1995). I am the domestic chronicler, they the horticulturists. There can be few gardens whose short history has been so well recorded, in family diaries, letters, notebooks, photographs, sketches and descriptions, notably Vita's *Observer* articles, many times anthologized, which did more to change the face of English gardening, as Anne Scott-James has written, than any writing since William Robinson's *The English Flower Garden*.

Sissinghurst suffered during the war but survived. A German bomber, crashing in flames, missed the tower by feet. The skeleton of the garden, formed by water, walls and hedges, was unalterable, and some of today's climbing roses are those which they planted in the early 1930s. Pamela Schwerdt and Sibylle Kreutzberger were the joint head gardeners during the last three years of Vita's life, and after her death till 1990, when Sarah Cook took over from them. Until I read Tony Lord's book, I had not realized that the post-war garden was in such decline. "Sissinghurst as it was in the late 1950s looked unlikely to survive," he writes. "Excessive freedom and informality were about to give way to chaotic ugliness and, before long, oblivion." From this fate Pam and Sibylle rescued it, "receiving few instructions from Vita, and almost none from Harold." If this was so, it can only refer to the short period when Vita was racked by back pains, for my recollection of the 1950s is that she would garden all day and write half the night, while Harold took complete charge of the spring garden, clipping the limes until two strokes debilitated him. But there can be no doubt that Pam's and Sibylle's contribution was almost as great as Vita's own. I relied totally on them when I came to inherit the castle in 1962, for I was no gardener, and they knew it.

THE NATIONAL TRUST

When Vita died, my main duty and desire was to preserve in perpetuity the garden, which together with her books, is the legacy of her imagination. Faced with heavy death duties, I inherited from her little capital with which to pay them. I had two options: to sell the farm, or to offer the whole property to the Treasury in part-payment of the duty, on the understanding that they would transfer it to the National Trust. There was no doubt in my mind, nor in Harold's, who lived another six years, that the latter solution was the better. If we sold the farm, the house and garden would be left in isolation in the middle of another person's property, and as access is by a private road which terminates at the castle, there would be constant disputes. In her lifetime, Vita had resisted my suggestion that she might give Sissinghurst to the National Trust ("Not that hard little metal plate at my door," she wrote in her diary), but she left a letter for me with her will to assure me that this would probably be my wish, and she would understand. She felt no hostility toward the Trust. For years she had served on its Gardens Committee, and Harold was Vice-Chairman of its Executive. But she had a deeper sense of family, privacy and ownership than I had. Knole, she considered, had been wrested from her by antiquated laws of inheritance; it had been "taken" from the Sackvilles (though her uncle gave it) and transferred to a public body. Sissinghurst was hers. She had bought it, rescued it, made it. I knew all this but felt justified by her letter in offering Sissinghurst to the Trust within a few weeks of her death.

But would the National Trust accept it? We had one advantage, that Harold and I, between us, were on friendly terms with successive Chairmen of the Trust, Lords Esher, Crawford, Antrim and Gibson, and latterly Dame Jennifer Jenkins and Lord Chorley, and with its directors, Jack Rathbone, John Winnifrith, Jack Boles, Angus Stirling and (today) Martin Drury. A second advantage was that Sissinghurst qualified in three ways—as an architectural treasure, for its literary associations, and as a famous twentieth-century garden. But there were two obstacles. A few influential members of its Council thought the garden slipped below the Trust's high standards, and I could afford almost no endowment to give with it.

Our most awkward and surprising opponent was Sir George Taylor, Director of the Botanic Garden at Kew and Chairman of the National Trust's Gardens Committee. He came to Sissinghurst on 25 July 1962 with Jack Rathbone. I described the visit to my wife:

Ursula Codrington [Vita's secretary] emerged from the porch looking like an Andalusian peasant in a striped apron. She fetched the *Mädchen* [Pam and Sibylle] and they made on the visitors the best possible impression—self-confident, charming, knowledgeable. We walked slowly round. "What I like so much about Sissinghurst," said Jack, "is that it is so untidy," The *Mädchen* registered horror. "Well, you know what I mean," said Jack, "it looks so romantic." He was amused by their indignation, but Sir George looked glum. I took them to the top of the tower. The whole Weald was bathed in sunshine. I have never seen it look lovelier. The clock struck one. It was at that moment that the fate of Sissinghurst was decided.

But it wasn't. At the October meeting of the Gardens Committee, Sir George said that he did not consider Sissinghurst among the great gardens of England, and advised that the Trust should not accept it. Then other members of the Committee chimed in, notably Hugh Euston (later Duke of Grafton), in defense of our garden, and the scales were tipped in our favor by Alvilde Lees-Milne, who is reported in the minutes of the meeting to have declared, "I and thousands of others put Sissinghurst way above such gardens as Sheffield Park. It is not only romantic and intimate, and full of interest, but it also happens to have been created by a great English poet and writer. To my way of thinking, it is everything a garden should be."

She won the day, and detailed negotiations began between myself, the Treasury and the National Trust, at the top level with Rathbone, at the local level with Ivor Blomfield, Director of the Trust's Kent and Sussex Region, for whose understanding I am eternally grateful. But the other obstacle remained: finance. I could offer the Trust no more than £15,000 as an endowment. Today they would demand several million, mindful of their formidable undertaking to maintain their properties in perfection forever. They asked me to pay a rent for the part of the buildings that I occupied myself. I was obliged to reply that if they insisted on this, the deal was off. It would be like mortgaging a valuable property for thousands of pounds and crippling my heirs. They relented. Then there were the delays imposed by the Treasury's procrastinations. They would take up to nine months to reply to a letter, and meanwhile charged me interest on "non-payment of duty." I complained to a friend of Oxford days, Niall MacDermot, who was Financial Secretary to the Treasury, but he could offer little help and slowly my reserves were exhausted. I was converting the south wing of the main building into a self-contained house, and this was considered an "improvement" which would attract more tax instead of counting as an extra asset that I was offering to the nation. So it went on. It was not until April 1967, five years after Vita's death and a year before Harold's, that the "hard little metal plate" went up over our door.

I have never regretted it. The "resident donor," as we are called, enjoys many advantages in return for the loss of his freehold. He is spared financial worry. The income of the property is tax free, since the National Trust is a registered charity. He has at his disposal the best technical advice in the country. If the lake leaks, the books fray, the pictures flake, the brickwork needs repointing, the Trust takes instant remedial action when a private owner might postpone these essential works year after year. Since 1967, the Trust has spent on Sissinghurst the million pounds which I did not have to give them. So grateful am I that I have often been moved to defend them when other ex-owners complain of minor changes, as at Kedleston, or discourage exterior filming, as at Knole. The donor's disadvantage is that he can advise but cannot decide. He does not employ the staff, so cannot command them. I noticed that when I could no longer give Pam and Sibylle instructions they were increasingly reluctant to accept my suggestions. This was natural. But before the Trust took over, I managed to initiate several improvements, in addition to reconstructing the interior of the south wing, like building the gazebo, repositioning the garden urns, installing the great Tuscan jars and reshaping the central terrace in the herb garden, with tiles laid on edge, an idea I copied from Lutyens.

After 1967, the Trust made changes on a more important scale. How could Vita, how could I, have afforded the service buildings—car-parks, lavatories, restaurants, shops—which the increasing number of visitors made essential? Would either of us have gone to the expense of wrapping the tower in scaffolding to repoint the bricks and replace the oak shingles on the turret tops? What owner would relay the entire sewage system, remake the lakes, or move the library bookshelves an inch from the walls to give the books space to breathe? Or when the statue of Dionysus starts to crumble, have an exact copy made? For all this I am grateful to the Trust's regional staff, specially Arland Kingston, Peter Griffiths and Dottie Owens, and to our administrators, Pamela Kilbane, Paul Wood, and now Bob Woods and Sarah Cook, who combine the role of head gardener with that of administrator of the whole property.

Sissinghurst has become one of the best-known gardens in England, and fame inevitably feeds fame. Eleven thousand visitors came in 1962: 199,500 in 1996. No private garden designed for the enjoyment of a family and their friends can stand such pressure. Lawns are worn away at places where people naturally congregate, delicate flowers are accidentally trodden on when a visitor steps aside to let another pass and the pleasure of every tourist is slightly diminished by the presence of every other. But how can one limit the numbers without offense? It is not acceptable to raise the entrance fee beyond the means of most people, or admit only National Trust members, or close the garden on the busiest days. The present solution, which inevitably causes disappointment, is to admit the public in groups, timed by tickets which they obtain at the entrance. Some may be obliged to wait more than an hour. Others go away because they cannot afford the time. This is the penalty we pay to protect a vulnerable work of art from excessive love.

I am often asked if I find the pressure of strangers disturbing. No more than a city dweller minds pedestrians passing his window, and in a garden there is no other traffic. Without visitors, the garden could not survive. They pay for its upkeep. With them we share a pleasure. To confine so sophisticated a garden to the few who live there would be like leaving a book unpublished or a painting unexhibited. It demands an audience.

So it gives me no pleasure when we close our gates to the public on 15 October each year. I miss them. We retreat to our privacies. The house is even more like a village than in Vita's day, for in making the south wing into a single residence, I released other parts of the scattered compound for occupation by the Trust's employees or tenants. We live separately, but our mutual help and friendship create a community. The Priest's House is tenanted by the distinguished medical research scientist, Dr. John Beale, the son of Vita's tenant farmer, Oswald Beale. His wife Rosemary affords us constant delight by her elegance of dress and fund of local knowledge. The Beale family extend beyond our gate, for Mary, John's sister, lives nearby, and is the mother of James Stearns, Sissinghurst's farmer, and of the clever Linda Clifford, who lives with her husband Brian in the other half of Mary's house. It is a tight-knit community.

The other cottage, known as the South Cottage, sits in the middle of the garden. It is where Vita and Harold had their bedrooms and is at the disposal of the Trust to let to outsiders. The first tenants were Kildare Bourke-Borrowes and his actress wife Pippa, one of the loveliest girls I have ever known. Then came Gila and Christopher Falkus, both closely associated with Weidenfeld. The next to take over the tenancy was the literary agent, Ed Victor, and his dynamic and eloquent wife Carol, who have contributed more to my enjoyment of life than any other couple. They made of the small cottage a center of intellectual life that it might have been, but never was, in my parents' days, inviting for a meal, or to stay for a week or more while they were away, writers like Stephen and Natasha Spender and Iris Murdoch, the publishers Christien Bourgois, Phyllis Grann of Putnam, Dick Snyder of Simon & Schuster, and Peter Mayer of Penguin, the architect Richard Rogers, the playwright David Hare, the film director Louis Malle and his wife Candice Bergen. Now the cottage has reverted to the family: it is leased by the Trust to my daughter Rebecca whose friends rejuvenate our slowly ageing community. Those who claim that the Trust's ownership of a house is the kiss of death should visit Sissinghurst to witness its vitality. The Trust is often accused of preserving its properties in the precise condition in which they found them. Not Sissinghurst, which is subject to constant change within the framework set by its creators.

COUNTRY HOUSES

My interest in domestic architecture was aroused as a child by our close family links with Edwin Lutyens. In his middle life he became the intimate friend of my grandmother, and was constantly in and out of her houses, adapting them, enlarging them, even building them, and as she was extravagant far beyond her ample means, and he, like all artists worth the name, encouraged extravagance in his clients, they planned together and sometimes executed architectural fantasies like the terrace which I described earlier, composed of ten thousand slates set on edge. My earliest memory of her Brighton house is carrying pails of pebbles from the beach to form the dark squares of the chessboard that he designed for the garden. How I hated it! "But McNed," I protested (his nickname among us), "there are only thirty-two black squares in chess. Here you have sixty-four!" "It's double-chess," he replied. "Like double-Dutch. Quick, another twelve pails!" Then he would reward me not with hugs or sweets but with funny drawings, one of an egg which, when unfolded, revealed the parent chicken, and another of a small boy peeing, which, when my mother approached, he quickly changed into a tulip growing in a pot. Once he showed me his plans for a great country house, and I asked him why the children's nursery was round. "So that they can't be stood in the corner," he explained. In another of his grand houses he pierced a peephole from the nursery into the hall so that they could watch the guests arriving for a dinner party. He adored children and we adored him.

His quarrels with Lady Sackville were always one-sided, her side. She would loudly complain when his clerk submitted bills for work completed, eventually pay them in tapestries and then declare that he had stolen them. Patiently he would explain that even architects, like peeresses, have to eat. Once she needed a blind to shield her loggia from the sun and pretended that she could not afford it. He suggested that she should place a box in the hallway inviting contributions from guests and tradesmen, labeled "For the Blind." This sort of thing delighted her, like his puns: "Toute Suite" for her flat, or "Is Lady Ida down?" when visiting the Sitwells at Renishaw. For the famous doll's house that he made for Queen Mary he scaled down some of our toy furniture to fit the royal apartments, and when the Queen asked him the meaning of the initials MG and GM on the pillows, he replied that the first stood for "May George?" and the second for "George May," but it is believed that the point escaped her.

Our family taste was largely formed by him. Mary Lutyens has listed her father's pet aversions—long-stemmed glasses, fish-knives, cut flowers, silk lampshades, pile carpets, the seaside and furniture place diagonally—all of which, except for cut flowers, were Vita's aversions too. His influence is apparent in every part of the gardens at Long Barn and Sissinghurst, in the use of indigenous materials, urns spaced equidistantly, and garden steps wide and shallow enough for two people to descend them side by side without interrupting their conversation.

His style has always attracted me more than modern architecture. When I came to write *Great Houses of Britain* I included among the forty houses none later than the Brighton Pavilion. The book was written in the summer of 1964. My photographer, an Australian named Kerry Dundas, was an exceptionally shy man. He was terrified by the grand and usually titled owners of the houses which we visited and could rarely bring himself to speak to them. As we were driving home after completing the last house on our list, he told me that he was getting married next week, never having mentioned any woman's name throughout the four months of our tour. I wrote each chapter in the house which it described, while Kerry took the photographs. The owners were naturally hesitant to offer us hospitality, not knowing what to expect, but sometimes we were asked to lunch, and sometimes to stay the night—at St. Michael's Mount with my uncle Sam St. Levan, at Castle Howard with George Howard and at Haddo with David Gordon. Our visit to Easton Neston was the happiest of these expeditions and the house my favorite. I described our hostess, Lady Hesketh, in a letter to my wife:

She seems to me the only worthy owner of a great house whom we have yet met. One of her likeable characteristics is the distance she puts between herself and strangers like us. It is most artfully done. I call her nothing but Lady H. She calls me nothing but Mr. N. But there is a great deal of banter and gossip, a rapid flow of classical and literary allusion which one misses at one's peril, hospitality flung at us like bouquets of flowers, great zest and, I suspect, a serious core. I think there is a profound religious sense back there somewhere. And of course this lovely house. Kerry is quite bowled over by all this. He collapsed into a silent Australian puddle, and I am left to play this exhilarating game with Lady H. alone.

Thirteen of our houses belonged to the National Trust. Most of the others were privately owned and occupied, and all were in superb condition. A great house is not dehumanized by polish but by the menacing presence of bored custodians, guard ropes, Don't Touch notices and drugget carpets on the Aubussons, all of which were absent in "our" houses. The patricians of the three great centuries, sixteenth to eighteenth, insisted on a perfect finish. At Holkham in Norfolk Lord Leicester took me to the last room in the enfilade of staterooms and told me to put my eye to the keyhole, through which, and through all ten intervening keyholes, I could see daylight at the far end, so perfect was the alignment and preservation of the mahogany doors. His library is one of the most beautiful rooms in England—and it was usually in the libraries that I wrote my chapters, like Bishop Ken's at Longleat, the long gallery at Blickling and the Robert Adam library at Mellerstain. When the book was published, Foyle's gave a luncheon at the Dorchester Hotel to celebrate it. A woman came up to me and, believing her to be Lady Haddington, the chatelaine of Mellerstain, I said that I thought her house one of the loveliest I have ever known. "What," she said, astonished, "25a Lansdowne Road?" She was Christina Foyle.

The showrooms in houses of this splendor were seldom used in their heyday. They were kept for weddings or occasional banquets. So they are today. I have attended three such occasions, all given for a dining society in the house of one of its members. The Society, which was founded in the early eighteenth century for lovers of the arts, admits, in spite of frequent attempts to change the rules, no women to its ordinary dinners, but on these rare occasions it seemed discourteous to exclude the hostess. When, at Lord Rothschild's invitation, the Society dined at Spencer House, Princess Diana was among the guests, because it had been her family's town house, the most beautiful in London. When we went to Chatsworth, the Duchess of Devonshire was our hostess. There were silver candelabra and maids in mob caps, and when we moved into the sculpture gallery, threading between the marbles, we were black against white, and in the drawing room, low-lit, low-cushioned, a Lucian Freud did not look incongruous beside the Reynolds of the Duchess Georgiana. At Petworth the doors were thrown open, room to room, creating a scintillating vista, and at dinner the young Caroline Egremont, dressed in scarlet, formed an exclamation mark between our sombre dinner jackets.

These houses benefit from rare manifestations of their original purpose, to entertain. Comparing them to the bleak furnishing and dismal guardians of French châteaux like Azay-le-Rideau, or the crumbling façades of some of the Palladian villas in Italy, the British have something to be thankful for. These houses are irreplaceable historical documents. There can never have been so wide a distribution of taste and craftsmanship as at the period when the gap between rich and poor was widest. Thousands of carpenters, masons, stuccoists, gilders, painters, metal workers, cabinet makers and weavers were creating works of art for the very few who could afford them. The cruel social system has left an astonishing legacy behind.

The house of this quality that I know best is Plas Newydd in Anglesey, now a property of the National Trust and still occupied by its donor, the Marquess of Anglesey and his wife Shirley. Like many other people, they found the house too large for them when their children left home, and created a single set of rooms along the top floor, leaving the rest of the house furnished and, on public days, open to visitors. It is like a sandwich, with the difference that here the filling is on top. Plas Newydd is not a "new place" as the Welsh name implies. It has a long history of building and rebuilding, of constant redecoration and of continuous occupation by a family which seldom remained satisfied with what they knew in their childhood. The compromise between privacy and display has never been better managed. To stay there for a night or two, and open the window in the morning upon the Menai Strait and a distant view of Snowdonia, gives me the sort of pleasure that is never staled by familiarity.

ARCHAEOLOGY

Archaeology is the poor relation of architecture. As it is mainly concerned with foundations and rubbish instead of buildings and works of art, its products are uglier. But excavation is often the only clue to how people lived in prehistoric times, and if the evidence is crude, battered and difficult to date, it pushes back the frontiers of our ignorance by half a million years, and traces the slow development of technology that raised man above the beast—how to turn fire to his advantage, how to domesticate wild animals, make pots, weave cloth, sail boats, turn wild grasses into wheat, pour molten metals into moulds, invent the wheel. Nobody will persuade me that to rediscover these discoveries is an otiose occupation. The very anonymity of the people who achieved all this—the first Briton whose name we know is Caesar's opponent, Cassivellaunus—brings us closer to them. Having left no written records, they have no history or genealogy. But we handle the things they handled every day. It is the domestic, not dynastic, scene that prehistory attempts to reconstruct.

George Tait, a classics master at Eton, first interested me in these things. His subject was Greek archaeology, and I would laboriously trace from published diagrams the ground plans of Tiryns or the Theseum. Then, while still at Oxford, I first met Mortimer Wheeler, the most dynamic and controversial archaeologist of his day. Our meeting came about in a strange way. In the summer of 1938, the coach of Balliol's rowing eight, R. C. Sherriff, who had an amateur's interest in archaeology, rented a field at Angmering, Sussex, which was known to contain the foundations of a Roman villa. The eight would provide the labor, but we needed a trained supervisor. He appealed to Wheeler, who recommended one of his star pupils, Leslie Scott. We were to meet this paragon in the Ritz, a venue chosen, of course, by Wheeler. He pretended that he could not join us himself, so we watched the entrance of the hotel for a likely-looking lad. None came. After half an hour, I said to Sherriff, "It couldn't be that girl over there, could it?" "Oh no," he replied, "he would never have sent a girl." But he had. She had been sitting in the corner of the foyer for the same half hour. She might have been someone's niece or fiancée. She was neither. She was Leslie Scott.

The next time that I saw her was at Angmering, in shorts and an Aertex shirt, grubbing up the remains of a hypocaust. She was not only supremely competent but devastatingly attractive. Wheeler, whose visits to the site were more frequent than were strictly necessary, was much in love with her, and so,

collectively, were the eight. I never knew if Leslie returned his love. Years after the war, when she was happily married, I plucked up the courage to ask her.
She smiled: "I'll tell you one day." She never did. A few months later, when
the youngest of her four sons died of leukemia, she killed herself and was
buried with him in the same grave.

I continued to know Wheeler. I published some of his books, and in the
1950s he invited me to join the Ancient Monuments Board, as its only lay
member. He was never one to believe that only the meek inherit the earth, let
alone dig in it. Politics, or big business, might have seemed more suited to his
maverick qualities, but it was to archaeology that he brought new energy, new
techniques, making a science out of treasure hunting, and investing his campaigns (Verulamium, Maiden Castle, India) with sexually charged excitement,
employing undergraduates to do the work, and attractive young women like
Leslie Scott, Tessa Verney (his first wife) and Thalassa Cruso as their supervi-
sors. His second wife, the dazzling Mavis de Vere Cole, was uninterested in archaeology except to the extent that her rare appearances on the site stopped all
work. His own performance was high-pitched in everything he undertook.
His management of ministers, mayors, students, press, civil servants, television, wars, was carried out with the maximum of audacity in the expectation
of inevitable success. His frequent flippancy, like Lutyens's, embarrassed people
who admired his genius, and his buccaneer reputation, his nomination as TV
Personality of the Year and his upstaging of colleagues in committee aroused
envy and distrust. His achievements as innovator, organizer, communicator,
scholar and gadfly were tarnished by the very qualities that made them possible.

In July 1956 I invited him to lunch at the Travellers Club with Patrick
Buchan-Hepburn, the Minister of Works, to discuss the preservation of
Hadrian's Wall, which I had revisited several times since my Newcastle days.
Wheeler was at his most expansive, imitating Syrian girls carrying wine jars
on their heads, telling the Minister what we should do for ancient sites in Jordan, and when finally I managed to introduce the subject of the Wall, he gave
us a brilliant lecture on what it had meant to Rome and what it should mean to
us, nailing down the Minister with such intensity that in the car on the way to
the House of Commons Patrick said to me, "I think we can do something,"
which, for a Minister, was going far. It was not an empty promise. The Wall is
now a World Heritage Site.

Wheeler was equally successful at Stonehenge and Dover Castle. He persuaded the Ancient Monuments Board to raise the great trilithon that had

fallen in an eighteenth-century gale, arguing that this was an accident that could be repaired with certainty, in contrast to the stones thrown down by the Romans, a significant incident in the monument's history, of which the evidence should be left untouched. At Dover we crawled through the semi-derelict tunnels and casemates constructed during the Napoleonic wars, Wheeler taking the lead like a ferret. The purpose of our visit was to decide whether they were worth preserving. Of course they were, and of course they have been. He was a histrionic, brilliant, dangerously attractive, persuasive man.

Archaeology has remained my nominated recreation in *Who's Who*, but recently it has taken a more sedentary form. I study Roman Britain more from books and maps than on foot, and in Greece I travel by cruise ship and bus to places like Phaistos in Crete (guided by Dr. Peter Jones), Santorini and Troy. Sissinghurst has not proved a rewarding site for excavation. A Roman coin dated *c.* AD 223 was found in the garden, but I was obliged to accept the explanation that it was accidentally dropped there by a wandering numismatist. I tried dendrochronology on our beams, but it came up with dates at variance with others authenticated by documents. Magnetrometry resulted in a confusing diagram of overlapping lines, none at right angles, and excavation was rightly vetoed by the gardeners. My only recent venture into this field has been to persuade the Kent Archaeological Society and Maidstone Museum to sponsor a simple monument at the point where Vespasian, as a young officer, led his legion across the Medway in AD 43, to fight the battle that led to the Roman occupation of British soil. The young Belgian archaeologist, Angélique Corthals, identified the crossing place at Snodland, the lowest point in Roman times where the river could be forded between Maidstone and Rochester. Her scholarship, and her company, have afforded me constant delight.

MAPS AND THE COUNTRYSIDE

When I was a boy, people often asked me what I would like to be when I grew up. To quell their impertinence, I invariably replied that I intended to be Director General of the Ordnance Survey, the most gratifying job in the world because its purpose is the most useful and its product the most pleasing.

I have always liked maps, the history of them and the history they contain. It astonishes me that people thought that our island looked like a squashed muffin until in 1579 Saxton published his atlas of England and Wales,

✑ 15. Vita and Harold at Sissinghurst in 1959. She died three years later, and Harold died in this cottage (the South Cottage) in 1968. ✑

❧ 16. (top) At the luncheon in honor
of U Thant, Secretary General of
the United Nations, in 1966. "I suggested
to Harold Wilson that I should invite
the Empire Loyalists, if they had come
to shout something, to shout it at me instead
of at our guest of honor." ❧

❧ 17. (right) Philippa with Rebecca
(aged 3) at Sissinghurst. ❧

❧ 18. (above) Philippa on her way
to the Shiant Islands in 1959. ❧

❦ 19. Ian Graham, Kit Macdonald, and Nigel in Vienna, 1967.
"Listen, Kit," said Ian. "They're playing our tune." ❧

❦ 20. With Joanne Trautmann in Virginia Woolf's bedroom at Rodmell in 1976. ❧

21. Nigel gives George Weidenfeld a present on his 60th birthday, September 1979. Mark Boxer at left.

22. Adam, Rebecca, and Juliet with their father at Sissinghurst in 1980.

23. Nigel and Adam on the Shiant Islands, with Mary Island in the distance between them.

24. Adam and Nigel meet in Dodge City, Kansas, on 13 June 1986,
having driven separately from Los Angeles and Miami, Florida. "When our cars met
bumper to bumper, I felt a greater awkwardness that I confessed at the time."

25. Benedict (Ben) Nicolson
by Rupert Shepherd, 1976.

26. At Sissinghurst, summer 1979. Quentin Bell, Edna O'Brien, and Nigel.

27. Shirley Anglesey and Nigel at his 70th birthday party, 1987.

28. Georgina and Nikolai Tolstoy at their house near Abingdon soon after the great trial of 1989. "Nobody who has pursued an argument for so long, so valiantly, is likely to be deterred by the warnings of his friends."

29. David Haig (as Harold) and Janet McTeer (as Vita) in the BBC's dramatization of *Portrait of a Marriage* in 1990.

30. A publisher's party at Sissinghurst in 1994. Left to right: Carlo Feltrinelli, Christien Bourgois, Ed Victor, and Nigel, with Ryan Victor in front.

31. Sissinghurst: "Its annual cycle is like a play, with acts and scenes." This is Act II, Scene 2, the White Garden at its best.

and its familiar outline swam suddenly into focus. I traced his achievement, and that of his successor, John Speed, in *The Counties of Britain,* a book I edited with the help of Alasdair Hawkyard for the British Map Library, where I studied Speed's astonishingly accurate originals. It was also there that I examined the map of western Russia that Napoleon used in his campaign of 1812, of which I wrote a history. In the Second World War my delight in cartography was fed by the detailed maps of North Africa and Italy supplied to us by the War Office and brought up to date, day by day, by air photographs. But my chief pleasure has been in modern Ordnance Survey maps of Britain, jumping from scale to scale like a zoom lens, for planning or making journeys. The OS has made us a nation of map lovers and in consequence a nation of walkers. In the United States it is rare to find in a country house the local $\frac{1}{25,000}$ map in their excellent USGS series. In England every stationery shop sells the OS maps. Why the difference? Because, an American has suggested to me, they think big, we think small. A more likely explanation is that we walk, they don't.

I enjoy driving through the countryside. I welcome the motorways because they have opened up parts of it which hitherto hid behind a maze of lanes. At the opposite extreme is the canoe, the slowest form of locomotion. I have twice traversed Kent by this method, once by the Hammer Brook, the River Beult and the Medway, from the foot of our fields, where Adam and I launched our double canoe, to Rochester, where we emerged dripping, three days later; and once, with Adam and Robert Sackville-West, from the highest point on the River Stour where we could float a canoe, through Ashford and Canterbury, to the tidal waters at Sandwich. Nobody challenged us on the Medway trip, but in crossing the Weald by the Stour, we were constantly abused by gamekeepers for upsetting their fish ("Not half as much as you intend to upset them," we replied, but to no avail), and for landing on the river bank to eat our sandwiches ("How would you like it if strangers casually wandered on to your property?" "Well, two hundred thousand people do exactly that every year," we replied, but the riposte was unfair and ineffectual). There is an ambiguity about the law of trespass on water. At one point we argued that something in constant motion like a flowing stream cannot belong to anyone since it is never the same except as a geographical expression, but we were repulsed by the doctrine of "riparian rights," and imaginary lines drawn down the center of a river and vertically to its bed. Gesticulating with sodden maps from the unstable base of a canoe is not the most persuasive method of dealing with angry fishermen, and we were usu-

ally obliged to carry our canoes along the bank to relaunch them at the next riparian boundary where the argument began again with the new owner.

No such obstacles confront the careful walker. The countryside is threaded
with rights of way, carefully mapped in the OS Pathfinder series, of which I
have accumulated a small library. I have walked almost the entire length of
Hadrian's Wall with Adam and Kildare Bourke-Borrowes, the Haworth section
of the Pennine Way with Adam and Edna O'Brien, and in the Lake District
with Julian and June Tower. He was our family doctor who cared for Vita and
Harold until their deaths, and for me until his retirement to Kendal in Cumbria.
They are friends to whom I owe much more than good health—him for his
gentleness and intelligence, her for her energy and ebullience, but it should not
be supposed that the qualities I attribute to one are deficient in the other.

It is mainly in Kent that I have walked. Its County Council has designated
long-distance paths like the North Downs Way, the Greensand Way and the
Pilgrims Way, and a skein of rights of way so thickly laid between farms and
villages that I sometimes wonder whether there are not too many of them,
paths that were formed in the Middle Ages to provide shortcuts for school-
children, but which are now redundant, since children travel by bus and car;
but they are still legally kept open through very seldom used, and form unjustified obstacles to a farmer's working of his land. The ramblers have too much
power. But I should not complain, for once a week I take the car to some
Wealden village, park it there, and walk the fields and woods for six or ten
miles in a circle. August is the best month for this, after the harvest. Then you
can follow the paths across immaculate land, stubble crackling underfoot, with
stiles and footbridges, and yellow arrows as discreet as winks, to guide you on
your way and make trespass legitimate.

In the nineteenth century John Clare was already lamenting that the countryside had lost something of is appeal. Even I, who make no claim to a Tom
Sawyer boyhood, would help load the wagons and pluck the hops. Today, few
of our village children take any part in the harvest, and few of them know in
any detail how bread and milk reach their tables. The agricultural process is
completed not by the year-long labor of a few men who lived on the farm (the
men whom Vita celebrated in *The Land*), but by huge machines hired from
distant garages for a few weeks. Yet the country looks little different than it did
in Clare's day. He would have noticed the hardened surfaces of the lanes, but
the woods and spinneys are unchanged, the fields still bounded by hedges
planted two centuries before he was born. If there is a loss of beauty in the

countryside, it is due to the insensitivity of people who can paint a cottage door pink, leave a derelict caravan or rusting car outside a farmhouse, or fill a gap in a hedge with part of an iron bedstead. These are offences that no legislation can control.

Kent is my county. I was brought up in it and have lived there permanently since 1962. It may not be England's loveliest county, for there are blemishes along its northern and eastern shores, but it is undoubtedly the most interesting. Geography has governed its history and history its appearance. It confronts continental Europe with a snub nose raised in defiance. If the kingdom is invaded, Kent suffers first. If we invade, it is from here that we take off. In the Channel ports, and now the Channel Tunnel, Kent has an immense commercial advantage over its neighbors. It has royal connections, and in Canterbury the focus of the Anglican Church worldwide. You might expect it to contain many ancestral seats, but there are no great estates in Kent, and only three houses of ducal stature, Knole, Cobham and Otford, the latter mostly in ruins. But it has more listed buildings than any other county, and two monuments, Canterbury Cathedral and Dover Castle, that are national symbols of ecclesiastical and secular power. The Weald, my Weald, is little spoiled. No industry except agriculture has penetrated it since the wool and iron trades abandoned it three centuries ago for the Midlands and the North, leaving behind countless manor houses built from their profits, farms spaced so close together that from any small eminence you are bound to see at least three, and towns like Tenterden, Cranbook and Edenbridge which are only villages writ large, their low houses withdrawn on either side of the market place and medieval churches at the hub.

All this I poured into the book which I wrote about the county in 1988. I knew little about the industrial towns when I started, or the holiday resorts like Margate and Ramsgate, or the marshes. I was guided round Romney Marsh by the painter John Doyle, who founded the society to preserve its many churches, but in the north and northeast, I wandered alone across dykes and along rain-soaked beaches, saddened by the nineteenth-century development of once pretty towns like Strood and Sittingbourne, and the tattiness of holiday resorts which their former patrons have mostly abandoned for the Costa Brava. For me there were many compensations in discovering small towns like Faversham. Sandwich and Lydd, and downland valleys that I detected from the map and explored on foot. All that is missing is a county museum worthy of Kent's history. It has some fifty town museums which display household and agricultural tools for which their owners no longer had a use, but there is no place where the county's unusual story is told by modern exhibition techniques. The museum should not be in the center of any town, but purpose-built on a green-field site, easily accessible by car, like the park of Leeds Castle. I bequeath the idea to my successors.

JANE AUSTEN

It was in gratitude to the Regency period, which gave us some of our loveliest architecture and landscapes, that I returned after many years to Jane Austen. She belongs in this chapter because it was in her day that the English countryside was most beautiful. Like many exiles, I read her novels during the war, telling myself that her idealized version of England was what we were fighting for. It was also the period of urban poverty, Botany Bay, cholera and satanic mills, but it is undeniable that England before the trains and trams, the tractor and the bus, looked its most serene. It was still largely rural, and in small towns like Guildford and Alton the neatness of the houses and dignity of the municipal buildings expressed a universal taste that we lost somewhere about 1830. Before then our forebears could not fashion a cottage chair or a pewter coffee pot without creating an object of utility and grace, and these things were taken so much for granted in Jane Austen's day that she never expresses any pleasure in them, or surprise. It is strange that to her, a vicar's daughter, a parish church was simply the place where you go to be married in the last chapter, not a place of worship or historical and aesthetic interest, and the beautiful country houses where she danced and sometimes stayed were just settings for the small conflicts between generations and classes, and the little moves that young people made, and still make, toward or away from each other, that she depicts so precisely in her books.

I wanted to discover more about the places she knew and how she used them in her novels. It would be a pleasant way of passing a summer. So in 1990 I drove around southern England with my photographer, Stephen Colover, and together we compiled the book which was published the following year under the title *The World of Jane Austen.*

Her birthplace, Steventon Rectory in Hampshire, where she spent the first twenty-five years of her short life, was pulled down soon after her death, but Chawton Cottage, near Alton, survives as her memorial. It was there that she revised her first three novels and wrote the last three, all in a period of seven years. It tells us little that we could not have gathered from her books and letters, except that she saw no need for a room of her own, sharing a tiny bedroom with her sister Cassandra and writing her novels on a little tripod table in the dining room after the breakfast things had been cleared away.

The more I studied her simple life, the more I liked her good nature, her inquisitiveness and humor. There is nothing in her letters to confirm the notion of a sour and unattractive spinster that we derive largely from Cassandra's unflattering watercolour sketch of her when Jane was aged about thirty-five. She and her siblings were much in demand as guests, particularly at country dances, which were held either in great houses like Hackwood (Lord Bolton), Hurstbourne Park (Lord Portsmouth) and The Vyne (John Chute), or more simply in Hartfield (*Emma*)–type houses near Steventon like Manydown, Deane House and Ashe Park. My favorite Hampshire house is Ibthorpe near Newbury where she often stayed with the Lloyds, and where, by coincidence, the painter Dora Carrington spent part of her childhood and youth, ignorant that Jane Austen had lived there too.

Although she never went abroad, and never to Scotland or even as far north as the Lake District, she knew southern England well, from Dover to Dawlish, lived for four years in Bath and three in Southampton, and paid frequent visits to London. But she was not an urban person. She was unhappy and unproductive in Bath, where I spent a whole week researching, with the help of Maggie Lane and Louise Ross, her connections with the city, but towns were then small, access to the countryside easy, even from Chelsea where she stayed with her brother Henry while writing part of *Persuasion*. She was a great walker, and I spent much of that summer tracing the paths that she had followed from village to village, farm to farm, which are easily identifiable from her letters. I stayed overnight in small hotels:

To Juliet (27 May 1990) from the Crest Hotel, Basingstoke.
It's a commercial hotel, but that's just what I prefer to old-fashioned inns. It has all the apparatus necessary for washing, eating, telephoning, writing. To stay privately on these expeditions (both Lords Portsmouth and Camrose invited me) would be more awkward. One would be apologizing the whole time for early rising, late returning, using the telephone, where's the loo?, can Stephen [Colover] come to breakfast?, and so on.

Basingstoke is a horrid town, full of office blocks and yuppified shops—no eighteenth-century part left at all. But the countryside is full of Georgian houses belonging to people who are doing well in the City and whose wives are Laura Ashley devotees. I like that sort of thing. Adam hates it. I like beautifully panelled rooms filled with flowers and chintzy chair-covers, with ancestral pictures on the walls, and little children bursting in, to be brought up short when they find an elderly, handsome stranger in their mother's sitting-room. It's astonishing how little is changed. 'We folded back the door between dining-room and parlour,' Jane would write to Cassandra. There is the dining-room, there the parlour, there the doors.

I was writing of Ashe House, but it was in Kent that I came nearest to understanding Jane Austen. For centuries her ancestors had owned farms near Horsmonden, and her brother Edward inherited the estate of Godmersham in the Stour valley between Ashford and Canterbury. I researched the history of this lovely house and published a small pamphlet about it. It was the focus of Jane's Kentish life, and from it I visited all the houses in the neighbourhood which she had known, like Goodnestone (Lord FitzWalter), Rowling, where she wrote some parts of her early novels, Godinton Park (George Plumptre) and Chilham Castle, disclaiming that any one of them was the model for Rosings, Pemberley or Mansfield Park, but deducing that she drew an architectural feature from this house, a horticultural expedient from that garden, and from all of them the social life of which the houses themselves are the best evidence.

The publication of my book drew me into the ambit of the Jane Austen Society. It had been run, almost owned, one might say, for the previous forty years by Sir Hugh Smiley and his wife Nancy. I had known him as a Grenadier major during the war, never associating him with a love of literature, and it came as no surprise to hear him proclaim that he had never read a single Jane Austen novel and didn't intend to. Yet he was a dedicated Janeite, a man of humor and determination, and he had built up a membership of about two thousand . But the Society's activities were virtually confined to an annual meeting at Chawton at which an address was given and subsequently printed in the Society's annual report, which contained little else. In contrast, the Jane Austen Society of North America held week-long seminars (I attended one at Santa Monica), had forty chapters (branches), arranged Jane Austen tours of England and published a book-length collection of essays every year. Could not

our Society emulate them? Our most popular novelist deserved the most energetic following. I put these suggestions to the annual meeting in 1992, to the
dismay of most of the platform and the approval of most of the members. I
was elected to the Committee by acclamation.

Then I made a grievous error of taste and tactics. My enthusiasm was in-
appropriate for the Committee's most junior member. Lady Smiley (her husband having recently died) was outraged by my presumption. I wanted to
update the Society's Constitution, make it a charity, increase its membership,
found new branches, investigate its finances and hold the annual meetings in
different parts of the country instead of always at Chawton. Most audacious
of all was my proposal, backed by Maggie Lane, that the Society should purchase the Austen's house in Bath, 4 Sydney Place, and open it as a museum.

Maggie had written several books about Jane Austen and was founder of
the Society's Bristol and Bath Branch. She and I pursued this project energet-
ically. We convened a meeting in Bath of architects, historians, accountants
and others; we had Sydney Place surveyed and photographed; and together
wrote a "feasibility study" within two months of being permitted, but not encouraged, by the Committee to do so. I also provisionally booked the Bath Assembly Rooms for the next annual meeting. This, for the Committee, was the
last straw. Our proposals for Sydney Place were turned down almost without
discussion and I was reprimanded for booking the Assembly Rooms without
authority. I was not asked to resign but did so, conscious of having given offence by overplaying my hand.

This incident had a happy sequel. Maggie Lane and I remained in close
contact. She dedicated to me her next Jane Austen book, and we lectured separately or together in Bath, Bristol and Kent as the fame of our author grew
with the dramatization of her novels for film and television. The Committee
acted with great vigor after my departure. They drew up a new Constitution,
increased the membership, held seminars in Manchester and Birmingham,
founded new branches. Slowly I was forgiven. The Chairman, Brian Southam,
joined a tour of the Kentish houses which I organized, and the President,
Richard Knight, gave me his help and support. The Society published my
booklet on Godmersham. I proposed the vote of thanks to Roy Hattersley, our
speaker at one annual meeting, and was invited, in the summer of 1997, to give
the address myself. My father lectured on the same occasion in 1956. Inexplicably, he called Jane Austen "a callous woman" and her novels "almost incon-
ceivably snobbish"; a judgment that I reversed.

NINE

THE TRAVELER

꿍 움

M y traveling has been extensive but only marginally adventurous.
Let me list the places where I have never been: China, Japan (in
fact, most of the Far East), South America, South and Central
Africa, and the Poles. As for adventures, I have walked the gorges of the Himalayas, Karakorams and the Hindu Kush, been benighted in Norway, nearly
drowned in Scotland and was on the point of falling down a well in Tunisia. I
have eaten pigs' lungs in Hungary and had two bad car accidents, both in Italy.
But apart from the war, I have never been in acute danger, never been in
prison, never starved, never found myself short of a bed, never fallen ill on my
travels and never been coshed or robbed. That is a feeble list of negatives. To
justify the title of this chapter, I can say that I have visited every country in
Europe except Bulgaria, every State of the United States except Iowa, the
Dakotas, Alaska and Hawaii, most of Canada below the wilderness line, Australia and New Zealand (once), northern India and respectable chunks of the
Middle East. That does not add up to much more than a modern businessman
would cover in a single year. Very few of my journeys were on business, unless writing and lecturing about them counts as business. They were for pleasure, but not relaxation for relaxation's sake. There was no lying on beaches,
but comfort certainly, in cruise ships, three yachts, a Ford Thunderbird on
American roads, sometimes cabin class in airplanes but never on Concorde,
curiously few trains.

I have been an inquisitive traveler, reading up the history of the places I visit, a guide-book addict, but a linguist only in French and German. Increasingly I have avoided roughing it, graduating upwards from open air to tent, tent to bed-and-breakfast, bed-and-breakfast to two- and three-star hotels, but there I have stopped, except for a Christmas self-treat at Lainston House near Winchester. Luxury palls; it demands smarter clothes, luggage and company than I possess, especially company, for I am by nature a solitary traveler, selfishly anxious to avoid the need to suit another person's convenience, hear their moans and cries of delight, and inflict on them my peculiarities like punctuality, dislike of queues and opera, and an inability to keep down anything but western cooking. It is within the British Isles that I have been most audacious—to be precise, within three of them, the Shiant Islands.

THE SHIANTS

My mother was the first to spot the advertisement in the *Daily Telegraph* in February 1937. "Uninhabited islands for sale. Outer Hebrides. 600 acres. 500ft basaltic cliffs. Puffins and seals. Cabin. Offers above £1200. Apply Col. Kenneth Macdonald, Portree, Skye." She sent me the cutting to Oxford, knowing my love of islands and that I could afford £1,500, having just inherited £11,000 from my grandmother. I immediately wrote to Colonel Macdonald, and he invited me to Skye. He hired a fishing boat to take me to the islands, but would not come himself. I could camp there for the night. This latter proposal was unexpectedly vetoed by Vita. I might be storm-bound there for days, with nothing to eat. I said that there were four hundred sheep on the islands. I could eat them. But no: it was to be a day visit only.

The Shiant Islands (their very name, in Gaelic, means "enchanted") fulfilled every hope aroused by the advertisement. I loved their remoteness, isolation, grandeur. Was it romanticism, or melancholy? Both, added to an atavistic desire to own land in the Hebrides (the Nicolsons were originally robber barons in the Minch), to have an escape hole, to enjoy nature in the wild. It would be something quite different from owning a farm or a moor, where you have to manage things, make improvements, prevent decay, have relations with authorities and neighbors. On me the difficulties of access to the Shiants acted as a magnet, on others as a deterrent. There would be some danger in total isolation—cliffs, tides, illness—when there was no form of communication to summon help. Of this I would boast, magnifying the risks. Looking back, I recognize an element of arrogance in my island mania. I would be different from other undergraduates. I would be the man who owned uninhabited islands and marooned himself there alone.

The Shiants lie in the Minch, the triangle of sea bounded by Skye, Lewis and Harris, and the Scottish mainland. Skye is fifteen miles to the south, the desolate coast of Lewis eight miles to the west, and the Highlands at three times the distance to the east. On fine days, the horizon, except to the north, is ringed by land, and there is traffic round the islands, by air and sea, but both at incommunicable distances. To reach the Shiants one must hire a fishing boat in Skye, or more usually at Tarbert in Harris, from where the trip across the Minch takes between two and three hours.

There are three islands, a little archipelago, two of them joined at sea level by a causeway of loose cobbles, which one can cross at all stages of the tide except when gales sweep over it, and a third, Mary Island, lying half a mile east of the others, and forming with them a lagoon in which yachts and fishing boats can ride at anchor. There is no jetty. You take a dinghy from the boat to the beach, and on Mary Island into a rocky cave, from where, as on all three islands, it is a stiff climb to reach the plateau and look down from the clifftops on circling birds and plunging seals. The "cabin" turned out to be a stone two-roomed cottage with a tin roof, the only man-made structure on the islands apart from sheep-fanks (pens) and the remains of old boundary walls.

The Shiants once had more permanent inhabitants. Two centuries ago, six families lived there. The lichened stones of their ruined bothies, the mattresses of soil ("lazy-beds") which they threw up to plant potatoes, can still be seen. By 1900 only one family was left—mother and father, a daughter named Marion, a deaf-and-dumb son, and a small girl who was said to be their incestuous child. In 1910, the mother died. It was mid-winter and her corpse lay in the cottage for six weeks before they could attract the attention of a passing lobster boat, for it was unthinkable to bury her in unconsecrated ground. The experience broke up the family. The father left for the Falklands to tend sheep in even greater solitude, and Marion to weave tweed in Harris, where forty years later I met her, an old crone by that time, who had never married and had never learned a word of English. I spoke to her through an interpreter. She told me that they caught puffins for food, ate their eggs and stuffed pillows with their feathers; that they kept a cow and three hundred sheep; and that the children never went to school. As she spoke, her eyes blurred with tears, but whether from self-pity or recollected emotion I could not determine.

In the early 1920s the Shiants formed part of Lord Leverhulme's Hebridean estates, and he planned to raise silver foxes on them, a madcap project from which he was dissuaded. On his death in 1925, the islands were bought by the novelist Compton Mackenzie, who married the two daughters of his tenant, Malcolm Macsween, the younger after the death of the elder. I only once met Mackenzie, but we corresponded, and in his memoirs he expressed "intense relief" that I had bought them from Colonel Macdonald, who held them for only a year as a commercial venture but never went there.

My solicitor, John Venning, was sympathetic, but as in 1937 I was not of legal age, he counseled caution. "I certainly do not consider your scheme wholly mad," he wrote, "but I fear your money may be locked up, and you might find it extremely difficult to dispose of the property if you wished to do so." His prediction was surprisingly wrong. The eventual price I paid was £1,400. In 1974 the islands were valued at £50,000; today, perhaps twice as much. It is the only sound investment I have ever made on my own initiative, and one which has turned out an unexpected patrimony, for I gave the Shiants to Adam when he was twenty-one, and he intends to give them to his son when Tom comes of age in 2002.

Conditions there have hardly changed in sixty years. There is still no jetty, no cultivation, no fresh water except for a single spring, and no regular communication with the Outer Hebrides. I have returned there many times, sometimes alone, sometimes with friends, then with my children, now with grandchildren. Typical was my second visit in 1937, when I spent a month there with only a dog for company, studying the Greek philosophers for my Oxford degree. On my return, I wrote to my brother Ben:

How lovely were the lovely moments; how bloody the bloody. I slept in a green tent beside the sea. Imagine my little tabernacle dimly lit by candles within, lashed by rain, shaken by gales, obscured by mist. The gloomy wail of the Harris foghorn occasionally breaks through the roar of the waves. I write my notes from Aristotle on a packing case full of potatoes on which some sympathetic fisherman has written the address: 'Mr. Nigel Nicolson, the lonely Shiant Isles.' One of the guy ropes snaps, the flap of the tent is wrenched aside, and an angry gust of wind and rain upsets my ink bottle, blows out the candles, soaks my sleeping bag. The matches are too damp to light a fire. I bury my head in my hands and almost sob, feeling for the muzzle of my sheep-dog under the camp-bed as the only source of comfort in an intolerably hostile world.

But—and this BUT should be written in letters a foot high—I wake up next morning to find the sun fixed in a pure sky. I lie all day with no clothes on, overlooking the sea. A seal raises its great dog's head a few feet away. And birds and birds and birds, kaleidoscopic clouds of them. One day I saw them floating in battalions, moving to the swell of the waves like a field of corn in the wind. Through my field-glasses I peer into the bridge of a Norwegian timber-boat, and would murder anyone who dared to land.

In fact, I rather hoped they would. A month alone is too long. I found myself declaiming to the sheep all the poetry I could remember and longed for human company. It was also on that visit that I nearly drowned. My only craft was a collapsible canoe in which I paddled over to Mary Island. On the way back, it disintegrated in mid-passage. The water was very cold, but I had little difficulty in swimming to the nearest rocks, towing the remains of the canoe behind me, but I did not have the strength to pull it ashore. When I told the fisherman of my adventure I realized how close to death I had come. For half an hour between the ebb and flow of the tide the water in the lagoon is quite slack. Had the tide turned, nothing would have saved me from being carried out to sea.

Next year, 1938, I took my first guest to the islands, Rohan Butler, and while he was there, my father and brother hired a ketch to visit us. It was a beautiful day. Harold wrote in his diary that night:

We cast anchor. We get into the dinghy, and hum along the placid waters, and all the little puffins rise in fury. As we approach the beach, two figures run down to it. Nigel and Rohan. We walk around to his

little shieling. Niggs is glad to have a day like this to show me his romance. It is like a Monet, all pink and green and shining. I have seldom in life felt so happy. After lunch we go round the islands in the
dinghy. The cliffs are terrible and romantic. We sing for the seals and
they pop up anxious little heads. It is lovelier than can be believed.

Visits did not always turn out so fortunately. After the war, I took the bold
step of inviting two of London's most glamorous débutantes, Margaret El-
phinstone and Elizabeth Lambart. Both were bridesmaids at Princess Elizabeth's wedding in the following year. I went to the islands a week ahead of
them to prepare the cottage, and in particular to poison the black rats, the rare
rattus rattus, which had colonized the Shiants since a shipwreck in 1876. My
fear was that the poisoned rats might leave behind unpoisoned babies which
would squeal with hunger in the night. To try it out, I slept in the room that
the girls were to occupy. Not a squeal. Next day they arrived. They behaved
like heroines. I put them to bed at midnight when the sun had scarcely set. At
3:30 I woke up to hear through the thin partition cries of distress. Three rats
were frolicking in the empty chest of drawers, making a noise like a tam-
bourine. The girls buried their faces in their blankets and refused my help,
thinking that if I released the rats from their prison they would jump into the
bed.

It was a night of horror, and also one of violent wind. In the morning I
discovered that our dinghy had been swept off the beach and smashed. When
the fishing boat returned to rescue us there was no means of reaching it except
by swimming. I swam out first and returned with a rope which I tied round
Elizabeth's waist, then Margaret's. In the water their skirts billowed out like
crinolines. Malcolm Macsween, whom I had inherited as my tenant from
Compton Mackenzie, said that they were the jolliest girls he had ever met: they
might have been born and bred in the Hebrides. When I told them this, they
were compensated for their ordeal.

Adam came to know the islands even better than myself. "At times in the
last two decades," he has written recently, "they have been the most valued
things in my life." Once, as we rounded the north cliffs on our way from Tarbert, he turned to me and said, "Buying these islands is the best thing you have
ever done." He described that journey in 1989:

The Shiants are about to spring their most theatrical gesture. Until now they have looked like pieces of moorland dropped rather carelessly in the sea. But at this point they reveal their other side: black basaltic cliffs, 500 foot from sea to lip, clustered into hexagonal columns, each ten foot wide, gathered like pencils in a box, their stubs dropped cleanly into the inky green water. The swell sucks and booms in the sea-caves at the cliff's foot. And above them in an endless, screeching pattern of flight and landing on ledges, are the birds, white specks spattered across the face of the cliff, a dazzling density of noise and movement.

It is exactly the scene depicted in a watercolor by William Daniell in 1819 (illus. 10).

I used the islands as a refuge, for solitude and summer holidays. I have never visited them in winter, which Macsween's sheep somehow survived unshepherded. In some years geological students camped ashore (the rocks are said to be among the oldest in Britain), and for several years in succession Cranbrook School sent parties there, one of which, in 1986, ended in tragedy. While the other children were unpacking their stores soon after landing, a boy, Simon Woollard, started to climb the low cliff behind the cottage, and as he grasped a slab of rock it came away in his hands, sliced through his helmet and killed him instantly. His body was flown out by a RAF helicopter from Lossiemouth. Two months later his parents visited the islands, and Adam and I were there to meet them. It was the first death on the islands since Marion's mother's in 1910.

From that melancholy scene I was rescued in the most pleasing manner. Peter Jay, who was cruising the Hebrides in his yacht, sailed into our lagoon, bringing with him Olivia Fane, Adam's first wife, who was eight months pregnant with William, and Guy Philipps, who married my younger daughter Rebecca. Peter lifted me off the islands and took me to Skye, where he landed me by rubber dinghy close to the spot where in 1746 Flora Macdonald beached her open boat after the most famous voyage in Hebridean history, bringing with her Prince Charles Edward disguised as her maid, Betty Burke.

My familiarity with the Hebrides, and the chance that I had come to know some of the directors of Unilever through publishing their magazine *Progress*, led me to write *Lord of the Isles*, an account of Leverhulme's purchase of Lewis and Harris at the end of the First World War. The cellars of Unilever

House disgorged the records of his extraordinary experiment, the only failure of his long career, and I spent several months in the luxury of its offices, before traveling north in the autumn of 1959 to read the files of the *Stornoway Gazette* and interview some of the crofters who had contributed to the old soap-boiler's downfall by refusing to accept his schemes. He had hoped to reverse the habits of centuries which had kept the Hebrides in medieval penury. He wished to amalgamate crofts to form sizeable farms, and introduce modern methods of fishing and tweed manufacture. His fishing port was actually constructed, off the southern tip of Harris, at a place called Obbe, a name which he changed to Leverburgh, like one of his new settlements on the Congo. Hebridean pride was outraged, and when English girls with bobbed hair, short skirts and silk stockings were brought over from Port Sunlight to run the office, the preacher denounced them in words typical of the islanders' deep religious faith and doom-laden fear of change. "Oh my dear friends," he said, "it is something awful to see the harlots and concubines of Lever Bros running about the streets of Obbe." Nevertheless, Leverhulme persisted in Harris, having failed in Lewis, and his great works at Leverburgh were only brought to an end when he died in 1925. Malcolm Macsween told me that having denounced him in his lifetime, the Harrismen worshipped him after his death.

ITALY

I have many associations with it. There were prewar family visits, to Pisa, Portofino and Rome; the long trudge up the peninsula from Naples to Austria in 1944–5; my honeymoon in 1953, when a farm tractor turned as I was passing it at sixty mph, smashing the car and sending me and my young wife into hospital at Verona; another accident in Sicily in 1970, when I overturned my car in avoiding another, and lay under Etna, both of us smoking heavily, I with three broken ribs. Then there was Ben's marriage to Luisa Vertova in Florence; a holiday as the guest of Marietta Tree in her Tuscan villa, and of Drue Heinz on Lake Como; a long drive from Rome to Venice with Adam and Caroline Mauduit when they were jointly compiling *An Architect in Italy* (1988); and celebrating Henry Anglesey's seventieth birthday in Venice. All these might deserve separate treatment, but I will focus on another, the start of a twenty-five-thousand-mile journey through Europe in 1967, when I was writing *Great Houses of the Western World*.

It was a companion volume to *Great Houses of Britain,* and infinitely better. My thirty-six houses were chosen from the United States, Britain and the whole of Europe west of Russia. I had as one of my two companions Ian Graham. He was not by profession a photographer but an archaeologist specializing in pre-Columbian civilizations of Central America, and in contrast to Kerry Dundas, who had taken the photographs for the earlier book, he was gregarious by nature, deeply interested in the arts, architecture, music and literature of the West, and so pleasing a guest in the many houses we visited that our hosts, and in particular our hostesses, welcomed us for his sake more than him for ours.

The third member of our party was an attractive American girl, Kit Macdonald, aged twenty-three. I first met her when she was working for the United Nations Association of the U.S.A. and later stayed with her parents in Gainesville, Florida, where her father was Professor of Law at the university. From there we drove to Cape Kennedy, and (very fast) along Daytona Beach. On our way back to Gainesville, I invited her to join Ian and me on our tour of the European houses. She accepted immediately, and her parents agreed. In subsequent correspondence I thought I must make one thing clear:

> My dear Kit, ABOUT MORALS. Your mother doesn't think that you will return a ruined woman, and my wife doesn't think that I will return an alienated husband. But other people may leap to both conclusions. We may be invited to stay in some of the houses, and I shall make it evident beyond doubt that you are travelling as secretary to our expedition, AND NOTHING ELSE. But you must be prepared for raised eyebrows and gentle sniggers. You must not mind this. You really mustn't.

She didn't. My secret fear was that she would fall in love with Ian, and I warned him of this, but he assured me that he would take care to see that she didn't and, again, she didn't.

I collected a brand-new Fiat in Turin, and Ian joined me in Padua. I wrote about, and he photographed, our first two houses, Malcontenta and the Villa Pisani, then we drove to Rome to pick up Kit, who had flown from New York that day and was waiting at the airport, spruce and slightly apprehensive. As she had never been to Rome before, in fact never to Europe, she could be excused for exclaiming at her first sight of the Victor Emmanuel monument at the base of the Capitol (1885), "Gee, how those old Romans knew how to build!" Ian remained ominously silent. But she was a quick learner and highly efficient. She typed out my chapters as fast as I wrote them, kept the accounts, paid the bills, sewed on buttons, bought us ice cream, acquired from local museums pictures of our houses as they had appeared in earlier centuries, and was allowed, occasionally, to drive the car.

The loveliest of our Italian houses was the Villa Lante, near Viterbo, and I described it in its garden, resting my manuscript on the stone table channeled for the flow of water which cooled our wine. From there we drove north on the most scenic road in the world, the Autostrada del Sole, and parked the Fiat outside the villa of its maker, Giovanni Agnelli. We were shown round the house by his wife, Marella, who was courteous but uncertain whether to treat us as journalists or guests. She said, "Now I am at your disposal for the interview. I have half an hour," but later she warmed to Ian, and his photographs of the house delighted her. But we were not asked to stay for lunch. Lunch there certainly was, because we smelled it, and there were a butler and footman in white coats laying the table. So I remarked to Signor Agnelli, who was now sipping cocktails on the terrace, "Well, we had better be going; it's probably your lunch-time." The hint was not taken. Ian suggested that he should open the bonnet of the Fiat, fiddle with the entrails, shake his head sadly, while I crawled underneath, all this within view of Signor Fiat himself. But we did none of this. The house, the Villa Perrosa, was reward enough.

Next day we drove four hundred fifty miles to Tarragona.

SPAIN

I have only twice been to Spain: once on this journey, when we described the Casa de Pilatos in Seville, and in 1993, when I took part in a conference on garden design at the Escorial. It was on that occasion that I saw the great monument to the fifty thousand who fell on both sides in the Civil War, a huge cross on a mountain top and a cathedral-size tomb hollowed out beneath it. Franco's grave is a stone slab in the very center, with just his name. A girl tossed a bunch of wild flowers on it, more from sympathy than reproach.

In my hotel bedroom I watched a *corrida* on television. They say that the experience is less dreadful in the arena because one is remote from the bloodshed and shares the emotions of the crowd. Seeing it alone, and in close-up, I found it horrifying. The performance did not follow the ritual that I had expected from reading Hemingway. There was no prodding of the bull with pikes, no padded horses, no climax with the sword. After the parade, a solitary horseman planted the *banderillas* into the bull's neck, first singly, then in pairs, prancing around the stupefied beast and raising his hat to invite applause after each successful strike. Then there was a business with scarlet capes which seemed to me a mere goading of the bull. I awaited the *coup de grâce*, but there was none. A team of six youths advanced in file, on foot and without weapons. The bull met them in a lumbering gallop and skewered the first four, flinging them to the ground, where the enraged animal turned on them with horns flailing like scimitars. I do not think that any were killed, but as they were carried off, the cameras zoomed in on their ghastly wounds. The bull was then despatched with daggers and its carcass hauled away by mules.

Spaniards have a stoical indifference to suffering and death which we lost some time in the seventeenth century. *Aficionados* say that there is beauty in matching human agility against brutish strength, Ariel against Caliban, and that it is more like a ballet than a fight. They claim that we are hypocritical in denouncing it, for the hunting of stags and foxes is just as cruel. I think this a false analogy. The true one is professional boxing. A century hence, people will think it extraordinary that we tolerated for so long the spectacle of two half-naked men slogging each other into insensibility. Both in boxing and bull-fighting, the paying of money to watch men and animals suffer abominably at each other's hands is deplorable.

FRANCE

We entered France from Spain at Biarritz and drove rapidly north to where the châteaux lie. When we reached Tours, we saw the Queen, our Queen. Kit insisted on this. Ian refused and began taking photographs of Azay-le-Rideau in pouring rain. I drove Kit to the airport to see Her Majesty arrive for an equine weekend. There were more gendarmes than people, and we had a front-row view of the simple little ceremony. A Caravelle fluttered in. We watched a huge Rolls-Royce being given its final polish and the royal standard straightened. This was a blind. The Queen suddenly appeared from behind the airport buildings in a tiny Austin and was driven rapidly to the stables. Kit said that she looked lovely. I warned her not to repeat these loyal sentiments to Ian.

Our French houses were Balleroy, which made the jacket picture of the book; Azay, disfigured by bored attendants; Château d'Oiron; Château d'Anet; and Montgeoffroy. My favorite was d'Anet, built by the greatest architect of the French Renaissance, Philibert Delorme for its most famous woman, Diane de Poitiers, and now owned by Charles de Yturbe, who gave us lunch. Ian took his most beautiful photograph there—of a door in the hall guarded by a *torchère* in the form of a Roman solider, wearing a wig beneath his gleaming helmet. This made the back of the jacket.

But France. It was the first foreign country that I ever visited, aged six, when Mlle Nadré (Goggy) took Ben and me on holiday to St. Quay in Brittany, where I disgraced myself by sticking my finger into a metal ring attached to the bedstead and couldn't get it out. I was released by a metallurgist with a saw. Vita once took me paddling in the Loire, and Mortimer Wheeler to excavate an iron-age fort on the Ile de Groix. Post-war, I went two or three times to St. Tropez to stay with Dan and Dorothy Silberberg, but I do not enjoy lounge-lizarding. My sightseeing must have a purpose, like my quick dash to the Invalides when I was writing my Napoleon book, and longer trips to Paris once the Channel Tunnel opened, of which one in particular is etched on my memory, when my daughter Juliet showed me parts of Paris (Malmaison, Bagatelle, Place des Vosges) which I had never seen before.

Only once have I walked seriously in France. It was in 1992, when I walked one hundred twenty miles in ten days through some of the wildest parts of the Cévennes. My companion was John Doyle, now President of the Royal Watercolour Society. He was walking from Canterbury to Rome, painting as he went, to make a book about St. Augustine's journey in the reverse direction in A.D. 597. As nobody can be sure of the saint's exact route, it was legitimate to assume that he, like us, took in the most historical parts of France. The Cévennes is stark country, more famous for Robert Louis Stevenson's *Travels with a Donkey* than any previous event and so, temporarily, we exchanged St. Augustine for Stevenson. He treated his donkey, Modestine, atrociously, whacking and goading her every step of the way. We were more fortunate: we had a car, driven by John's son Christopher and his friend Cathi Davis, who ferried our luggage ahead to the next inn on our route, while we walked in comfort, carrying nothing but a map and a stick, and arrived each evening to find dry clothes, a bath, dinner and a bed.

Sometimes, like Stevenson, we lost our way. Inexplicably, a well-trodden path would suddenly terminate in a cataract of boulders, fatal to a weak ankle, and Cathi would guide me over them as carefully as Nausicaa once guided the exhausted Odysseus. John Doyle's only defect as a companion was that he was stronger and fitter than me, and could talk while walking up steep hills. I couldn't respond. So we devised a code. He would hold his walking stick aloft if he had something interesting to say, and I could accept it or not. But if he had something of supreme importance to indicate or say (like a swallow-tailed butterfly or a sudden illumination into the character of his wife Elizabeth), he would agitate his stick, and then I had no choice but to stop and listen. Being a man brimming with stories and remembered verse, out of kindness to me he would only release them on level ground. He was the map reader of our expedition, the water carrier, the morale booster, the historian, guide and goad, the perfect companion.

I have walked distances with Adam in Brittany and the Pyrenees while he was writing his book *Long Walks in France* (1983), but the Cévennes walk will be my last. From now on, France will mean the car, the Tunnel and the train.

GERMANY

My first visits were in 1928–9, when we spent school holidays with my father, then chargé d'affaires in the Berlin Embassy. One summer he rented a house on the Wannsee outside Potsdam, where we were joined by Maurice Bowra and John Sparrow, and put us under the tutelage of a youth who was to teach us German. The holiday was memorable for two reasons: a cautionary tale and a near-disaster.

The tale was told to us by Sparrow. He was then twenty-two, a double-first at Oxford, and Bowra had just been elected Warden of Wadham College. They had taken a night train from Warsaw, traveling west, and their compartment contained four berths which they hoped to keep to themselves. At the last moment, a lady joined them and decorously put herself to bed in an upper berth. John and Maurice, taking her for a Polish widow, proceeded to taunt her. "She's combing her hair with a golden comb," said John (she was doing nothing of the sort). "She's fast asleep," said Maurice (she was wide awake). In the morning, the jokes continued: "She's painting her toenails green" (totally untrue). As the train began to draw into Berlin, the lady, who had not hitherto spoken a word, said in clear Cambridge accents, "Would you mind helping me down with my suitcase, Professor Bowra?"

The near-disaster occurred when Ben and I went swimming in the lake under the eye of the German youth. I thought to surprise them by diving under the punt where they were sitting and coming up on the far side. I started on this perilous exploit by taking a deep breath, and only surfaced when my breath was exhausted and I thought myself well clear of the punt. I wasn't. My head bumped its flat bottom. Nobody knew of my distress and it could have been ten minutes later or more before the tutor said, "When did you last see your brother?" or, very carefully, the same in German. I remember the desperate flailing of arms and legs that saved me. It was the moment when I came nearest to sudden death, apart from the incident of the Tunisian well (p. 89).

There were month-long visits to Hanover, Göttingen and Berlin as a student in the late 1930s, then a long gap till the Königswinter conferences of the fifties, and a tour of the British Army on the Rhine to prepare for a House of Commons debate on army education overseas. But my most extensive tour of Germany was the Ian-Kit tour of 1967. By now it was mid-summer, the weather continuously fine, and every bar and night-club was playing "Puppet on a String" that had won Sandie Shaw the European Song Contest of that year. Our German houses included Benrath near Düsseldorf, Schloss Fasanerie at Fulda (the property of Prince Philip of Hesse) and the mad King Ludwig's Herrenchiemsee in Bavaria. The best (because our visit there was the most enjoyable) was Schloss Langenburg. Only four years earlier this great twelfth-century castle had caught fire and the family wing was totally destroyed. In the interval, the Hohenlohes had rebuilt it. It was a house that I had chosen from an illustration in a tourist brochure. It looked lovely, and I had not known about the fire, because the rebuilding was so authentic. Nor did I know the family, but they invited us to stay. We were shown into a nest of bedrooms in a tower. The telephone rang. "Mr. Nicolson?" "Yes." "I am Charlotte Hohenlohe. I thought I would ring to say hullo." The English was perfect. I longed to meet its owner. Half an hour later we crossed the courtyard, and went up another tower in a lift and found her. She *was* English. She cannot have been much more than twenty-five. They had been married only a year and she was expecting her first baby. Kit was thrilled. She was beginning to stand up to Ian. "One thing I can't bear," he said, "is the idea of women in hair-curlers in the early morning." "Well," said Kit sweetly, "that's one thing you are never likely to have to put up with."

From Bavaria we entered Austria, found an amazing castle, Hochoster-witz, to replace the preselected house which disappointed us, and drove to Vienna. We dined in an open-air restaurant where our photograph was taken (illus. 19) by a wandering paparazzo. The band struck up "The Blue Danube." "Listen, Kit," said Ian, "they are playing our tune." He had had his revenge.

East Europe

Kit, as an American, could not be risked behind the Iron Curtain, and she returned happily to Rome where she had an admirer, while Ian and I drove to Budapest. We lived in luxury for a night as the guests of the Ambassador, Sir Alexander Morley, but even he failed to obtain a Polish visa for me. At the Polish consulate I sat for an hour opposite a gloomy bureaucrat who had obviously received instructions not to admit me, possibly because I had written unfavorably about Warsaw after a visit there in 1963. Eventually I took from the table a leaflet headed, in English, "Welcome to Poland," inserted the word "Not," and passed it across to him. He acknowledged it with a wintry smile. So we had no Polish house for the book, but to compensate, two splendid houses in Czechoslovakia, Vranov and Buchlovice, and I spent a night in Prague. Ian took the car for a week-long holiday somewhere (he could be mysterious), and I flew to Berlin, where Kit rejoined me. For a child of the space age she was surprisingly scared of flying. She announced that the runway at the Tempelhof airport was the shortest in the world, and Pan Am's "Whisper Jet" required the longest. We must go to Hanover by train. But we would need visas to cross East Germany and it would take ages to obtain them. So we flew. Kit gripped my arm as we took off, but once aloft, she had no fear, and none, paradoxically, as we were landing in Hanover, where the Whisper Jet, having abandoned its natural element, was trying desperately to stop.

Scandinavia

Ian joined us in Hanover and we drove across the Danish frontier on 4 August. It was Kit's twenty-fourth birthday. As she was attempting to slim, Ian wrote a poem in her honor, of which I can remember only two lines,

Now for the first time since her birth,
Will her age exceed her girth?

but she refused to swim with us in the Kattegat, saying that she was too shy to expose herself to our ridicule. She was consoled when the owner of "our" house, Borreby, gazed into her eyes as he raised his glass to celebrate her birthday.

In Sweden the house was Skokloster, and it was the last, because Norway, we were told, did not wish to compete in the Great Houses stakes. Ian flew from Oslo to London, bearing with him a precious cargo, his films and my manuscripts. The journey, and the book, were finished. Kit wept at his departure. Then it was her turn. Adam and Juliet, with two friends, Joanna Doubleday and Andrew Till, flew to Bergen to join me for a holiday. Kit and I met them at the airport, and she returned, again in tears, to America. I met her several times in later years, and spent three days with her in 1986, during my *Dodge City* trip. By then she was a wife, a mother, a divorceé and a highly successful lawyer. I think of her with gratitude and delight, and hope that she will forgive Ian Graham and me for her youthful initiation.

With the children I drove north to Narvik, naming geographical features as we went—Juliet River, Adam Falls, Bubbles (Joanna) Glacier and Andrew Pass. We stayed the first night at an inn near Lom, where we found English tourists scarcely daring to speak aloud for fear of being overheard, and into this morgue erupted four shattering children demanding reindeer steak for tea, bear rugs beside their beds and jam with their cornflakes, all of which an entranced management provided. The place began to wake up. The piano was uncovered; Juliet played her tune; Adam danced. The other guests were astonished by our setup. Who was this grave gentleman with the four bouncing children? Where was their mother? She was at St. Tropez, sunning herself with the catfish and forming an increasing intimacy with Sir Robin McAlpine, whom she married *en secondes noces.*

So we drove through Namsos and Trondheim, and by a fifty-mile loop into Sweden. We came to a kiosk where the children could buy sweets. Andrew asked the attendant, "What have you got that's typically Swedish?" "Swedish!" she cried. "This is Lapland!" That required some explanation. Our favorite game was to throw pine trees into torrents. I carried one end of a log of vast dimensions, the children the other, and together we hurled it into the abyss. The fun was to keep pace with it along the bank as it hurtled over waterfalls. Then we crossed the Arctic Circle, and put the Fiat on board the *Mitnatsol* at Narvik, from where we cruised back to Bergen and thence, by another ship, to Newcastle. Why do I devote so much space to this one holiday? Because it was the happiest of my life.

Less happy was our Norwegian visit ten years earlier, just before the Suez affair reached its culmination. I was taking the chair at a meeting of the Cultural Committee of the Council of Europe in Oslo, and when it was finished my wife and I fled to the mountains. We stayed at Flam on the Sognefiord. I planned to walk alone from the head of the valley at Myrdal down to Flam, across uninhabited country, starting at noon. At first it was easy going, and I knew that I was well within the five-hour limit that I had estimated for the walk, all in daylight. After three hours I came to a small lake, clearly marked on the map, but I had not realized that the cliffs fell sheer into the water, and I was obliged to climb two thousand feet to bypass them over the shoulder of the mountain. This added two hours to my walk, and in the gathering darkness I came to another lake. Again the same problem: the path led to the shore, but no further. The cliff stopped all progress. Fully clothed, I slipped into the freezing water to swim around it. Landing safely on the far side, I could see the lights of the village, Steine, which was my destination, but between me and it was a river in spate. I tried to ford it in several places but could not stand upright on the slippery stones, and remained, shivering, on the near bank, waiting for the distant dawn. I could see headlights of cars only two hundred yards away, but the torrent drowned my cries for help. An hour later I heard shouting on my side of the river and two Norwegians made their way toward me with torches, and led me to a bridge which I had not spotted in the darkness. A police car took me from Steine to Flam, where I rejoined my distraught wife. She had sensibly alerted the mountain-rescue team to find the missing MP. It was the moment when my doomed marriage came closest to an indissoluble bond.

GREECE

It is my favorite country after my own, although I cannot speak a word of new Greek and have forgotten almost every word of the old. My philhellenism took root at school under the influence of George Tait, was encouraged by my father, with whom I first visited Greece in 1935, and expanded during my undergraduate years, when I spent every long vacation walking alone through Attica and the Peloponnese. After the war I formed closer links with the country through the Freedom from Hunger Campaign, organizing projects like the cheese factory at Igoumenitsa and the honey farm in Crete. But I returned again and again with no other motive than to recapture the Hellenic pleasures of my youth.

Two such expeditions were made in the luxury of a crewed yacht hired by my American friend, Dan Silberberg. One year it was the Cyclades; the next a circumnavigation of the Peloponnese. The captain would bring us the chart as we sat at dinner, like a menu, and invite us to select a destination for the next day's cruise. Often I would be put ashore at dawn to walk across an island or a peninsula to rejoin the yacht at dusk. Once I landed on the southern tip of Ithaca, and having struggled through the maquis on one of the hottest days that I can remember, I emerged at the northern tip to find the yacht moored just where we had arranged, and swam out to it. Dan reached down a glass of ice-cold wine to greet me. That was a great moment.

Another ended in the manner that I would rather forget. We landed at Kardamyli in the Peloponnese to visit Patrick Leigh Fermor. I expected to find a low-slung cottage above the sea; I found a small monastery of pink stone which he had built himself. Here he lived with his wife Joan, a piratical, immensely companionable figure, hero, scholar, traveler, writer, with a touch of Hemingway, a hint of Falstaff, the look of Pan, rugged, sensitive, ebullient and tough. Quick to anger, quick to laughter, he both exalts and diminishes his friends. I went with him to a café in Kalamata, where men came up to him, and there was a burst of machine-gun banter and ribaldry, incomprehensible to me, but in feeling all too clear. They loved him, admired him, followed him, perhaps feared him.

Next day he gave a lunch party. The British Ambassador, Michael Stewart, was passing through with his wife and two friends on their way to Mani. Ties, then coats, were discarded. Paddy was nervous about his lunch (Joan being away in Athens), and when it came at 3 P.M., it consisted of a few Aristophanic fish in tomato sauce. He sang us an improvised ballad about King Cogidubnus, thumping his flagon on the table to beat time. It was a Dionysiac potation. All went very merrily until Dan Silberberg, entranced by the scene and a bit tight, said to him, "Paddy, how would you feel if a friendly American bought a piece of land next to yours and built a villa on it?" Paddy, appalled, replied: "There is nothing I would hate more." He then realized, too late, that the friendly American was Dan himself.

My later cruises were more conventional. For several years, including the year of this book's publication. I have traveled through the Aegean with Swan Hellenic, choosing their ships for their convenience and comfort, and the information which we are fed on board and ashore by classical scholars of the eminence of Lord Renfrew (Kos, Samos), Peter Jones (Crete, Athens), Sir Anthony Kenny and Nigel Spivey. One's fellow passengers are elderly. Only we need the luxury and can afford the fare. On one *Orpheus* cruise there was but one passenger under the age of fifty, the twenty-three-year-old daughter of a lecturer, and I contrived to abandon the table which I had been made to share with seven widows to join her family at theirs. On one warm day at sea she appeared on deck in a bikini. The officer of the watch approached her: "Excuse me, miss, we do not permit two-piece bathing suits." "Oh, you don't, do you?" she replied. "Then which piece would you like me to take off?" Her *mot* spread round the ship like wildfire, to the horrified delight of the widows.

My best Mediterranean cruise, and the longest, was with the travel firm Serenissima in 1982. It was a Crusader cruise. Wherever there was a crusader castle, chapel or relic to see, we must see it, in Italy, Yugoslavia, Turkey, Syria, Israel, Crete or Malta. Spiritually it was less uplifting than socially, for, as one of our fellow passengers, John Ryle, wrote, "The duplicity and greed of the medieval adventurers in their slow rapacious advance on the generally benign caliphate of Jerusalem must be one of the least edifying episodes in the history of the Church." John Julius Norwich was our chief lecturer, his knowledge universal. Asked to summarize the whole of the Old Testament in an hour, he gave it to us, without a note. Freya Stark was also on board, very old and wise, and Stuart Preston, Alvilde Lees-Milne, and John Julius's wife Mollie and his daughter Artemis Cooper. And Sue Baring. It was with her, whom I had never met before, that I spent most of my time. We walked across Kos together and that night I wrote in my diary:

We wander on, meeting wild flowers, Greek peasants, donkeys, goats, in barely cultivated country, ascending slowly to the hills, and I told her about my life, and she told me about hers. All this in Kos, with the sea around us, a tortoise underfoot among the thyme, and the sun setting behind the hills where the young English soldiers died in 1944, knowing nothing of Kos, Hippocrates or Aesculapius, or why they were there, victims of Winston's romanticism.

We came off the hill as it was growing dark, and when we reached the coast, I found paths between the brambles which would not scratch her legs, and we came to a smooth stretch of sand. We both wanted to bathe. 'You go behind that bush,' I said, 'and I'll go behind this one,' and we parted agreeing to meet swimming in the Aegean. The water was deliciously warm—all the summer's heat contained in it. I saw her head bobbing some 100 yards away, and we swam towards each other under the moon. This is the best moment of 1982.

On the last day of the cruise, at six in the morning, she banged on my cabin door to fetch me to witness an unforgettable sight, our entry into Malta. The captain let us stand beside him on the bridge as he coached *Stella Maris* through the narrow entrance to Valletta harbor. I found it amazing that those honey-coloured walls could have survived, apparently intact, the bombardment of the Second War. From there the whole party flew back to London, and we resumed our separate, unromantic lives.

RUSSIA

I have been there only twice. The second visit was on a National Trust Baltic cruise which touched for a night at St. Petersburg, and we were taken by bus to Peterhof and the Hermitage. It was too quick a visit to leave much impression. The first, in 1984, was more extended but less pleasant. I was writing a book on Napoleon's Russian campaign and was determined to visit at least the Kremlin, where he stayed before the fire, and Borodino, where he fought his main battle. It was the period immediately before Gorbachev's revolution and the officials were still hostile to Westerners, caring only for their cash. At Moscow airport a surly youth demanded that I empty all my pockets and lay their contents on a table in view of all the other passengers, who stared at me with suspicion and distaste. Finding nothing to which even he could take objection, he turned away with a sneer and no apology. That was my introduction to Russia. Then I took a taxi. The driver disdained my roubles, insisted on

dollars. I had no dollars. We began bargaining. Without any common language, I scribbled figures on the margins of a newspaper. He threatened to put
me out, miles from my hotel. In the end we compromised, vastly in excess of
my fare. We reached the hotel. It was horrible, a vast scoop of masonry, and
the food was almost uneatable.

That was how it started. Much as I tried, I could not like Moscow. The
people were hostile. Never a smile; never a gesture of help. But watching them
with each other, they seemed affectionate, the younger ones loving, all un-
afraid, busy, happy, but when they came into contact with a foreigner they
turned sour. We were the enemy. In no other country have I felt more a foreigner. Intourist told me that it was forbidden to visit Smolensk, and the Museum of Moscow (where there was the best evidence of who or what caused
the fire) was closed for two years. I had lunch (my only good meal of the trip)
with the Swedish Ambassador, and put my questions to him and a British journalist, Mark Wood. Why does one never see in the streets people of a middle
class? They travel in cars. Everyone seems dressed the same? They are shy of
appearing superior. Why is there so much queuing at food shops? The supply
system is curiously primitive, given the efficiency of the transport. How do
they react to Mrs. Thatcher? With increasing admiration.

Day after day I applied to visit Borodino, which lies only seventy miles
west of Moscow and is listed as an historic site, accessible to tourists. Intourist
said that I should have arranged it in London. I would need a special visa to go
there. Nobody had told me that. In despair, I gave the lady a sachet of Sissinghurst potpourri. Surprisingly, that did the trick. Were they expecting a
bribe all along, as in India?

It was my best day. I hired a car and was given an English-speaking guide,
Lena Krudyaskova, about twenty-eight, fair hair knotted, thinnish, intelligent, friendly. When we reached the battlefield she let me explore it thoroughly. It is about as large as the field of Waterloo, still rumpled with the
earthworks which the Russians threw up in 1812, and again in 1941, for it is a
palimpsest of two great campaigns. In the center lies the Great Redoubt,
which contains the grave of Russia's most romantic general, Bagration, who
was buried there after the battle, having died of wounds. Lena and I stood beside it in silence, and I plucked a wild marigold, letting it fall beside his name.
I think she trusted me after that. On our way back to Moscow we talked politics. She described very well the problems of the Russian economy and was
sensible about Scargill's miners' strike, accepting that uneconomic coal pits

must close but protesting that the police should not join the minority to break the strike. On arriving back at the hotel, she refused to join me for a drink at the bar, and refused a tip.

Next day I boarded a British Airways plane for London. We sat for an hour motionless on the tarmac. At Heathrow that would mean that we hadn't received the signal to take off. In Moscow, things are different. Two uniformed men entered the plane and removed a struggling passenger who appealed to us for help. We looked down at our English newspapers to read the latest news from the Olympics at Los Angeles.

INDIA

Twice. Once for a WFUNA conference in New Delhi, memorable for a visit to Agra, a reception in Lutyens's Viceroy's House, and the sudden call on me, as leader of the British delegation, to speak on Winston Churchill, the news of whose death was whispered to the chairman.

My second visit was in 1973. Time-Life invited me to contribute to their series of books on "The World's Wild Places" and suggested that I might "undertake" the Himalayas. Undertake? Would I be expected to climb? No, I could keep to the foothills and look at the peaks, but I must venture into places that *look* wild. There must be no people in the photographs and no human structures. There could be animals if they were undomesticated, like crocodiles. I doubted whether there were any crocodiles in the Himalayas. But there are in the Ganges? Yes. Well, you can see the Himalayas from the Ganges? Perhaps, on a very clear day. So, in the finished book there is a double-page spread photograph, very beautiful, of a crocodile. That was the trouble. My photographer, Terry Spencer, took three thousand photographs during our trip, of which only eighteen were used, all of the Kali Gandaki gorge in Nepal, of which no other photographs were obtained from the agencies. His other photographs, though excellent as a record, were discarded because they were not dramatic enough. Time-Life wanted animals like the snow leopard which we had never seen, gentians which were not in flower and summits which we never trod. Illustrations were bought in from previous expeditions more adventurous than ours, from Kew Gardens, from Japan, and the editors were equally daring with my text, adding stories from other men's books and improving my prose to make it more colorful. My inaccuracies were corrected by a team of advisers whom I never met, among them Lord Hunt, who led the successful assault on Everest in 1953. I complained then, but I do not complain now. It made out of our four-month journey a saga of heroic proportions, and a lovely-looking book.

The Himalayas extend much further than India. We started in Nepal and ended in Afghanistan. I will extract but two adventures. Adventures? I experienced nothing beyond the range of a reasonably active tourist, like Byron:

> Perils he sought not, but ne'er shrank to meet:
> The scene was savage, but the scene was new;
> This made the ceaseless toil of travel sweet.

In Kathmandu we hired a light aeroplane, being on a Time-Life expense account, and flew in an hour to Everest. The mountain is not humbled by its present-day accessibility, any more than it was diminished by surrendering to the British the blue riband of mountaineering. It still exacts its penalties. It stands aloof, stern more than beautiful, graceless even. Nobody has ever loved Everest as they might love Nanda Devi. "It is a place to have been to, not to go to" an American said to me, and he had stood on the summit. Our Swiss pilot flew us close to it. I watched the altimeter climb: 15,000 16,000 18,000 feet. He handed me his oxygen mask. Terry Spencer, sitting behind me, was busy taking photographs from the cabin door, which he had opened above this stupendous drop, insisting that nothing, not even a sheet of clear perspex, should come between his lens and the amazing view. We flew to the head of the valley, a mosquito among wedding cakes, and our Swiss floated us away from Lhotse's ice-wall with a falcon's ease. Then we turned back to Namche Bazar, the Sherpa village, where there was a joke of an airstrip, a finger held out waist-high, on which we took our chance to perch.

There is a hotel there, at 12,000 feet. It was built by the Japanese before the air route was established, every part of it, except wood and stone, carried by Sherpas on the seventeen-day trek from Kathmandu. I was told that one exhausted porter, on arrival, put down his burden, a sheet of plate-glass, on the rocks and shattered it. The hotelier offered us the choice of oxygen or a cocktail: we took both. From my bedroom window I had a clear view of Everest. A cloud broke its outline halfway up, to its advantage, for mountains need clouds to assert their height, and a cloud's movement to emphasize their immobility. At dinner that night we were joined unexpectedly by Robert McNamara, the head of the World Bank and formerly U.S. Defense Secretary. With his wife and two friends, he had trekked to Everest's base camp. It was Thanksgiving Day, and the manager had contrived turkey and all its trimmings for his distinguished guest.

After spending Christmas in Delhi, writing hard, I traveled through the Hunza region as far as the Chinese border. Travel in mid-winter is fairly hazardous. My little plane from Rawalpindi turned back four times before we eventually made it, and as I sat beside the pilot I could understand why: clouds huger than the mountains blocked our route, and if he risked flying through one of them he might find Nanga Parbat (26,600 ft) lurking like a tiger inside. On the fifth attempt we landed at Gilgit, which became my headquarters for a week. It is a grim little town, and its rest house bitterly cold, but I owed Time-Life a little hardship and spent a night in a forester's hut at 14,000 feet, and trod, for the only time in this expedition, unravished snow.

The road through the Hunza valley was still under construction by Chinese coolies, and for most of the way we followed in our jeep a track cut into the cliff face scarcely wider than the jeep itself. Curzon and Peter Fleming rode this way, I thought, and soon (that day has now come) the road would be finished and tourists would ride in comfort to the Pamirs. Beyond Pasu we were halted by a barrier. It was not the Chinese frontier, which lay a few miles ahead, but a Pakistani check point where we were told, courteously and with many jokes, that we could go no further. The soldiers sent a guide to lead us half a mile on foot to see the confluence of the Hunza River and the Shimsal. I recorded the scene for the book:

Lord, this is a dreadful place. I began to understand why our ancestors pictured Hell as cold. Night was falling. The wind increased in force and bitterness, and all around us the cliffs turned menacing and sullen-yellow. Two great glaciers, ending in dirty snouts, were faintly visible in the gloom, and other ice-falls were clamped to chutes of fallen rock. Mist canopied the valley. There were no birds, no trees, no plants, no animals, and no people except the soldiers in their unenviable outpost. Ahead of us we could hear the roar of the Hunza river, and when we reached it, we saw the Shimsal forcing its way through the opposite cliff. This was no confluence: it was an ejaculation. The anger of the Hunza was simply doubled. As we turned back across the stones, the sky surrendered the last of the day's light, and all that remained to guide us were the vast shapes of the Karakorams, blacker than the blackness that surrounded them.

There was more to come: Chitral, Peshawar, the Khyber (the very name has a cutlass ring about it), Kabul, where the Ambassador, John Drinkall, mercifully invited me to stay three nights in the Embassy, and finally a short walk in the Hindu Kush, before returning home via Teheran, where I slept in Harold's old bedroom as the guest of the Counsellor, Richard Ellingworth. Back in England, I began to protect my prose against the remorseless improvements of the Time-Life editors in New York.

AUSTRALIA AND NEW ZEALAND

I wondered if I would ever go there. Then in April 1992, *The Times* travel editor asked me if there was anywhere in the world where I had never been and would like to go. If so, *The Times* would send me there and I would write about it. On the spur of the moment I nominated the South Island of New Zealand, because it was furthest away, and its club foot was an undeveloped wilderness of fiords and mountains, one of the wonders of the world. On the way, I could stop in Sydney to stay with Dick and Mary Paget-Cooke.

I had not reckoned with jet lag. On my many trips to and from America it had caused me no problem, and I assumed that a flight treble the distance in the opposite direction would be equally placid. But hours and hours of flying, gobbling up the darkness without a single stop till Singapore, is infinitely wearying. I revived slightly as we flew over the Northern Territory of Australia, wondering what sort of country this could be, when you can cross the first two thousand miles without seeing a single house. Then the desert breaks into scrub, the scrub into forest, and the forest into fields and neat rows of houses. This is Sydney. Our huge untiring machine wheeled over the harbor, and I spotted the pretty piece of Meccano and the group of broken eggshells that stand for all Australia in the minds of people who have never been there. My friends were there to meet me and took me to their pleasant house at Bayview.

Next day we crossed the great bridge several times, climbed into the opera house, visited two museums, took a boat trip round the harbor, had lunch, had dinner, bathed, talked, laughed, and walked, ran—and then I collapsed.

It was a terrible disappointment for the Paget-Cookes. They had taken much trouble to entertain me, and on the second day drove me to the Blue Mountains, while I slumped in the backseat, scarcely able to talk. I was led, protesting, to the lip of a great canyon; to me it was just a stupid hole in the ground. Taken to see the famous Three Sisters, pinnacles of rock, I said that freaks of nature, human or mineral, bored me. I was thoroughly unpleasant. When, to my relief, we returned to Sydney, I slept for fourteen hours and awoke restored, able to express something of my gratitude and remorse to Dick, my oldest friend, and Mary, the light of his later age.

I was ready for New Zealand. How did the legend arise that it is a boring country full of boring people? It may have something to do with all those sheep. There are sixty million of them, and only 3.5 million humans, and the assumption is that constant association with the gentlest and most gullible of domestic animals must lend to the New Zealand character something of their ineffectiveness, although only a tiny proportion of the population have any-thing to do with them. It is a libel. If a single European city, with a population as large as the whole of New Zealand's had produced Katherine Mansfield, Rutherford, Hillary, Freyberg and Te Kanawa, we would call it astonishing.

The tourist, however, does not meet many sheep or people. He goes to the South Island because it is the only part of the civilized world which remains, though mapped, partly unexplored, and the inhabited parts of the island are extremely beautiful. In a small church on Lake Tekapok a large window is cut in the east wall where a reredos ought to be, and you look through it on to a panorama so lovely that you are tricked into thinking it painted. I joined a coach tour of a dozen people in order to see as much as possible, and we drove from Christchurch to Dunedin, to Milford Sound and Queenstown. For a small sum I circled Mount Cook in a helicopter and landed on the snow just beneath the summit. I felt guilty in doing so. Should the wilderness be made so accessible that it ceases to be wilderness? Should the helicopters, the jet boats and the bungy jumping be prohibited for the sake of peace? But tourism for so remote a country is a necessity. It will always be a luxury destination, expen-sive to reach, and there is nowhere to go afterwards except back again. So it must advertise its attractions. It is estimated that by the year 2000 the annual number of visitors will equal the population. But let them keep the fiordland empty. Leave to the hikers a sense of exploration. Let some of the wild waters fall unheard.

It is the wonderful paradox of New Zealand that it reveals its innermost secrets to strangers, and has turned its very awkwardness to advantage. The obstacles of mountain, lakes, rainforest, gorges, and river torrents have become playgrounds, or tests of skill or endurance, for people who do not belong there. If you imagine the Scottish highlands without roads, double the length of its sea-lochs, and treble the height of its mountains, you will have some idea of this wilderness. To penetrate it by land, making use of the few trails and huts that the National Park rangers have created, requires a hardihood that exceeds mere tourism.

TEN

THE AMERICANOPHIL

❧ ☙

THE LINDBERGHS

The first and most remarkable American I have ever met was Charles Lindbergh. All men's characters and all men's achievements are unique, but his character and his achievement were outstanding for a man who owed his immense fame to a single thirty-three-hour act of daring when he was aged twenty-five. Throughout his life, he would occasionally creep into the Smithsonian in Washington to gaze at *The Spirit of St Louis*, the little plane in which he had flown solo across the Atlantic in 1927. He told the story in a book of the same title which surprised everyone by its narrative skill and intensity of feeling, correcting the legend that he was nothing but an inspired mechanic with charming looks. The flight (which he would call "my trip to Purris") was the central event of his life. Then came the kidnapping and murder of his baby. The story had everything—mystery, pathos, glamour, terror, detection, and, ultimately, for Bruno Hauptmann, the electric chair, a fate, as Ludovic Kennedy demonstrated in his book *The Airman and the Carpenter*, which was wholly undeserved. He was framed by the police.

Charles and his wife Anne were so hounded by the American Press that in 1935 they fled with their second son to England, and rented our Wealden house,

Long Barn, soon after we had left it for Sissinghurst. My father had known the Lindberghs in America, when he was staying with Anne's mother, and researching the life of her father, Dwight Morrow. I met them several times at Long Barn and they lunched twice at Sissinghurst. Lindbergh was reserved, formidable. I was startled by his treatment of his son, Jon, aged four, whom he would swing by his ankle around his head, while Anne looked on white-faced. "He's got to learn," Lindbergh grimly explained. "He's got to learn."

His reputation was temporarily tarnished by his pro-German, anti-Semitic, isolationist stance before Pearl Harbor, and my father wrote a critical article about him which destroyed their friendship. When Harold's diaries were published in 1966, Lindbergh threatened to sue him for comments about his prewar attitudes, such as "he believes in Nazi theology. . . . He hates democracy" and for "exaggerations" like "He vaulted through the French windows," when he merely walked through them, and claiming that the Luftwaffe was "ten times stronger" than the RAF. He took a literal view of hyperboles natural to a writer and diarist. I was obliged to handle the dispute on my father's behalf, because I had edited the diaries for publication, and Harold, after two strokes, was no longer capable of sustaining an argument. My chief defence, which I was reluctant but obliged to use, was that I had sent the relevant pages of the edited diary to Anne Lindbergh before publication, asking for her approval. She had replied in writing, "I do not find anything which need be deleted from our point of view," and was sure that her husband, who was temporarily away from home, would not wish to change or omit anything. For some reason she failed to show the pages to him on his return and, when I met her in New York some five months later, she confirmed her (by implication, their) consent. There was no denying this and my later letters of justification remained unanswered. The correspondence caused all of us much distress. It is the only fight I have ever had with an American, apart from Louise De Salvo, whom I would not allow to write the introduction to the Vita–Virginia correspondence because she was a Socialist-feminist, and Vita wasn't.

DODGE CITY

I first saw the United States in 1954 as the guest of Haverford College, Pennsylvania. My wife and I flew to New York, where we stayed a night with the

Silberbergs. "So it really does exist?" I said to Dan. "Does what exist?" "New York." "Well, in fact it doesn't. It's all a myth." It has remained a myth to me ever since. It is not quite of America, not quite of this world.

We were hustled by train to Philadelphia, and my long love affair with the United States began with an explosion—Hurricane Hazel, which burst on us in the middle of a lecture I was giving at Swarthmore College about the British Empire. It was like the ringing of the bell at the end of a gruelling round of boxing, saving me from a mauling by students who had been brought up to regard our colonial record as one of unmitigated horror and disgrace.

I have returned to America almost every year since then, always by air until 1996, when I traveled on the *Queen Elizabeth 2,* gratis in return for a single lecture delivered on board to a group from the Royal Oak Foundation, the U.S. supporters club for the English National Trust. Why do not more people cross the Atlantic by sea? It is luxurious, companionable, interesting and convenient. Modern communications bring the world to the ship, the ship to the world. You could run a major business from your cabin. But we all think that sea travel wastes time, and time is the most important asset we have. Not for me it isn't. For me what counts is variety, and nothing better illustrates that preference than a book which Adam and I wrote together in 1986 called *Two Roads to Dodge City.*

We undertook to visit between us every state in the continental United States except Alaska, and parts of Canada. *En route* we would write to each other letters which would be published as the record of a father–son relationship and a voyage of discovery. The idea was not quite original. In 1955 Jacquetta Hawkes and her husband, J. B. Priestley had written to each other while separated in different parts of the Southwest, and published their letters under the title *Journey Down a Rainbow.* But they had not moved from fixed locations. We intended to move, fast and far. On the same day, 15 March 1986, Adam flew from London to Los Angeles and I to Miami. From these starting points we drove north along our respective coasts until we hit and entered Canada from where we turned south, I to the Gulf, he to Mexico, then north again, to meet, three months after we started, in Dodge City, Kansas, the approximate center of the United States. We posted our letters by Express Mail once a week to prearranged addresses.

It would never have worked if we had traveled together. We would not have a book to show for it, and we would not have got on. Our habits were too different. I enjoyed comfortable houses and dinner parties. Adam, who was only twenty-eight and scarcely knew America, found it no hardship to sleep in his car beside a desert road, having a looser itinerary and a more relaxed attitude to travel. I planned ahead, knowing where I would sleep each night of the thirteen weeks, while he left it to chance encounters, apart from the weekly letter-drops, seeking the excitement of the unexpected and discovering his lodging, if any, more by serendipity than by choice. His was the West, the young man's country; mine the East, the settled regions where I already had many friends. When we met on the Plains, it was on neutral ground.

The double journey worked out as planned. Neither of us fell ill. Our cars stood up to great exertions. Mine was a Ford Thunderbird; Adam's a clapped-out Pontiac Catalina which survived twelve thousand miles. We did not cover quite every state. I skipped Iowa; Adam the Dakotas. We never missed a letter, for although the normal U.S. postal service is as slow as a dromedary, the Express lives up to its name, and delivers anything from anywhere to anywhere in twenty-four hours. When we had to signal a change of date or destination, we communicated through Adam's sister, Juliet, then living in New York, and through her we sent copies of our letters to Mike Bessie of Harper & Row, who kept a careful track of our journey and monitored our Anglo-Americanisms.

It was a joy to know that after a long day's drive I would find at the Howard Johnson Inn, Boston, for example, a letter from Adam written from Tillamook, Oregon. His letters were lively, funny, provocative. When he considered that our correspondence was sinking to the level of separate travel diaries, he decided to raise the stakes by accusing me of being a bad father and a conservative clinging to outworn ideas, while he was the enlightened young iconoclast. I replied, robustly, as in this letter from Louisville, Kentucky, where I was having a great time during Derby Week:

> Why do you find Butte, Montana, "the sort of place I like more than any in the world"? I think that paradoxical or perverse. It makes me think that you would enter the Owsley Brown house [in Louisville] with reluctance or a sneer. Is it that you consider great affluence in some way improper, when there are still so many poor in this land? But consider, Adam, that these people, or their grandfathers, were once poor too. America was created by the poor. Log cabin to this

white house. It is not as if the present generation are idle or impo-
tent. . . . And you are wrong to say that I refuse to recognise any subconscious part of the mind. That's my whole point, that Americans
draw subconsciously on the past to stimulate their present. I see evidence of it everywhere. History *is* the subconscious.

Adam answered a week later from Utah:

I have a great appetite and longing to immerse myself in lives that
don't remind me of my own, in experiences that show me more of
what I'm like. The obverse of that is a sense of frustration and discomfort when I find myself contained and restrained inside a polite
and comfortable situation with which I am already familiar. I know
that I would have gone crazy with that string of parties you had up the
East Coast. I would have become rude and riotous, not because the
people were rich (I have no trouble in accepting that people should
enjoy the rewards they have earned), but because the situation would
have been polite.

Earlier he had written from Santa Cruz:

There is a heaviness, like an overweight jogger, in English culture,
which makes life singular and slow. I'm impatient with the steerage
way you claim we have; stability is a boring virtue, and consistency all
too often the mask for the lack of invention. I'm for variety with the
chance of failure or vulgarity, if that's what's required. The English
suffer from taste and a lack of daring.

He spoke like a young American. There was much more of this mutual
bruising. As Valerie Grove wrote in a review of the book, "It is perhaps typical of an English upper-class family that a father and son should have to travel
several thousand miles from home in order to begin talking honestly to each

other," and when our cars met bumper to bumper in Dodge City on 13 June, I felt a greater awkwardness than I confessed at the time. To lower the tension I said, "It doesn't matter how much we insult each other in public, so long as we are nice in private," and we were. Next day we flew to New York, to be greeted by Juliet in a limousine at the airport, and a celebration dinner with Marietta Tree.

The book was a flop. The *New York Times* thought it snobbish (we had both avoided Disneyland), and prejudiced against America (good heavens!). The *Boston Globe* didn't know "who's more irritating, the horribly self-conscious Adam, or the stupidly self-possessed Nigel." That killed it. The *Washington Post* was kinder: "The book is personal, reflective, funny, carefully observed, wonderfully discursive." I thought so too. Adam was more critical. It was done in too much of a hurry. We should have revised it. But to me its point was its spontaneity. It was sad that Mike Bessie, who had done so much to promote the book, could not justify a paperback edition, which, in publishing terms, is the ultimate ignominy.

Next year we returned to the United States on a week's "author tour," trundling from one radio or TV station to another, and were awarded "segments" of a minute each. The last segment was with the radio program of the *Christian Science Monitor.* Adam described the interview for the *Spectator:*

Our host, Bob, said we could refer to him, if we liked, in the course of our remarks. He gave an example: "That's a very interesting question, Bob, and I would like to answer it in the following way." But for some reason neither of us did.

If only the interviewers had been as sophisticated as the reviewers, and we were given an opportunity to hit back at our critics, the book might have stood a better chance. It was a good idea, I thought, not badly executed, and as representatives of our two generations we had performed in character and not to our discredit.

LECTURING

In one way or another, most of my visits to the United States and Canada have involved a lecture. Sometimes I was attending another person's, as when I took the chair for Alistair Cooke in New York. I had never met him before, and such was my pent-up admiration for his achievement that I spoke too fulsomely and too long in proposing a vote of thanks, only to find when I eventually turned toward him that he had left the platform for his next appointment. But normally I was giving the lecture. In England a visiting American, unless unusually distinguished, would barely fill a quarter of a town hall. In America they are not only more tolerant of an hour-long lecture, but hungry for it. They are infinitely generous to their guests. They are prepared to stand in line for an hour afterwards to shake the lecturer's hand, and while they wait they prepare their introductory sentences, like "I had a cousin who once lived in Sevenoaks," thereby reassuring me that while I might be a long way from home, the world, all things considered, is a very small place. I did not much enjoy these greetings. A lady in the queue at Baltimore said to me, when she reached the saluting base, "It must be so nice for you to be able to relax," little realizing that for me it was the moment of maximum tension.

My audiences, they assured me, enjoyed not only my English accent but my English manner, and with practice, I became adept at exploiting both. Malcolm Muggeridge had advised me that to gain and hold attention, a lecture, whether it be delivered at Benenden School or Des Moines, should be composed eighty-five percent of anecdotes and jokes, and fifteen percent of sense. Once I had grasped that truth, I polished my subjects and undertook a tour of ladies' clubs under arrangements made by the lecture agency, Colston Leigh. I had four subjects, the Law of Obscenity, Bloomsbury, Biography and Class. This last was the most popular, but I felt instinctive guilt in repeating it so often. A well-known singer would not be in the least embarrassed to sing "Maybe This Time" in Las Vegas one night and repeat it in Palm Beach the next, when she hadn't written either the words or the music, but the lecturer, who has taken great pains with "Class" is under an uneasy impression that his lecture should be struck only once from its die.

I soon gave up the clubs for the universities. Although the fees were less, the understanding was greater. My happiest recollection is of Stanford University, California, where I stayed with Lucio Ruotolo, Chairman of the English Department, whom I had known when he rented Monk's House one winter and was driven out of it by the cold. My hosts for the lecture (on Virginia Woolf) were Peter Stansky and William Abrahams, co-authors of *Journey to the Frontier*, a biography of Julian Bell. It was pouring with rain, and as we drove to the hall, Abrahams warned me that there might be a slim audience owing to the weather. It was packed with six hundred students and faculty, a laughing, colorful, expectant semicircle of youth. I asked for a glass of water. This created consternation. None was to be had. So I began: "Here is this great University, which licks the Bears 21–3 [I had just attended their ball game against the University of California, Berkeley], which has built the only nuclear accelerator in the world, which numbers in its faculty six winners of the Nobel Prize, but cannot produce a glass of water for a wandering Englishman, though the stuff is teeming down outside." I have never given a more successful lecture to a more responsive audience. Among them, to my surprise and pleasure, was Ann Getty, and together we attended a students' reception afterwards. It was one of those rare occasions when, inflated by success, drink and the attention of the young, one feels lifted, as if by a dirigible, from sullen earth to sing hymns at heaven's gate.

It was not always so. When I lectured on feminism at Boulder, Colorado, and said that middle-class Victorian women were fortunate to have been cared for so well by their menfolk but made no use of their opportunities, half the student audience, the female half, walked out. At Norman, Oklahoma, only six students attended my lecture (*Lolita*) out of twenty thousand, and six in an auditorium designed for four hundred have a depressing effect upon the lecturer and each other. The university is better known for its football than its academic pretensions, and illustrates both the aspirations and shortcomings of higher education in the U.S. It is their justifiable boast that almost any young Oklahoman who wishes can enter the university, but half of them sink into apathy and drop out. The faculty are discouraged, some in despair. Clever people, they are stuck to Norman like clams, having once obtained tenure there. Why not arrange exchange visits with professors from Harvard, Yale or Stanford? Because none of the professors at Harvard, Yale or Stanford would want to spend a year at Norman, Oklahoma. I found the same at Louisiana State University at Baton Rouge. There the authorities were intending to reduce the student body by some four thousand in order to raise the standard and lower the expectations of young people who, if they graduate at all, will not find jobs worthy of their graduation.

THE AMERICAN DRAMA

In December 1987 I flew with my daughter Rebecca from Nassau to San Salvador (Watling Island) to see where Columbus landed. All the Bahamas lie very low, having risen from depths of three and a half miles and stopped growing as soon as they surfaced. Columbus must have wondered whether these insignificant slices of land would yield to another vast ocean. On the tiny runway we were met by a man wearing a hat with the legend, "Property of Sing-Sing Penitentiary," where he had been an inmate for ten years, and he led us to a beach where a white cross stood in the center of a ring of flag poles. The pure sand shelved sharply under the surf, and a ridge of coral lay half a mile off-shore. Did Columbus's three ships ride like cockleshells within it? Possibly. The inscription below the cross read: "Christopher Columbus made the first recorded landing in the New World on this beach, October 12, 1492." It is a reasonable guess, and the word "recorded" is an ingenious reference to the strong supposition that the Vikings in the eleventh century settled temporarily in "Vinland," thought to be Nova Scotia, and to the certainty that thousands of years before them, American Indians colonized both continents from Siberia. Still, for most people San Salvador is the beginning. That cry from *Pinta*'s forecastle, '*Tierra! Tierra!*' is one of the most evocative signals ever uttered from a human throat.

I went, too, to Jamestown, where Lord De La Warr, sailing in, met the survivors of the colony sailing out, turned them back and saved it. And to Plymouth Rock where the Pilgrims landed. Then, with Kathy Hill-Miller, to Ellis Island, where her grandmother, as a girl of seventeen, was one of a crowd of immigrants from Poland. The discovery and settlement of America captivated me. I read and traveled extensively, wondering why Americans care so little for their history when it is the most concertinaed, the most triumphant, history of any people. I once drove across the State of Washington from Seattle to Pullman, a remote university town which houses the Woolf library from Monk's House, and arrived full of wonder for the audacity of the first explorers and settlers, to find that T. S. Eliot meant infinitely more to the students than Lewis and Clark, just as in Texas few young people cared about La Salle. When I reached the plains, I drove at ten mph across the grass where once the wagons rolled, to get the feel of it. Every ten miles a village, every hundred, a town, but the lovely architecture of colonial Virginia and New England never spread west of the Appalachians. It is impossible to imagine small towns like Nantucket or Guilford, Connecticut, or a city like Savannah, Georgia, transplanted to the mid-West. It was discovered too late, and life was too hard, for such architectural niceties, until the boom years of the nineteenth century loaded the land with encrusted stone instead of the light clapboarding and brick of the East Coast. I must make exceptions. Buildings like the Capitol in Austin, Texas, and the Frenchified town houses of Mobile, Alabama, and on a smaller scale, Ste Genevieve on the Mississippi, are great achievements. In our own century (soon to be called "the last century") some modern buildings are admirably dramatic. Take downtown Dallas, for example. Or Chicago.

In a way, Chicago does justify its reputation for toughness, but this applies to any city where the stresses build up. As soon as the traffic lights turn green, cars streak off the stop line, indifferent to scuttling pedestrians, and receptionists in offices and hotels look up angrily from their personal telephone calls, which they have no business to be making, as you approach the desk. But the city is beautiful. When I was last there, in the spring of 1986, I walked across the lawns beside Lake Michigan, looking up at the glass skyscrapers which reflect each other down a long, shimmering avenue, and entered one of them, the Amoco building, an eighty-story pillar of infinite grace. The main hall is split into different levels, broad stairways and escalators connecting them, a marble ice rink of a floor. I stayed with Charles and Susan Meyer in Lake Forest, a suburb so exclusive that a stranger inquiring the way is looked on with intense suspicion. You either know your way about Lake Forest, or you don't go there. It is a happy, stratified society. Money counts. But there is no looking disdainfully down or enviously up. Segregation by wealth gives no offence. It stimulates ambition. My lecture on Class greatly benefited from my visit.

My association with Chicago originated with my biography of Mary Curzon, who was born and brought up there. She was the daughter of the self-made millionaire Levi Leiter, the co-founder of the great emporium, Marshall Field. After a brilliant début in Washington, Paris and London, she married George Curzon, three years before he was appointed Viceroy of India, and at twenty-eight she became Vicereine, the youngest in history, and the only American. Her daughter, Lady Alexandra ("Baba") Metcalfe, had invited me to write the life of her father, but after reading the Ronaldshay, Dilks and Rose biographies, I pleaded that there was too little to add, and suggested that the letters and diaries of her mother, hitherto a shadowy figure who had died when Baba was two, would provide excellent material for a new angle on the great proconsul. So off I went to Chicago in 1975 to study her childhood. Through Jo Trautmann, I discovered a post-graduate student from the University of Virginia called Amy Henderson whom I engaged for four months to search the files of the Chicago newspapers, the Chicago Historical Society and the Library of Congress for Leiter references, particularly concerning the Chicago fire of 1871, when his great store was totally destroyed, and Mary's early successes in society. Amy did her work with pertinacity and care, and I met her for the first time in New York where she handed me the product of her research. I had imagined her a shy, thin student. I had not expected a beautiful young woman with Titian hair and a marvelously shaped face and eyes. We often met in later years. She became the resident historian at the National Portrait Gallery in Washington, specializing in the history of film, music and drama, and she twice arranged for me to lecture there. Once it was about American heiresses who married impoverished English noblemen, of whom Mary Leiter was one.

The trouble was that I did not admire Mary to the degree that her daughter hoped. She was spoiled by money and social success, was subservient to Curzon, contemptuous of men like Asquith, Balfour and Kitchener who rivaled him, and made too little of her opportunities in India. As an American, who was adulated for her youth and beauty, she could have softened the impact of British Imperialism, but never made an Indian friend and took few initiatives to discover, as her husband did, the culture of the country. Curzon came to love her, though he undoubtedly married her for her father's money, and during the first three years when they lived in London he treated her coldly. For Baba's sake, I exaggerated Mary's grace and played down his unkindness and her snobbishness. Her death, aged thirty-six, was very touching. Baba told me that on finishing the book her pillow was wet with tears.

My many trips throughout the United States have left behind many acquaintances with whom, for a time, I continued to communicate through Christmas cards, but there were others who became friends. The places where they live, many of which I managed to thread on the string I called *Dodge*, are stars among the stripes. In Washington there was Susan Mary Alsop, who wrote Lady Sackville's life and in whose house in Georgetown I stayed several times, marveling at her ability to bring together politicians, writers, artists, journalists and museum people in a way that even Lady Colefax never managed in London. Also Roger and Frances Kennedy, with whom I enjoyed a *Dodge* visit. He was Director of the Museum of American History, and taught me, through his talk and books, to look at American architecture in a new way, while Susan cured me of smoking, for when we attended a dinner party of twenty together, nobody smoked, nineteen because they didn't wish to and I because she caught my eye.

In New York the stars were the Silberbergs, Marietta Tree, Drue Heinz and the Frick Collection. There was a little cluster in Louisville, Kentucky. Kate Stout came from there, and on one of my lecture circuits for the U.N. my host was Cyrus MacKinnon, manager of the Louisville *Courier-Journal*, who gave a dinner party the night of my arrival, and Roberta and Ian Henderson were among the other guests. Both families came to represent for me all that I liked most about America. With the MacKinnons, Cyrus ("Cy") and his wife Wig, I ate a Thanksgiving dinner, sang in public for the only time in my life, spent the week of the Kentucky Derby, and Christmas in the Bahamas. The Hendersons I once enticed to Sissinghurst with their sons, telling them that they should be photographed together for a poster advertising the charm of America, and when they protested that there were a million other families like theirs I said that they would do nicely as a sample, praise modulated to suit their taste. Through the MacKinnons I came to know some of the Binghams, who owned the *Courier*, from Mary the grandmother to Emily the granddaughter (but her only once, in the rain at Chapel Hill, North Carolina), and between them, Sallie, the adventurous, thrice-married, maverick novelist, whom alone among my smarter friends Adam was anxious to meet. "I like the sound of Sallie Bingham," he wrote from Springdale, Utah. "She's just my type. And I know, for God's sake, that she's just your type too." I liked that, for it was true.

There is one star in Texas, appropriately for the Lone Star State, a lady of ninety, Mildred Robertson, who lives in a curtained house in Galveston and finds her way almost annually to Kent, brimming with anecdotes of her latest conquests and adventures. In California there is Madeline Moore of the University of Santa Cruz, Jane Lancellotti and Suzanne Stroh, and higher up, in Washington State, Anne Wombach, garden architect and horticulturist, who acts from time to time as Christopher Lloyd's assistant at Great Dixter. At Bloomington, Indiana, there is Bill Cagle, the librarian of the Lilly Library, which guards the Vita–Harold letters. In Florida, Kit Macdonald and (star of stars) Joanne Trautmann, who lives with her husband, Sam Banks, at Tierra Verde. In Massachusetts, John and Valerie Henderson. Back in New York, or really outside it, for they live in a lovely wooden house, painted white, half-buried in the forest but only an hour's drive from Manhattan, Tony Robinson and his wife Roxana, who writes stories of domestic felicity and infelicity, too true to life to be fictional, though they are.

I must say something about the blacks, for although I have no black friends, I am troubled by them. Once, in Tennessee, I paused to ask a group of students why they were demonstrating against apartheid in South Africa when there was the unadmitted equivalent in the United States. They were shocked by the question. Again, in Washington, D.C., I asked a Republican Senator, Charles Mathias, whether the poorest blacks feel they have the respect of the whites and he replied, "I genuinely think they do ... My own children have no anti-black prejudice whatever. They're absolutely color-blind." I wish that I could believe this. The semi-ghettos of Dallas and Cleveland, the statistics of black unemployment, illiteracy, murder and illegitimacy, contradict it. There is, to be sure, a burgeoning black middle class, but one hardly ever meets them. A black judge in Florida, the only one in his circuit, told me that the momentum imparted by Martin Luther King has slackened. It was not only the whites who drew apart; he did too. "If I go to a meeting where there are twenty whites and five blacks present, I instinctively gravitate towards the five." Who was I to condemn it? We in Britain have experienced, stage by stage, in the last twenty years, what America has struggled to master for more than a century, and we are no nearer a solution.

CANADA

I first went to Ottawa for the Alexander biography (*Alex*) as he was Governor-General of Canada after the Second War, and later to Toronto and Montreal for lectures and interviews during the six-year publication span of the Virginia Woolf letters, mainly under the direction of Pat Rosenbaum, the greatest Bloomsbury scholar of them all. To give an idea of the whole episode, this is taken from my letter to Richard Tower, aged thirteen, from the Sheraton Hotel, Toronto, in November 1977:

I am writing in part of this enormous hotel which is called, believe it or not (I expect not), 'Richard Tower'. I have a suite, something I have never had before, with two bathrooms, two TV sets, a vast sitting-room and a bed for six. This morning I was woken up at 6.30 by the telephone. A young voice said: 'Good morning, Mr Nicolson. It's time to open your eyes and drink a cup of coffee. See you in thirty-five minutes.' It was the girl from the TV station. So I got up, sleepily switched on the TV and watched the opening of the show in which I was to appear. I was billed as 'the last surviving member of the Bloomsbury Group.' So, thus fortified, I taxied out to the TV station, to be seated on arrival by the make-up artist, who took ten years off my age.

Looking like Antonia Fraser, I was conducted into a vast garage, with monster machines like dinosaurs crawling across the floor. I was led up to a lady called Helen Hutchinson, the chief interviewer. We established instant intimacy. A dinosaur crawled up, and Helen said, 'Well, Nigel, it's dandy to have you on the show again.' Again? I'd never been in Toronto in my life. But this show goes out all over Canada, and it seems that I appeared on it in Montreal four years ago. So it's Nigel and Helen for the next ten minutes, she surreptitiously reading about me from notes supplied by her staff. As soon as it's over, Helen's smile flattens to a mask, and she turns away from me to talk to a man about Christmas cards. I'm shooed off to another show in a different part of the city, and am given a new face, and a new interviewer called Tom, who makes jokes like, 'Who's afraid of Virginia Woolf?' to show off his culture. The show was taped, and I watched it re-run later that day. 'Who's that handsome man?' I asked myself, hoping that it was me. It was Tom.

Nine years later I was back in Toronto with Honey Thomas, who drove me around the city and up the CN Tower. My purpose on that trip was not to lecture other people about Bloomsbury but to discover the difference between Canadians and Americans. Toronto had few clues to offer, since it is metropolitan, not urban, but when I went on to Kingston, Ontario, I put the question to the Principal of Queen's University, Ronald Watts. "We're more American than the British," he said, "but more British than the Americans." When asked to amplify this definition, the other guests (I was dining with Donald and Frances Holman) assured me of Canada's attachment to the Crown, and of Canadian sobriety. "We are less prone to violence and emotional upsets than the Americans," they said. But American habits do creep in. Visiting one of the university's tutors, Kay Dick, I picked up a dissertation by a student on "The Contemporary Symbolic Novel" and opened it on the following sentence:

> The realistic novel strives, above all, in Gombrich's sense of realism, to render a mimesis of appearance.

I asked Dr Dick what that meant. She explained that "mimesis" meant "imitation." Then why not use the more normal word? And why "render"? Why "appearance"? For that matter, why Gombrich? Her colleagues said that students wrote like that because they thought it was expected of them. I had another silent thought: they wrote like that because American academics do.

In 1979 I flew from London to Calgary, and from there took the famous railroad to Vancouver through the Rockies. I had a night's "roomette" on the train. It's a comfortable ride through uncomfortable country. Tiny ledges cut out of a canyon for a tiny train. And then, suddenly, sea birds, and wonderful Vancouver! It is the most beautiful combination of the works of man and the works of God that I have ever seen. The sea slides into the city center, and mountains encircle it. I found it extraordinary that the same people, or at least the same race, who created an American monstrosity like Calgary ("the fastest-growing city in the West") could build this beautiful place from scratch in ninety years, a mixture of gleaming high-rise buildings, parks, shining expressways, little yachts in the harbor and a whole university, Simon Fraser, perched on a mountain top. I went there for a seminar and was so taken with it that I hoped Rebecca would want to complete her education there, and I made inquiries whether she would be welcome. She would be. But one cannot shuffle one's children half way round the world like pieces on a chess-board. She didn't want to go there, and didn't. O Canada! O Rebecca!

ELEVEN

THE FAMILY MAN

This is the most difficult chapter to write, for it requires self-analysis and references to people who would much prefer not to be mentioned, or, if at all, obliquely. Particularly does that apply to love affairs. None of mine were very intense, none lasted very long and none ended in mutual hostility. My relationship with the three women whom I have most loved outside marriage was physically innocent, and the names of the few others which occur in this book are given without further clues and with a brevity which will please them more than disappoint. But let me begin with my brother.

BEN

I suppose that in childhood many siblings have a closer bond with each other than with their parents, and this was certainly so in the case of Ben and myself. Although he was two and a half years older than me, we were inseparable. We shared bedrooms, expeditions, wickedness and jokes, particularly jokes, often at the expense of our parents, with whom we spent far less time than with our successive nannies. Vita and Harold had strange conceptions about us. I have recently come across a letter from my father to his mother, Lady Carnock, written from Berlin in 1928, in which he sketches our characters. I come out of his analysis with an undeserved advantage:

High spirits in place of Ben's gloom. He sees the funny side of everything. Immense daring, and adventure-love. He is passionately affectionate. Gay, untidy, brilliant and keen, and interested in everything. He likes animals and flowers, whereas Ben loathes them. He is interested in the servants and the people in the village, whereas Ben treats them as if they didn't exist. He is full of his own amusements, whereas Ben moons about, rather bored. I think his zest and industry will mitigate his impulsiveness and slap-dash habits. He will not be an intellectual, but will probably become a very witty, hard-working, ambitious lawyer.

It is a father's idealized picture of a son he scarcely knew. Ben, in contrast, was "dreamy, very reserved, proud, rather slow-minded, affectionate in a deep undemonstrative way, impatient, tidy, rather a nut." But Harold also allowed him to be "truthful, interested in people far older than himself [this was Bloomsbury], a good brain, a good heart and a decent character . . . His faults are his dislike of doing anything at which he can't excel, a possible selfishness, and lack of physical, and I suppose moral, courage."

Harold came closer in his forecast of the adult Ben than of the adult Nigel, apart from "rather a nut" and Ben's alleged lack of moral courage, for he showed more independence of his parents' values than I did. He was the first to break with the domesticity of Sissinghurst and Neville Terrace. At Oxford, his friends were among the most brilliant of his generation. He chose his own profession, art history, while I followed, to some extent, my father's. Ben's three major books on the artists Terbrugghen, Wright of Derby and Georges de La Tour are classics, and his editorship of the *Burlington Magazine* for over thirty years made it the most respected art-historical journal in the English language, and probably in the world.

To the *Burlington* he attracted writers of distinction by his own distinction, slowly developing qualities of tact, humor and self-confidence. Without any formal training in art history, he became a scholar of the first rank. The gentleness of his nature was stiffened, when his professional interests were engaged, by a steely determination to discover and express the truth. His friends would often be startled by the candor with which he would expose a fake, in a painting or a person. But Harold was right to detect his dreaminess, which at times came close to *naïveté*. He was indifferent to appearances, dressed with the utmost disregard for convention, hated smart parties and entertained his friends in a manner which bordered on the eccentric, as illustrated by my own experience of one of his dinner parties in his grim little flat in Holland Park. I wrote to my wife:

The other guests were Shirley Anglesey, Terry and Joanna Kilmartin, Jocelyn Baines and his beautiful silent American wife. Ben showed me round his flat with pride. It did not take long. When we got to the kitchen, there was no sign of any preparation for the dinner party. 'Where's the cooking?' I asked. 'Oh,' said Ben. 'It's all cold.' So in the dining-room ('Philip's spare bedroom', he explained), there was the dinner all set out—half an avocado each, spam, a few lettuce-leaves and some raspberries. 'Isn't it delicious?' said Ben. We agreed it was.

There was the occasion when as Deputy-Surveyor of the King's Pictures under Kenneth Clark, he was ordered, much against his will, to join a weekend party at Windsor Castle. After dinner the family played "murders." All the lights were turned out in the drawing room, and Ben, chosen to be the murderer, crawled between the sofas and tables until he found something which he took to be a cushion, and poked it. It was Queen Mary's bosom. Nobody was less of a natural courtier, and he resigned soon afterwards, telling our present Queen that no living artist was good enough to paint her portrait, "but there are some excellent photographers."

He was, as Harold noted, a man of deep affections, and from his friends like Philip Toynbee, Francis Haskell, John Bury and Richard Shone I learned more about him after his death than I knew in his lifetime. They would tell me of his austere integrity, as when, having bought a picture for £800, he refused an offer of £1,600, because it would be "profiteering." His secretary at the *Burlington* told me that although their desks stood side by side, he would pass her notes like, "Sally, I'd like a cup of coffee. Would you? Ben." Yet he could manfully resist assaults on his editorial authority by enraged contributors, among them his old friend John Pope-Hennessy, and particularly Douglas Cooper, who encouraged the editor with such comments as, "The magazine has to my mind sunk to a depth where I hardly dare recommend any of my continental friends to read it," and once stormed into the office, addressing himself to Sally, "Will you tell the editor," who sat three feet away, "that I shall never again contribute to his despicable journal." Of course he did. As his successor in the editorial chair, Caroline Elam, has said, "Ben's correspondents were curiously wide of the mark. His years at the *Burlington* are seen as the apex, not the nadir, of the magazine's fortunes."

In 1955, when he was forty-one, Ben married Luisa Vertova, a Florentine, herself an eminent art historian. The marriage ended not in disaster but in mutual agreement to part. Ben was not a domesticated person. But he cared deeply for their only child, Vanessa, whom I have come to know and love in later life, for she lives with her husband, Andrew Davidson, her two daughters, only half a mile from my own house.

I saw Ben all too seldom in our busiest years. He gave me valuable moral support in the controversy over *Portrait of a Marriage*, and we would sometimes meet in the Beefsteak Club. On the last occasion, as I entered the room, he looked up at me, his face irradiated with such welcome and delight that I was moved to take him by both his shoulders in reciprocated affection. He dined there on the last night of his life, 22 May 1978, apparently in perfect health, and left to catch the last train to Holland Park. In the booking hall of the Leicester Square tube station he collapsed and died instantly of a massive stroke. He was only sixty-three. Five hundred people attended his memorial service in St James's, Piccadilly, and Kenneth Clark gave the address.

MY MARRIAGE

As the newly elected MP for Bournemouth East and Christchurch, I was not looking for a wife, but I found one in Philippa, who lived in the New Forest with her parents Sir Gervais and Pamela Tennyson-d'Eyncourt just outside the constituency. She was twenty-four, a very attractive girl, as coltish as a New Forest pony, as stubborn as a mule, unsophisticated, charming. Looking again at the photograph of her when she was young [illus. 12], I wonder how I could ever have ceased to love her. Her mother, the stronger-willed of her parents, was not convinced that a literary MP was a suitable husband for her daughter, and told me bluntly at our first meeting that there were two types of people whom she despised, politicians and writers. That was a poor start to my courtship, but it resulted, within two months, in our engagement, and within five we were married. That caused further trouble with my in-laws. They paid a formal visit to Sissinghurst without Philippa or me, and at lunch Vita remarked that she was looking forward to the wedding in Christchurch Priory, where I wanted to be married, since it was beautiful, fairly modest and in the middle of the constituency. "Christchurch Priory!" said Pamela. "No, it's to be in St Margaret's, Westminster," and, as the d'Eyncourts were paying for it, there could be no further argument. After lunch Harold took my future father-in-law for a walk. "Tell me, Gervais," he said. "What sort of sum were you thinking of settling on Philippa?" "Settling on her? I don't understand what you mean. Can't Nigel afford to keep her?" "Well, the dowry." "My dear Harold, dowries went out with the First World War." They returned to the house somewhat subdued, to find Vita and Pamela sitting in silence.

So, on 30 July 1953, we were married in St Margaret's. There were two further problems. Pamela was persuaded, much against her will, to invite to the wedding members of my Executive Committee, but not their spouses, which caused great offence in Bournemouth. And when she heard that I had asked Rab Butler, an old family friend, to propose the health of bride and bridegroom at the reception in Fishmongers Hall, she refused to let him jump the queue. "But he's very busy," I said. "He's acting Prime Minister" (Churchill was ill). "I don't care if he is acting God," she replied. "He must wait, like everyone else," and waiting meant behind six hundred other people. I was saved by the sudden death of Rab's mother. He sent his apologies, and Ben made the speech. Harold and Vita, knowing very few of the guests, looked pathetically out of place, Vita hating her smart clothes, as timorous as a doe.

We stayed the first night of our honeymoon at Sissinghurst, then at South Wraxhall, a lovely Elizabethan house lent to us by Lady Glyn. From there we drove to Italy, crashing the car outside Verona. In Venice we spotted a cruise liner in the harbor and begged a lift back to Southampton. Early in October our doctor, Robert Howard, whom we had called to Philippa's aid when she complained of nausea, came downstairs to where I was waiting and said, "She's going to have a child." That is the moment which no father ever forgets.

The night when Juliet was born was the only time in my life when my mother-in-law and I felt any mutual affection. I telephoned her in panic and she came to sit with me. We played dominoes for hours. The drama unfolded its normal course, but to me it was a unique event. I was dreadfully worried and, like many fathers, felt guilty: I should be suffering, not Philippa. At 3 a.m. the nurse leaned over the banisters to say, "Mr Nicolson, you have a baby daughter." I wept with relief, clasped Pamela in an unprecedented hug and behaved as if this miracle had never happened to anyone before.

We were then living at Shirley House, an old farmhouse which I had bought some months before, at Bransgore, on the edge of the New Forest, near enough for me to get at my constituents, but not near enough for them to get at me. For months we had lived there by the light of oil lamps, while workmen laid the cables and the wires, and then came the great moment, just in time for Juliet's birth, when it was finished. I had spent all evening in Christchurch and drove back after dark to see, where our house had been, an ocean liner standing in the meadows, every light ablaze. Philippa had switched on the whole system to surprise me. I rushed indoors, found her in bed, embraced her. It was a moment of complete happiness.

It must have seemed that I was the most fortunate of mortals, with the brightest of futures. I was thirty-seven, co-founder of a publishing firm which was beginning to prosper. I had a seat in Parliament with an impregnable majority. I was married to a lovely young wife and we had a child. I was in the best of health. I had no financial worries, no scandals to cover up. We had holidays together on the Shiant Islands, on the Isle of Adlerney where we followed the Russian Sputnik round the world, and once at Calvi, in Corsica, where we dined on board *Surprise* with Lord Mountbatten. In the Election of 1955, I was reelected with another five thousand added to my majority. And on 12 September 1957, Adam was born, again at Shirley House.

So what went wrong? I must blame myself. I came to dislike what Cyril Connolly called "the wear and tear of proximity." It was with increasing relief that I sought the privacy of my own bedroom. But Philippa, were she still alive (she died in 1987), would not deny her share of our misfortune. She was bored by constituency duties. Some of them bored me, too, but my pleas that it was necessary for us to attend social functions fell on her deaf ears. I believe that her mother encouraged her to shirk them. Our first tiff came when I invited two leading constituents to tea at Shirley House. It was important that Philippa should be there too. She refused. She hid upstairs with Juliet and I made some lying excuse. Afterwards, to quell my anger, I drove alone for hours round the New Forest. These incidents always ended in reconciliations but cumulatively they weakened the tissue of our marriage. For a period she was ill with tuberculosis and, although she recovered in time to give me moral support during my personal Suez crisis, she suffered a permanent loss of energy, and I found myself acting increasingly without her. We had few interests in common apart from the house, the children and the dogs. I was unsympathetic. I turned away from her.

After I lost my seat in Parliament, we sold Shirley House and moved to London, where Rebecca was born on 10 April 1963. For some years we lived at 79 Limerston Street, Chelsea, and Lord Sackville lent us the Kennels in Knole Park as a weekend cottage. When Vita died in 1962 we moved to Sissinghurst and kept Limerston Street for only a few more years.

Philippa was kind to Harold in his last lingering years and began to take an interest in the garden, but it was not sustained. We drifted apart. She had separate friends, including my cousin Patrick Plunket, and we took separate holidays. In the summer of 1967 she met Robin McAlpine, a widower, while she was staying with the Silberbergs at St Tropez, and on her return she told me that she wished to divorce me and marry him. I begged her to reconsider. Was this not simply a new excitement to diversify her empty life? Robin was twenty-two years older than her. But he was Chairman of the great civil-engineering firm, a multimillionaire. She would have three houses, servants, cars, horses and a title (he was knighted in 1969). It was a gas-filled balloon, I thought, which would lift her into a stratosphere of luxury and freedom from worry. No more household budgets to guard our limited income. No more intellectual visitors. A husband who was attentive and generous, and would be out of the house most of the day. I did not oppose her wishes for long. I gave her grounds for a divorce, but for as long as possible we kept it dark. Harold never knew of the collapse of our marriage before he died. At the moment of our separation, I took the elder children on holiday to Ireland, without telling them the reason. As we were bicycling through the Isle of Aran, I thought of Philippa moving into the London flat which Robin had rented for her, and I took the children there on our return. The divorce was unopposed and was declared absolute in March 1970. Three days later, Philippa and Robin were married. What did I feel? Sorrow, humiliation and much self-reproach for not having shown her more affection. After a time, I saw the advantages of the single state and have never been tempted to marry a second time.

MY CHILDREN

As a family our marital record is dismal. Ben and I, and my three children, have all been divorced, and until now (1997), only Adam has married again. His second wife, Sarah Raven, has created new bonds between us. Her nature combines rare opposites, energy and calm, from which we are all beneficiaries. She represents stability, generosity and love. She and Adam have two children, Rosie and Mollie, and by his first marriage to Olivia Fane he had three boys, Tom, William and Ben. Juliet, who married James Macmillan-Scott, has two girls, Clementine (Clemmie) and Flora. Our progeny will stretch far into the twenty-first century. It is strange to think that Vita and Harold will be to them figures as vague as my great grandfather, Admiral Sir William Nicolson, a choleric and disappointed man, is to me.

I am neither choleric nor disappointed. My children have given me great happiness and much cause for pride. They do not consider that I have been as good a father to them as Harold was to me and often tell me so. In their childhood they were not so central to my life as Adam's and Juliet's children are in theirs. The "spaces in our togetherness" which Vita advocated as the secret of a happy family life have sometimes been too wide. I have excused myself by saying that when you are young, you are too busy to pay enough attention to your children, and when you are old, they are too busy to pay much attention to you. But I did try:

Nigel (in London) to Philippa (in Nassau) 12 March 1962
Verity [an au pair girl] is rather nice. She looks like sin itself, with a long hank of black hair hanging over one shoulder and a pint-sized face, very wicked, but she is considerate and sweet, and Adam [aged five] adores her. 'I want Verity to bath me.' 'Well, she can't. She's going out for the evening.' 'Who will bath me, then?' 'I will.' 'But I don't want to be seen by you.' I insisted, and there was a lot of hiding behind towels, and loud complaints that the water was too hot, then too cold, and I had chosen the wrong-coloured bath-mat, and the pyjama jacket goes on *first*, Dadda, didn't you know that?

That was the trouble. I didn't always know that. Adam's headmaster at Summer Fields had gently to remind me that he was the least-visited boy in the school. We had holidays together (Hadrian's Wall, Norway, the Shiants, canoeing the Kent rivers), but there wasn't enough of that cuddling in babyhood, story-telling in childhood, wood chopping, fishing, sailing and climbing in adolescence that Adam gives his sons. I regret this. Then there was my divorce, which hurt him more than I suspected at the time. At Eton he developed fast, made friends easily in college to which he had won a scholarship, enjoyed his work, and if he went through periods of distress, self-distrust and even jealousy of other boys' talents, as I had, he did not tell me. I wrote to him regularly, and he replied, but we did not communicate on an intimate level.

When he left Cambridge, he was tempted for a time to adopt a career in the Third World (I suggested the U.N.), but while these ideas were simmering he was approached by Weidenfeld to write a book about long walks through Britain, then a companion volume on France, which launched him on his career as writer, journalist and part-time publisher in partnership with his cousin, Robert Sackville-West.

His walk books developed his love of the countryside, poetry, history, architecture and wild life, and his innate literary talent expanded rapidly. He has enviable gifts. He can write in a couple of hours a one-thousand-word article colored by imagery and wit, but nothing that he writes seems good enough for him. His book, *Frontiers,* for example, which won the Somerset Maugham Prize, he considered "near-worthless," and when I asked him why (for I much admired it), he didn't want to explain. Our relationship is one of cautious affection. The caution on my part is due to my knowledge that I can easily upset him. He is a private person. He has a capacity for flaring indignation, but also for great tenderness, as when he was present at the birth of his children (not sitting downstairs like me), scattering his mother's ashes on a Swiss hillside as she had requested, and attending the High Court not from duty or curiosity but from sympathy, when I was giving my evidence in the Tolstoy trial. Like Ben, whom he resembles in many ways, he is contemptuous of fakes, snobs and smartness, rejecting more of my inheritance than I rejected of Vita's. He is efficient but does not make punctuality, except for deadlines, or dressing up for an occasion, a high priority in his life. He is more tolerant than I am of the gaps in people's interests. "You don't like classical music," he will say. "Francis, or Annabelle, is uninterested in politics. What's the difference? Why does it matter?" To my surprise, he looks forward to inheriting my grandfather's title from our cousin, David Carnock, who made a great success of his career as a solicitor. I had imagined that Adam would consider an hereditary peerage anachronistic. But he is not suspicious of tradition, nor indifferent to privilege. He wishes to justify them by effort and an honorable life.

When Juliet left Oxford she worked in publishing for Hamish Hamilton, then for Chatto & Windus under Carmen Callil. After her marriage to James Macmillan-Scott she moved with him to New York. He won increasingly responsible and lucrative jobs in finance houses, and she again worked in publishing, first in the American branch of Weidenfeld & Nicolson which George formed with Ann Getty, and afterwards in the Atlantic Monthly Press. She remained in New York for ten years. During that time we corresponded every week, and either she would come to England, or I to America, at least twice a year. After her divorce from James in 1995, she returned to London with her two daughters and set up a literary agency in her Belgravia house with the advice and support of Ed Victor.

In her various jobs, Juliet has made her name by unflagging energy and friendliness, from which I have benefited as much as anyone. She brought into my life friends like Susan and William Boyd. I like her generation. I enjoy being a grandfather. I owe to Juliet not only her affection but her gift for organizing my life, and in some sense replacing what I never had from her mother, an interest in the people, books, places, subjects and activities that interest me. She has been my stoutest stake in my later life.

Rebecca, her younger sister, as she grew up, was increasingly attractive, adventurous, independent and surrounded by friends. In her later childhood she took a serious interest in riding, encouraged by her step-father, Robin McAlpine. Once, in 1982, I watched her perform at a one-day event at Iping, Sussex, and was amazed by her audacity, calm, modesty and skill. I had not realized that she had attained such heights in that competitive world. I urged her to aim for the British Olympic equestrian team, but it was a choice between that and Oxford, and wisely—and to my secret delight—she chose Oxford. In her vacations she traveled to Russia, Japan, China and Sri Lanka. Though she sometimes accuses me of neglect, we see an increasing amount of each other. I admired the way she took her first steps in journalism, disdaining my suggestions of junior jobs in the National Trust, the National Gallery or the BBC, and walking without appointment into newspaper offices to gain a toe hold in her chosen profession. There was a spell with Eddie Shah, then with the *Mail on Sunday*, *The Times*, the *Sunday Correspondent*, the *Spectator*, and now with the *Sunday Telegraph*, where she edits the review section, to which I contribute a weekly column. By a process of nepotism-in-reverse, she persuaded her editor, Dominic Lawson, to employ me on the *Spectator* and, when both of them moved to the *Sunday Telegraph*, I went with them.

Between Rebecca and me there is still a certain reserve. Her marriage to Guy Philipps failed. He is a successful young barrister, whom I admire and slightly fear. Their wedding at Sissinghurst was the most elaborate event we have ever staged there, the more dramatic because it took place in pouring rain. There must be other dramas in Rebecca's life of which I am ignorant. Both of us enjoy our teasing, withdrawn yet provocative relationship. To me my children are like Columbus's fleet of caravels—the *Santa Maria* (Adam), the *Pinta* (Juliet) and the *Niña* (Rebecca), breasting the ocean waves, sometimes out of sight but never out of mind, heading for the horizon.

REQUIESCAT

Rest in peace. Well, not quite yet. I am now eighty. I have not spent a day in bed through illness for thirty years. Loss of hair, nobody much minds. Loss of vigor has not in my case been a problem, for I no longer wish to climb mountains and can walk ten or twelve miles across country with more joy than suffering. Loss of friends is painful: in the last year Fred Warner, Baba Metcalfe, Quentin Bell, Marietta Tree, Christopher Falkus, Stephen Spender, Rohan Butler, Cyrus Mackinnon and my aunt Gwen have died. I have reached the age when I open the obituary pages with trepidation. Loss of hearing has been a disadvantage, for while I can hear one-to-one conversation without difficulty, no hearing aid that I have yet discovered can eliminate background noise in a crowded room. Loss of vision is compensated by spectacles, of teeth by dentures, of appetite by abstinence, of sleep by reading far into the night.

I live in one wing of the front range of buildings at Sissinghurst. It is more comfortable than Vita would have thought decent, for I have central heating, eight bedrooms and four bathrooms. Externally it is maintained by the National Trust; internally by me. Once every twenty years I give the house a face lift, in a rural but not rustic manner, leaving chunky oak doors to warp, tapestries to fade, carpets to fray. I do not trust my own taste sufficiently to undertake these redecorations without expert advice. On the last occasion I employed Emily Todhunter, who toured the house with me and, on entering the only elegant bedroom, pointed to an exquisite woollen bedspread that I had bought at Betwys-y-Coed and declared, "Well, that must go for a start." It went, but only as far as my own bedroom, and when Emily had finished, I had to admit that by subtle touches (a lampshade here, a chair cover there) she had transformed a house that might have been mistaken for the retirement home of a tea planter into an agreeable residence fit for a judge in his old age.

It is a place made for entertainment. One great advantage is that guests have only to open an outside door to step into one of the most beautiful, and probably the most famous, gardens in England, which is maintained for my delight, and the public's, by a team of seven gardeners under Sarah Cook, at no expense to myself. My relationship with the National Trust, as I have indicated in an earlier chapter, is excellent. As I employ nobody except a lady, Eileen Cook, who comes once a week to clean and tidy the house, and I own no land, I am on the best of terms with the Trust's tenants, being one myself, never having to refuse a rise in wages or impose a rise in rent. I am spoiled.

Kent is not as neighborly a county as, say, Gloucestershire or Hereford, lying so close to London, where many of us work and tend to make our friends, whom we invite to the country for the weekend. But we are not unsociable. I have neighbors with whom I have more or less grown up, the Beales and the Stearns, Betty Hussey of Scotney Castle, Frank and Elizabeth Longford, Pat and Dione Gibson, my cousins from Knole, Jane and Richard Carr; and newer friends like David and Catherine Barham, John and Caroline Ure (ex-ambassador and traveler), Mary Villiers who is Chairman of the Kent and Sussex Region of the National Trust, Kirsty and Christopher Hudson, George Plumptre and his wife Ra, Mark and Rose Collins—I could go on but not indefinitely, for I am not extravagantly hospitable nor famously popular. A summer lunch for twelve is my annual apogee; a winter dinner for eight not unusual.

More fleeting visitors are students and scholars who come to consult the family archive, garden writers, friends of friends, people benighted by snow or lassitude, eminent visitors, chiefly from abroad, to whom the National Trust wishes to extend a special courtesy, and two hundred thousand members of the public. The place, in summer, hums with activity, and I welcome this, enjoying seclusion but not solitude. It happens from time to time that I entertain people whom I hardly know, or have never met, like Joanna Lumley whom I invited to dinner to meet John Updike and Victoria Glendinning, a blind date that turned out successfully; or when John Gunther asked if he could bring to lunch a lady whose name was so famous that he couldn't possibly mention it on the telephone: it was Greta Garbo. Princess Grace of Monaco came once, the Queen of Norway on another day, Prince Charles on yet another. I act as host for them for an hour or two, conscious that I am not the attraction but the garden which my mother made.

It is time to draw this book to a close. When Harold was eighty, Ben and I, and Kenneth Rose, who was our guest that night, asked him what he most regretted in his life. After a moment's thought, he replied, "That Vita died first." My answer would be sadly comparable, that I made a failure of my marriage. I have had other disappointments—in politics, in business, in the law courts—but all had their compensations. I was thrown out of the House of Commons, but not with dishonor; I lost money in business, but in the process helped to found one of the most successful postwar publishers; I have no regrets for the part I played in the Tolstoy–Aldington dispute, though Tolstoy lost it. I have written books that have achieved some success, and made myself into a confident lecturer. For periods at a time I have been lazy, thinking, as Harold once wrote in his diary, "I am attempting nothing; therefore I cannot fail," an excuse which both of us knew to be fundamentally flawed. I would like to have written Holroyd's book on Lytton Strachey. I would like to have remained in Parliament long enough to achieve office. But this is retrospective daydreaming.

It has not been a wasted life. It is studded with a few triumphs, and many moments of delight: winning my house colors; Harold's visit to the Shiant Islands; the capture of Perugia; the night when Juliet was born; my lecture at Stanford University; my walk with Sue Baring over Kos. These were moments that made me suddenly aware of my own nature. This is what I like doing most. These are the people whose company I most enjoy. This is what I am like. This is what I want to remember.

CHRONOLOGY

(Titles of books by N.N. italicized, and dated by year of publication)

1947–50	Demobilised. Conservative candidate for N.-W. Leicester
1949	Founding of Weidenfeld & Nicolson Ltd. *The Grenadier Guards 1939–45*
1950	Contests N.-W. Leicester in General Election
1951	Contests Falmouth and Camborne in General Election
1952	Elected MP for Bournemouth East and Christchurch
1953	Marries Philippa Tennyson-d'Eyncourt
1954	Juliet born at Shirley House, Bransgore, Hampshire
1955	Reelected for Bournemouth East. Visit to Israel. Debates on capital punishment
1956	Suez crisis. N.N. de-selected
1957	Adam born. Member of Council of Europe. Königswinter conferences
1958	*People and Parliament*
1959	*Lolita* crisis. Unseated by Bournemouth ballot
1960	*Lord of the Isles* (Lord Leverhulme)
1960–63	Returns to full-time publishing. Sells Shirley House. Moves to London
1961–6	Chairman of the United Nations Association
1962	Vita dies at Sissinghurst
1963	Rebecca born
1964	Retires from Weidenfeld & Nicolson
1965	*Great Houses of Britain*
1966–8	Edits Harold Nicolson's *Diaries and Letters* (3 vols.)
1967	Sissinghurst becomes property of the National Trust. 20,000-mile tour of Europe with Ian Graham and Kit Macdonald
1968	Harold dies at Sissinghurst. *Great Houses of the Western World*
1970	Divorced from Philippa, who marries Robin McAlpine
1971–81	Chairman of the Governors of Cranbrook School

1973   *Alex: The Life of Field Marshal Earl Alexander of Tunis* and *Portrait of a Marriage*

1974   Journey through Nepal, India, Pakistan, and Afghanistan. *The Himalayas*

1974–80   Edits *Letters of Virginia Woolf*, 6 vols., with Joanne Trautmann

1975   European Referendum. Research in Chicago

1977   *Mary Curzon* (Whitbread Prize for Biography). Journey to Canada

1978   Ben dies

1979   Six-week lecture tour of Canada and United States

1981   Lecture on Suez at Yale University. Southern TV film on Vita and Harold

1982   "Crusader Cruise" in Mediterranean

1983   Publication of Victoria Glendinning's biography of Vita

1984   Bloomsbury Symposium in Dallas, Texas. Chairman of Charleston Committee

1985   *Napoleon: 1812*

1986   *Two Roads to Dodge City* (with Adam Nicolson)

1987   Philippa dies

1988   *Kent. The Counties of Britain* (Speed maps). Christmas in Tunisia

1989   Tolstoy–Aldington trial

1990   BBC dramatization of *Portrait of a Marriage*

1991   *The World of Jane Austen*

1992   *Vita and Harold* (Letters). Visit to Australia and New Zealand. Cévennes walk

1992–7   Weekly column for *Spectator* and *Sunday Telegraph*

1994   *Vita and Virginia* (play) in New York

1996   Lectures on *Queen Elizabeth 2*

1997   *Long Life*

INDEX

Abbreviations: NN. Nigel Nicolson
HN. Harold Nicolson
V.S-W. Vita Sackville-West